FININT

A Trader's Field Manual for Public-Source Financial Intelligence

Zachary Handa

Demeter Academy Press · 2026

FININT: A Trader's Field Manual for Public-Source Financial Intelligence

First published 2026

Published by Demeter Academy Press, Los Angeles

ISBN: 978-1-971093-04-8 (print)

Printed in the United States of America

10 9 8 7 6 5 4 3 2 1

Important Disclaimer

This book is for educational and informational purposes only. Nothing in this publication constitutes investment advice, legal advice, tax advice, or a recommendation to buy, sell, or hold any security, financial instrument, or asset of any kind.

The author is not a registered investment adviser, broker-dealer, attorney, or accountant. The frameworks, techniques, and methodologies described in this book reflect the author's research and perspective and are not guaranteed to produce any particular result.

Past performance of any strategy, technique, or analytical approach discussed does not guarantee or imply future results. All investing involves risk, including the possible loss of principal. Financial markets are inherently unpredictable, and no methodology — however rigorous — eliminates uncertainty.

Readers are responsible for independently verifying all information before making any financial, legal, or investment decision. Nothing in this book should substitute for qualified professional advice tailored to your specific circumstances. Consult a licensed financial advisor, attorney, or accountant before acting on any information presented here.

The author and publisher make no representations or warranties, express or implied, about the completeness, accuracy, reliability, suitability, or availability of the information, tools, or related materials contained in this book. Any reliance placed on such information is at the reader's own risk.

The author and publisher disclaim all liability for any losses, damages, or adverse outcomes — financial or otherwise — incurred as a direct or indirect result of applying the information, techniques, or frameworks described in this book.

References to specific companies, securities, regulatory cases, or market events are included solely for educational illustration. They do not constitute endorsements or recommendations regarding those companies or securities.

Table of Contents

Introduction: Why Public Information Is Enough

Every trading edge the market respects was built on something someone else could have found.

The Wirecard fraud sat hiding in publicly available filings for years. Nikola's inoperable trucks were documented in SEC disclosures anyone could have read. Enron's collapse was telegraphed in footnotes that most investors scrolled past. In each case, the information was there. The question was never access — it was method.

That is what this book is about.

What This Book Is

FININT: A Trader's Field Manual for Public-Source Financial Intelligence is a practical guide to systematic market research using only legally available, publicly accessible information. It covers the full research workflow: how to define what you need to know, where to find it, how to verify it across independent sources, how to build a structured investment thesis, and how to maintain the discipline required to do this consistently.

The word "field manual" is deliberate. This is not a survey of financial theory or an academic treatment of market microstructure. It is an operational reference — the kind of book you keep open while you work. It describes specific sources, specific techniques, and specific workflows. When it tells you to compare consecutive MDA sections side by side and calculate the change in hedge ratio language, that is exactly what it means. When it describes building a fraud red flags checklist from Form 10-K footnotes, it means that too.

Who This Book Is For

This manual was written for three types of readers:

The self-directed trader or investor who is serious about research but has never been taught how to read a 10-K systematically, work through regulatory filing databases, or build a reproducible research process from scratch. You know that analysis matters, but your current process is mostly reactive — news articles, earnings recaps, and analyst summaries written by people whose incentives you can't fully verify. This book replaces that with a primary-source methodology.

The aspiring analyst or researcher entering the financial industry who wants to build the investigative skills that separate strong analysts from average ones. The techniques covered here — forensic filing analysis, source triangulation, activist report evaluation, alternative data interpretation — are the foundations of institutional-grade research. Most are never formally taught. This book teaches them.

The experienced practitioner looking to systematize and extend an existing process. You likely already use many of these sources. This manual offers a structured framework for integrating them, reducing analytical blind spots, and building the documentation and feedback systems that transform ad hoc research into a repeatable professional practice.

If you are looking for stock picks, trading signals, or a system that replaces judgment with rules, this is not that book. This is a book about developing the judgment to do the research yourself.

What Problem This Solves

Most retail investors and independent researchers are outgunned — not because they lack access to information, but because they lack a framework for using it. They face the same SEC filings, the same earnings transcripts, the same regulatory databases as institutional analysts. The difference is methodology.

Institutional research teams have structured processes for everything: how to evaluate a filing, how to weight conflicting sources, how to document an investment thesis, how to conduct a postmortem. These processes exist because unstructured research fails at scale. They work not because they guarantee correct conclusions, but because they make errors detectable and correctable.

This book describes those processes. It adapts the methodological discipline of professional financial intelligence work for the individual researcher who may be working alone, without a Bloomberg terminal, and without a compliance department telling them where to look.

What Background This Book Assumes

You should be comfortable reading basic financial statements — income statement, balance sheet, cash flow statement — and understand what revenue, operating income, and earnings per share represent at a conceptual level. You do not need to be an accountant or a CFA charterholder. The book explains specialized concepts as they arise and includes a full glossary at the back.

You should also be familiar with how public stock markets function at a basic level: what it means for a company to be publicly traded, what the SEC requires of public companies, and what the difference is between buying a stock and holding a bond. Beyond that, the manual is self-contained.

How to Use This Book

As a sequential read: Parts 1 and 2 build the conceptual and technical foundations—the intelligence cycle, the legal framework, and the core filing types. Parts 3 and 4 extend into advanced collection techniques, international sources, fraud detection, and alternative data. Part 5 adds the policy intelligence layer: lobbying, federal contracting, and congressional trading. Part 6 integrates everything into a professional practice: research organization, thesis construction, monitoring systems, case studies, and skill development. Reading in order gives you the full system.

As a reference manual: Each chapter and subsection is written to stand independently. If you need to understand 13D and 13G filing mechanics, go directly to Chapter 7. If you need guidance on reading activist short-seller reports, go to Chapter 11. If you want a checklist of accounting red flags, go to Appendix B. The Glossary at the back defines every technical term used in the text.

As a practice guide: The most valuable use of this book is alongside active research. Open a real 10-K while reading the filing analysis chapters. Pull an actual earnings transcript while working through the MDA and tone analysis sections. Apply the company dossier template (Appendix A) to a company you're currently investigating. The techniques become useful through application, not memorization.

A Map of What Follows

Part 1 establishes the foundations: what FININT is and how it differs from casual research, the five-phase intelligence cycle that structures the entire methodology, the legal and ethical framework governing public-source research, and how to evaluate and weight different types of information sources.

Part 2 covers the core U.S. regulatory filing system: how to read and extract intelligence from 10-Ks, 10-Qs, 8-Ks, proxy statements, and beneficial ownership disclosures. It teaches reading between the lines — footnote analysis, auditor flags, accounting red flags, and MDA interpretation.

Part 3 addresses advanced data collection: government macro data, short interest, options market signals, activist and short-seller report analysis, insider filing patterns, court records, and central bank communications.

Part 4 extends the toolkit internationally and into fraud detection: international filing sources, offshore structure identification, alternative data interpretation (satellite imagery, job postings, web traffic), and the investigative workflows used to verify or challenge corporate claims.

Part 5 adds the policy intelligence layer: lobbying disclosure analysis, federal contracting data, and congressional trading patterns. These chapters show how government spending, regulatory influence, and legislative insider activity create tradable information flows that most equity analysts overlook entirely.

Part 6 integrates everything into a professional practice: research organization, thesis memo construction, monitoring systems, real-world case studies (GameStop, Wirecard, Enron, Archegos), and the postmortem and skill development frameworks that separate systematic practitioners from one-trade analysts.

The appendices provide working tools: a company dossier template, a fraud red flags checklist, a key databases reference, a sample monitoring routine, and a research postmortem template. The glossary defines all technical terms used throughout the text.

The public record is a vast, underutilized asset. Most of what professionals know about any public company sits in documents anyone can download for free. The edge is not in the data. It is in knowing what to look for, how to verify it, and how to build that knowledge into a reliable process.

That is what the rest of this book teaches.

PART 1

FOUNDATIONS — WHAT FININT IS AND KEY DISTINCTIONS

Most investment research fails not because the data is missing, but because the method is. Financial intelligence is a discipline before it is a toolkit, and that discipline has to be in place before the first database is opened. This section lays the foundation: what separates systematic financial intelligence from casual research, how the intelligence cycle moves the work from question to conclusion, where the legal and ethical boundaries of public-source investigation actually sit, and how to assign weight to sources that differ sharply in reliability and timing.

These are the chapters readers are most likely to skip in order to get to the techniques. That impulse is understandable, but it is usually costly. Later failures of overcollection, weak sourcing, or analytical overconfidence almost always trace back to something that was not learned, or not taken seriously enough, in the foundations.

CHAPTER 1

Defining Financial OSINT and FININT

A trader sees a competitor's stock move on no obvious news. The usual response is to scan the headlines for an explanation. But sometimes there is none. That does not mean the move is random. More often, it means the market is reacting to information that has not yet been packaged into a headline: a quiet change in supplier relationships, a regulatory filing buried in a foreign jurisdiction, or a technical development visible only to people who know where to look.

Financial intelligence offers a way past reactive news consumption. It shifts the trader's role from passive consumer of financial media to active investigator of the public record. The aim is not to find a single silver bullet. It is to assemble a mosaic from legally available fragments: corporate registries, patent databases, executive biographies, satellite imagery, regulatory dockets. Any one piece may seem trivial. Taken together, they can reveal the story behind price action before it hardens into conventional wisdom.

The task here is to draw the line between systematic intelligence gathering and casual research, and to show how raw public data becomes a structured investment thesis through a disciplined process.

What Financial OSINT Is and Is Not

Financial OSINT is not casual web browsing for stock tips. It is a systematic method for collecting and analyzing legally available information to produce actionable market insight. The difference is one of process and intent. A retail investor who reads a news article about a company's new product is doing research. A financial intelligence analyst who cross-references that announcement with patent filings, executive LinkedIn profiles for relevant experience, and satellite imagery of factory parking lots is doing OSINT. The second approach builds a mosaic from scattered public points to form a picture the market has not yet priced.

At its core, the work involves mapping relationships and verifying claims through primary sources. Tracking funds through layers of offshore entities, for example, may require pulling records from corporate registries such as OpenCorporates, property records, and leaked datasets like the Panama Papers. The goal is to identify ultimate beneficial owners that formal filings may conceal. Scattered records become intelligence about hidden financial relationships or fraud risk. The questions are concrete: Who actually controls this network of companies? Do the claimed business operations have physical evidence behind them?

Two assumptions often narrow the way people understand financial OSINT. One is that it depends entirely on free tools and public websites. In practice, professional workflows often rely on commercial aggregators as well. Services such as Moody's Maxsight compile structured data on hundreds of millions of entities worldwide, making due diligence far more efficient than manual collection ever could.

The second assumption is that OSINT is mainly reactive, something used only after a red flag appears. In practice, its proactive uses are often more powerful. Financial institutions screen counterparties against sanctions lists and adverse media before transacting, not after. For a trader, the parallel is screening a company's officers, corporate structure, and disclosed relationships before committing capital—not after a short report or enforcement action forces the issue.

It is just as important to define what financial OSINT is not. It does not involve accessing non-public information or crossing legal boundaries. Scraping the dark web for illegal trade data or hacking tools is outside ethical intelligence work. Those activities belong to criminal reconnaissance, not market analysis. The same is true of using Shodan to identify exposed corporate servers or doxxing individuals for blackmail. The boundary is material non-public information. Analyzing a CEO's published travel schedule on social media to infer merger discussions is OSINT. Receiving a tip about those discussions from an insider is not.

The method also differs from simple data collection. Raw data becomes intelligence only after processing and analysis. Pulling every SEC filing for a company is only a start. The real work lies in reading between the lines of the

Management Discussion and Analysis section, tracking changes in risk-factor language across quarters, and cross-referencing executive compensation details with insider trading filings. That analytical layer can reveal subtle changes in corporate narrative or incentives that may signal future performance. It is what separates signal from the noise of modern disclosure.

Financial OSINT is also a double-edged tool. The same methods investigators use to uncover fraud can be used by criminals to find weaknesses. Bad actors scrape public data to identify low-compliance jurisdictions or exploit social media leaks from compliance officers. That reality is one reason legal and ethical discipline matters so much in professional practice. It also helps explain why the market for these tools and services has grown so rapidly, driven by anti-money-laundering requirements and cybersecurity demands across the financial sector.

In the end, financial OSINT is a structured way of answering questions the market has not yet learned to ask. Through disciplined collection planning and critical analysis, it turns the sheer volume of public information from a burden into an advantage.

FININT vs. Casual Financial Research

Consider two analysts looking at the same semiconductor company after a surprise quarterly earnings miss. The casual researcher opens the latest 10-Q, reads the press release summary, checks a few analyst ratings, and concludes that the miss came from "supply chain issues" because management used that phrase twice on the earnings call. The FININT practitioner works differently. They cross-reference the geographic revenue breakdown with export data from the company's manufacturing hubs, compare inventory turnover over the last eight quarters, examine whether competitors in the same supply chain reported similar problems, and review changes in executive compensation language that may point to deeper operational strain. Same company, same public information, very different depth of analysis.

The difference between FININT and casual financial research turns on methodology, verification, and scope. Casual research treats public information as an answer. If a company reports fifteen percent revenue growth, that number becomes the conclusion. FININT treats the same figure as the beginning of an inquiry. Where did that growth come from? Which segments produced it? How does the revenue-recognition policy compare with peers? Are accounts receivable rising faster than sales? That kind of questioning turns surface data into intelligence about business quality and sustainability.

Verification is where the gap becomes most visible. A casual trader reads that a retail chain plans to open fifty new stores and takes management at its word. A FININT analyst checks job postings for store managers in the target markets, commercial real estate filings in those regions, and capital-expenditure guidance in the cash-flow statement. They look for construction permits and compare the proposed expansion timeline with competitor store closures in the same areas. If the expansion story lacks corroboration from independent sources, it is no longer a growth catalyst. It is a warning sign.

Scope is the third difference. Casual research tends to stay inside a single domain. Stock screeners identify companies with low price-to-earnings ratios. Technical charts show support and resistance levels. Neither says much about the other. FININT pulls together multiple streams of data on purpose. The same semiconductor company may look attractive on valuation and bullish on the chart. But a broader intelligence picture might show increased related-party transactions in regulatory filings, patent records indicating key engineers have left for competitors, and shipping data pointing to falling exports to major customers. The mosaic suggests deteriorating fundamentals that valuation metrics alone will not catch.

Take a pharmaceutical company trading at a discount to peers. Casual research may frame it as a value opportunity based on relative P/E multiples. FININT asks why the market is assigning a lower multiple in the first place. The analyst checks FDA advisory committee calendars for pending drug-approval decisions, reviews clinical trial databases for success rates in similar therapies, maps patent expiration timelines across the company's revenue base, and examines management's record on past drug launches. They find that the discount reflects a legitimate, probability-adjusted risk tied to an approaching patent cliff, not market inefficiency. The casual researcher had access to the same public information. The difference lies in knowing which questions matter and where to find the evidence.

The same gap appears in earnings-call analysis. Casual observers listen for headline guidance and general tone. FININT practitioners prepare before the call. They review the prior quarter's transcript to see which analyst questions were dodged or left unanswered. They build a checklist of operational metrics management discussed before but may avoid now. During the call, they track not only what management says, but what it avoids saying. Afterward, they compare the prepared remarks with the Q&A for consistency, note which topics triggered defensive language, and measure how much time management spent on forward guidance rather than explaining past results. Over time, this approach extracts signals from patterns that casual listening misses.

One common misconception is that FININT depends on expensive terminals or proprietary databases. Professional tools help, but they are not the core distinction. An independent analyst can do real FININT with SEC EDGAR, investor-relations pages, government economic databases, patent offices, and court records, all of them free. The barrier is not access to information. It is discipline: knowing how to frame research questions, which sources can validate which claims, and how to build an evidence chain that holds up under scrutiny. Bloomberg may accelerate collection. It does not substitute for systematic thought.

Another misconception is that correlation is enough. Two metrics moving together does not tell you why they move together, or whether the relationship will survive. Casual research often stops at spotting the pattern. FININT keeps going and looks for the mechanism. If a retailer's same-store sales correlate with regional employment rates, the FININT practitioner asks whether that relationship reflects real changes in customer behavior, whether it holds across different cycles, and whether leading indicators such as job postings begin to signal the shift before it appears in sales data. That is how you find out whether the pattern is a tradable signal or a coincidence waiting to break.

Financial intelligence turns public information from a commodity into an edge through method. The same SEC filings, earnings calls, and regulatory databases are available to everyone. The difference lies in how closely those sources are examined, how carefully their claims are tested against independent evidence, and how far their implications are traced across connected data points. Casual research treats information gathering as a box to check. FININT treats it as a disciplined process for producing insights others miss, not through privileged access, but through careful investigative work on the public record.

Key Takeaways

- ☐ FININT is not about having better data. It is about applying a structured methodology — source triangulation, cross-referencing, and evidence chains — to the same public information available to every market participant. The edge comes from process, not access.
- ☐ The gap between casual research and financial intelligence lies in three dimensions: methodology (systematic questioning vs. accepting reported figures), verification (testing claims against independent sources vs. taking management at their word), and scope (integrating multiple data streams vs. staying inside a single domain).

Fieldwork

- ☐ Choose a company you currently hold or follow. Write down the three most important claims management made in the most recent earnings call or press release. For each claim, identify one independent public source that could confirm or contradict it — a regulatory filing, a patent database entry, a job posting pattern, or an industry data point. This is the core FININT habit: treating management assertions as hypotheses, not conclusions.
- ☐ Pull the most recent 10-K for any company and read the first two pages of the MD&A section. Then read a recent news article about the same company. Note where the two accounts agree and where they diverge. The divergence is where intelligence work begins.

Apply This

When evaluating any company, ask: What is management claiming? What public evidence exists to verify that claim? And what would I expect to see in the public record if the claim were false? If you cannot answer the third question, you have not yet defined your research requirements.

CHAPTER 2

The FININT Methodology Framework

A trader may identify a promising company and gather a great deal of relevant data, yet still fail to turn that work into a profitable position. The problem is usually not access to information. It is methodology: the structured process that converts raw material into a coherent investment thesis and an actionable trade. Without that structure, research remains a pile of interesting facts rather than a systematic investigation with clear objectives, collection rules, and ways to test what is true.

Financial intelligence methodology provides the structure that lifts research out of casual browsing and into professional analysis. It starts with disciplined planning, defining specific intelligence requirements before any collection begins. That step avoids a common mistake: gathering everything available with no real purpose. From there, the method guides how collected data is processed into usable form, and how analytical frameworks test hypotheses against multiple streams of evidence.

What follows is the operating logic of that process: how the intelligence cycle structures research from question to conclusion, how collection planning directs effort toward the highest-value sources, how processing turns raw material into analyzable inputs, how analysis separates signal from noise, and how dissemination connects insight to decisions. The point is not to produce speculative narratives, but repeatable, evidence-based investment theses.

The Five-Phase Intelligence Cycle

The intelligence cycle provides a structured way to turn scattered public data into a coherent investment thesis. It replaces reactive news-chasing with a disciplined workflow. The standard model has five phases, but they work less as a straight line than as a loop. Each phase solves a different problem in the intelligence process.

Planning and Direction establishes the research requirement. It starts by identifying intelligence gaps: specific questions current information cannot answer. A trader looking at a pharmaceutical company, for example, may need to understand the regulatory timeline for approval of a key drug. Planning turns that gap into a collection strategy. It determines which sources to consult, how to prioritize them, and where research time should go. Without that direction, collection quickly turns into aimless data hoarding.

Collection is the gathering of raw information from the sources identified in the plan. In the pharmaceutical example, that may include FDA advisory committee calendars, clinical trial registries, and patent filings. At this stage, the job is to retrieve material, not interpret it. Good collection depends on understanding source reliability and knowing how to reach specialized databases beyond ordinary web searches. Many researchers start here without doing the planning first, which usually means time wasted on irrelevant material.

Processing and Exploitation organizes raw information into forms that can actually be analyzed. The material arrives in many shapes: PDF filings, spreadsheet downloads, audio transcripts. Processing standardizes it. That may mean extracting financial tables from SEC filings into spreadsheet models, timestamping management comments from earnings calls, or geotagging facility locations from corporate disclosures. The result is a set of structured inputs for analysis. Skip this step, and the analyst ends up repeatedly digging through the same disorderly source material.

Analysis and Production is where the real intellectual work begins. Analysts examine processed information for patterns, relationships, and implications. They use several forms of reasoning.

Deduction applies known rules to reach firm conclusions. If SEC rules require disclosure of all material contracts, and a company's joint venture agreement clearly meets the materiality threshold, deduction tells you the filing is mandatory.

Induction works the other way. It moves from repeated observation to probable trend. If management has repeatedly cited supply-chain delays on earnings calls and the stock has regularly sold off afterward, the analyst can infer a likely market reaction when similar language appears again.

Abduction is different. It asks for the most plausible explanation for a set of observations. If a stock falls on heavy volume while options activity spikes and a competitor files a new patent, the best explanation may be that the market expects a loss of share. The conclusion is not certain. It is simply the most convincing account that fits the facts.

In the pharmaceutical example, analysis may show that management's comments about manufacturing capacity do not match patent-expiration timelines. From that, the analyst produces finished intelligence: a concise assessment answering the original question about regulatory timing, backed by evidence. This is the phase that separates information gathering from actual insight.

Dissemination and Integration delivers the intelligence to the point where decisions get made and folds the result back into future work. The output may take the form of a written memo, a dashboard update, or a verbal briefing. Good dissemination matches the format to the audience. A portfolio manager needs a different level of detail than a risk committee. Integration happens when the intelligence changes a trading decision, risk posture, or research priority. Once that happens, new questions emerge, and the cycle begins again.

A common mistake is to think the cycle ends once findings are delivered. It does not. Feedback makes the process iterative. Intelligence consumers react. Markets move. A thesis gets implemented and then challenged by events the analyst did not expect. Those reactions sharpen future collection requirements and expose what the original work missed. That continuous refinement is what makes systematic financial intelligence different from one-off research. Its strength lies not in producing definitive answers once and for all, but in managing uncertainty through repetition, adjustment, and better questions.

Collection Planning and Requirements

Collection planning turns vague curiosity into targeted data gathering. It starts by defining priority intelligence requirements: specific questions ranked by their importance to the investment thesis. One requirement might ask whether reported revenue growth is consistent with import and export patterns. Another might focus on whether executive stock sales tend to cluster before negative announcements.

These requirements come before source selection. The analyst first decides what needs to be known, then determines where that information is likely to be found. That order is crucial. It avoids one of the most common mistakes in research: collecting everything simply because it is available. A trader looking at a retail chain should define requirements around store traffic, inventory turnover, and competitor pricing before deciding whether to use satellite imagery, job postings, or supplier filings.

In practice, analysts often record these requirements in a priority intelligence requirements register. This is a living document that ranks the key questions and breaks them into sub-requirements. It becomes the foundation of the collection plan. The plan then maps each requirement to particular sources, collection methods, and resource commitments. It serves both as an authority document and as a guide to workflow.

Collection plans in financial intelligence often follow formal structures. One common model uses three steps. First, the analyst carries stakeholder needs into the plan. Second, those needs are converted into specific questions attached to each priority requirement. Third, a resource matrix is built showing source coverage, vendors, and available expertise. The point is to justify resource allocation while making sure coverage is wide enough to answer the actual question.

Transaction reporting offers a concrete example. Financial crime investigators, who specialize in tracing illicit fund flows and building evidence chains from public records, define requirements around suspicious activity patterns. Their plans prioritize queries against databases containing millions of transaction reports. Parameters include dates, report types, countries, industries, and locations. The outputs may range from summary reports to detailed transaction lists. The contrast with unfocused data gathering is obvious.

Fraud detection offers another example. Here the requirement is to identify anomalous patterns that may signal deception. Teams concentrate on real-time transaction analysis and pull data from many sources: transaction records, behavioral data, regulatory filings, and more. Standardized models and automated pipelines handle much of the processing. When the planning is sound, these systems can improve fraud detection while lowering operational cost.

A collection plan is never static. It has to change as new information appears and priorities shift. Another common mistake is to gather data without clear requirements at all. That produces noise, not signal. In practice, good financial intelligence uses both internal and external material. Public records, regulatory filings, and transaction databases add context that traditional financial statements cannot provide on their own.

The collection plan is where the mission becomes operational. For an independent researcher, that means defining scope, time horizon, freshness requirements, and legal constraints. Scope determines which companies, sectors, or issues fall inside the inquiry. Time horizon sets the historical depth needed for trend analysis. Freshness distinguishes between real-time alerting and periodic review. Legal constraints ensure that every step relies on publicly available information.

Good planning also balances backward-looking and forward-looking work. Financial intelligence has to reconstruct the past in order to understand the present, but it also has to identify indicators that may point to what comes next. A sound plan includes both: requirements for building historical baselines and requirements for monitoring forward indicators. That is what separates systematic research from reactive information gathering.

The collection plan is the bridge between research questions and actionable insight. It turns abstract needs into specific tasks. Without it, even sophisticated tools end up processing irrelevant material. The difference between data hoarding and intelligence production begins here.

Processing Raw Data into Intelligence

Raw data becomes intelligence only after a process adds structure, context, and meaning. Imagine a stack of SEC filings running to thousands of pages. In raw form, they contain financial statements, footnotes, management commentary. Processing isolates important relationships: revenue-recognition policies against cash-flow patterns, capital expenditures against depreciation schedules, narrative changes against financial strain. The output is not more data. It is a structured assessment of earnings quality.

Financial intelligence analysts usually move through a defined pipeline. The first stage is data preparation and cleansing. Raw transaction records and corporate filings have to be standardized, deduplicated, and enriched. Addresses, phone numbers, and currency figures need to align across sources. Timestamps must follow one format. This work is foundational. Without it, later analysis rests on corrupted or mismatched inputs. Tools such as Python, Pandas, and Scikit-learn make that process scalable.

Pandas DataFrames provide the tabular structure for much of this work. Analysts can load CSV exports from financial APIs, clean and merge them, then filter and aggregate the data to produce metrics such as sector volatility. The advantage is scale: vectorized operations replace manual spreadsheet work and support larger, repeatable data pipelines.

Once the data is clean, the next step is feature engineering. This is where analysts extract patterns that matter from transaction data and corporate records. Features may capture anomalies in transaction velocity, unusual geographic spending, or shifts in behavior over time. In corporate analysis, they may include debt-to-equity, return on investment, or trends in revenue and profitability that raw figures alone do not reveal.

Statistical methods then turn those features into analytical signals. Regression can test how strongly one variable moves with another, such as stock price changes against earnings per share. Clustering can group similar data points, such as stocks with comparable risk or performance profiles. Time-series methods can model longer-term patterns through techniques such as exponential smoothing. Classification models can predict outcomes from labeled historical data, whether loan default risk or the probability of a given stock-price direction.

The last stage is communication. Insights have to be expressed in forms people can use: visualizations, dashboards, structured reports. Business intelligence platforms serve this purpose. They aggregate raw financial data into interactive dashboards for real-time monitoring and trend analysis, often without requiring deep coding knowledge.

Power BI and Tableau are common examples. Power BI is especially useful for connecting to public data sources such as Excel files and APIs inside Microsoft-heavy environments. Independent traders may use it to build dashboards tracking economic indicators and their effect on particular sectors. Tableau is stronger on advanced visualization and can be especially useful when patterns are hidden in blended datasets. A position trader, for instance, might build heat maps showing clusters of insider trading across biotech firms.

Automation extends the process. Scripts can pull daily stock-performance data from databases through APIs, clean it with Pandas, and generate formatted reports without manual intervention. That shift is significant. It turns repetitive data handling into a scalable intelligence process.

Still, aggregation alone is not intelligence. Collecting more SEC filings does not, by itself, produce insight. Another common error is to apply statistical tools without enough business understanding to interpret the output. Regression on poorly cleaned data produces elegant nonsense. Intelligence work requires both technical processing and domain judgment.

That is why processing typically sits inside a broader data-governance framework. These systems define ownership, quality standards, and access controls. Automated pipelines continuously ingest, validate, and transform data from filings, transaction systems, and market feeds. The point is consistency. Raw information becomes actionable intelligence not through ad hoc tinkering, but through repeatable processes that can be trusted. That transformation is the real value-add in financial intelligence work.

Analysis Techniques and Critical Thinking

A quarterly earnings report shows revenue growth of fifteen percent. The casual observer accepts the number. The financial intelligence analyst starts asking questions. Why did accounts receivable rise forty percent while cash flow from operations fell? Which product lines drove the increase, and are they sustainable? The shift from passive acceptance to active interrogation marks the analytical phase.

Critical thinking in financial intelligence means taking information apart in a disciplined way to test both its validity and its implications. The Five Whys is a simple example. A company reports a sharp rise in operating expenses. Why? Marketing costs increased. Why? The company launched a new digital advertising campaign. Why did that campaign require more spending? Because the targeting performed poorly. Why was the targeting poor? Because the underlying market research was flawed. Why was the research flawed? Because management was under pressure to show growth at any cost. The exercise forces the analyst past symptoms and down toward cause.

Structured argumentation does similar work at a higher level. An investment thesis should be built from evidence chains, not intuition. Every claim needs support, and each piece of evidence has to be linked through logic. Suppose an analyst believes a retail chain has inventory problems. They might begin with filings showing declining inventory-turnover ratios for three straight quarters. They then notice footnotes showing supplier payment terms extended from thirty to sixty days. Finally, they see increased hiring for warehouse-management roles in job-posting data. The conclusion does not rest on any one indicator. It emerges from the convergence of several independent signals.

Scenario planning provides another discipline. Rather than framing the future as simply bullish or bearish, it builds several plausible paths and tests the thesis against all of them. A pharmaceutical company facing a key drug-approval decision may be modeled in three scenarios: a base case with approval and moderate sales, an upside case with rapid adoption and label expansion, and a downside case with delays and competitive pressure. Each case receives a probability weighting based on trial data, precedent, and market conditions. The exercise clarifies which variables matter most and where monitoring should be concentrated.

Ratio analysis adds quantitative structure, but the numbers need context. Liquidity measures such as the current ratio speak to near-term financial health. Solvency measures such as debt-to-equity bear on long-term stability. Profitability measures such as return on equity say something about management effectiveness. But ratios do not explain themselves. A decline in gross margin may reflect pricing pressure, cost inflation, or a shift in product mix. The metric is useful only when compared across time, against peers, and against the company's own stated targets.

Financial models and simulations create controlled settings for testing decisions. A portfolio manager may simulate different interest-rate paths to gauge the sensitivity of a bond portfolio. A corporate analyst may run commodity-price scenarios to estimate earnings volatility. The value is not in pretending to predict the future with precision. It lies in showing which variables drive outcomes and where a thesis is most exposed.

Analytical work gets distorted in predictable ways. Some people mistake critical thinking for simple number crunching. But financial analysis requires understanding how liquidity, solvency, and profitability interact, not merely calculating each in isolation. Others treat analysis as backward-looking by definition. In practice, good analysis always contains a forward element. It compares the company not only with its own past, but with industry trends and management's guidance about what lies ahead. Budgeting and forecasting are useful only when they reflect present conditions rather than mechanically extending old ones.

The analytical phase turns processed data into insight through disciplined questioning and structured reasoning. It separates signal from noise by testing assumptions against multiple evidence streams. That skepticism is essential. It keeps confirmation bias from quietly shaping the thesis. Some of the most valuable insights arise from contradiction: management commentary that clashes with the numbers, regulatory filings that tell a different story from the press release. Those tensions are not obstacles to analysis. They are where analysis begins.

Dissemination and Feedback Loops

A financial intelligence analyst completes a detailed report on a company's worsening working-capital position. The report runs twenty pages and lays out the evidence: declining inventory-turnover ratios, stretched accounts payable, troubling changes in supplier-contract language. The analyst emails it to themself under the subject line "Research Complete" and moves on. Six weeks later, the company announces a liquidity crisis. The analysis was right. The intelligence went unused. That is why dissemination is crucial.

Dissemination means delivering intelligence to the point of decision in a form that makes action possible. In an institution, that may mean a formal report sent to portfolio managers. For an independent trader, the decision-maker is often the same person who did the work, but at a different point in time. The problem then is not communication across departments. It is building a system that puts the right intelligence back in front of you when the moment for action arrives. A trade thesis developed in January has to remain available and usable when the trigger appears in March.

The format depends on the decision context and the time horizon. A position trader watching a pharmaceutical name ahead of FDA approval may need a dashboard that shows the catalyst calendar, thesis summary, entry conditions, and exit criteria at a glance. A value investor following a list of distressed situations may need a spreadsheet ranking them by discount to intrinsic value, catalyst timing, and downside protection. A swing trader running overnight risk may need alerts tied to specific technical or fundamental thresholds. The underlying intelligence may be the same. The packaging cannot be.

For systematic traders, the core dissemination tool is often the investment-thesis memo. A useful memo answers five questions: What is the opportunity? Why does it exist? What evidence supports it? What would disprove it? What action follows from it? A well-built memo allows a trader to revisit an idea months later without having to reconstruct the original reasoning from scratch. It preserves not only the conclusion, but the assumptions and evidence chain beneath it.

Feedback loops make dissemination part of a learning system rather than a one-way transmission. The simplest version compares prediction with outcome. A trader records a price target derived from a sum-of-the-parts valuation. Three months later, they check whether the stock moved as expected. If it did not, why not? Was the analysis wrong, the timing wrong, or did new information invalidate the thesis? That review creates lessons that improve future work.

For solo traders and small teams, feedback has to be built deliberately. Otherwise it usually never happens. Most people move straight to the next opportunity without reviewing the last one. A more disciplined approach is to hold quarterly postmortems on both winners and losers. Which signals were missed? Which sources turned out to matter? Did the thesis hold while execution failed, or was the logic itself flawed? Over time, those reviews turn isolated trade outcomes into pattern recognition about the strengths and weaknesses of the research process itself.

Trade journals are one way to capture that feedback. Each entry records the thesis, the evidence, the entry rationale, and the original risk parameters. Later entries track how the thesis changes as new information comes in. The final entry records the outcome and the lesson. Read in sequence, those records expose patterns that are easy to miss when looking at trades one by one. A trader may discover, for example, that they repeatedly enter too early, before catalysts mature, or that their strongest trades share the same evidence profile.

Monitoring systems create another feedback loop while the position is still open. A trader long a semiconductor stock because of a supply-shortage thesis might set alerts for competitor earnings, industry inventory reports, and capacity-expansion announcements. When one of those alerts fires, the trader returns to the original thesis memo and asks whether the new information strengthens or weakens the case. That process guards against a common failure: holding positions based on stale assumptions because no one formally revisits the reasoning.

Even small teams can create institutional-grade feedback with simple routines. A weekly half-hour review of one completed investment thesis from the last quarter can be enough. The team asks what was knowable at the time but missed, which collection sources were redundant, and whether the analytical framework tested the thesis rigorously enough. Over time, those sessions build organizational memory without requiring much infrastructure.

Another mistake is to treat feedback as optional, something done only after the trade is over. Effective feedback runs continuously. It is also a mistake to study only losses. That creates a bias toward failure analysis while leaving success unexamined. Some of the most useful lessons come from trades that worked for the wrong reasons, when the thesis was right but the evidence supporting it was merely correlated, not causal. Those cases expose analytical blind spots that simple profit-and-loss accounting would miss.

Dissemination and feedback complete the intelligence cycle. They connect analysis to action, and action back to better analysis. Without dissemination, good research sits forgotten in notes and folders. Without feedback, the same analytical mistakes recur across positions without ever being named. Professional intelligence work treats both as operating essentials. The goal is a research process that improves through repetition, not a pile of disconnected one-off analyses.

Key Takeaways

- ☐ The five-phase intelligence cycle — planning, collection, processing, analysis, and dissemination — is a loop, not a line. Feedback from each phase refines the others. Starting with collection before defining what you need to know is the most common methodological error.
- ☐ Priority intelligence requirements (PIRs) focus your research before you touch a single document. A PIR is a specific, ranked question that drives everything downstream: which sources you consult, which data you process, and what analytical framework you apply.
- ☐ Dissemination is not optional. Intelligence that never reaches a decision point — even if that decision point is your own trade journal — has zero value regardless of its analytical quality. Build the habit of packaging findings into formats you can act on later.

Fieldwork

- ☐ Write three PIRs for a company you are currently evaluating. Frame each as a specific question: "Is the reported 20% revenue growth in Segment X supported by corresponding increases in accounts receivable and cash collections?" not "Is this company growing?" Rank the three by importance to your thesis.
- ☐ Set up a basic dissemination system for yourself. This can be as simple as a folder structure: one folder per company, with subfolders for source documents, analysis notes, and thesis memos. The goal is to ensure that research you do today is retrievable and actionable three months from now.
- ☐ After your next completed analysis of any company, write a one-paragraph thesis memo answering five questions: What is the opportunity? Why does it exist? What evidence supports it? What could prove it wrong? What action follows?

APPLY THIS

Before beginning any new research project, spend ten minutes writing your PIRs. If you cannot articulate what you need to know, you are not ready to start collecting data. The planning phase prevents the most expensive analytical error: gathering everything available without purpose.

CHAPTER 3

Legal and Ethical Foundations

Methodology gives research its structure, but structure alone does not solve the legal and ethical problems that define legitimate investigation. A trader can follow every procedural step correctly and still cross a line by pulling information from the wrong source or failing to keep public and private data streams separate. The point of this chapter is to set the guardrails: to show how research can stay within permissible bounds without giving up analytical rigor.

The legal framework draws a sharp distinction between skilled analysis of public records and improper access to confidential corporate information. That distinction protects market integrity while still leaving room for sophisticated investigative work. Recent cases involving expert networks and mosaic theory defenses show how regulators apply these principles in practice. The ethical dimension goes further. It is not just about compliance. It also covers the professional standards that govern how investigators handle sensitive information and manage conflicts of interest.

These rules define the environment in which financial intelligence operates. They mark the line between fair competition through insight and unfair advantage through access. Knowing where that line runs allows researchers to push their analysis hard without crossing into conduct that will not withstand scrutiny.

Legal Boundaries of Public-Source Research

One trader combines satellite images of retailer parking lots with quarterly sales data from SEC filings and builds a model for forecasting earnings. Another receives a text from a company executive about an upcoming merger before it is announced. The first is operating within the law. The second is not. The difference lies in the source and character of the information, not in the sophistication of the analysis.

The main legal boundary is material non-public information. MNPI is confidential information about a company or a security that has not been released to the market and would likely matter to an investor's decision. The standard for materiality comes from long-standing case law: information is material if a reasonable investor would see it as significantly altering the total mix of available information. Unreleased earnings, pending mergers, major management changes, and significant litigation outcomes all fit the category. Information is non-public when it has not been broadly disseminated through channels such as press releases or SEC filings.

Regulation FD, adopted by the SEC, is meant to prevent selective disclosure. When a company intentionally discloses material information to analysts or other favored parties, it must also disclose that information to the public, either at the same time or promptly afterward. But the rule also protects legitimate research. A company may share non-material pieces of public information without triggering a disclosure obligation, even if an analyst later combines those fragments into a material insight. That protection underlies the mosaic theory of investment research.

Mosaic theory allows an analyst to assemble many small pieces of public information into a conclusion that may itself move the market. A researcher may legally use shipping manifests, job postings, patent filings, and regulatory submissions to forecast a pharmaceutical approval timeline. Each underlying data point is public. The finished insight may be valuable, even highly valuable, but it is not MNPI because it comes from lawful synthesis rather than confidential access. Courts have generally upheld this distinction, protecting diligent public-source analysis while prohibiting trading based on secret corporate knowledge.

The case law matters here. In *Dirks*, the Supreme Court made clear that insider-trading liability depends not just on possession of confidential information, but on a breach of duty by the source and, in many cases, a personal benefit to the tipper. *Newman* reinforced the point that public-source, mosaic-based research does not become unlawful simply because it produces useful conclusions. These decisions are part of what protects analysts who work from public records rather than illicit relationships.

Researchers sometimes become too cautious because they misunderstand this framework. Some assume that any predictive analysis built from public data is legally risky. It is not. The legal question turns on the source of the information, not on whether the conclusion proves accurate or market-moving. The same misunderstanding appears around expert networks. Paying industry specialists for consultations is generally lawful so long as the discussion stays away from confidential company information and remains grounded in public or general industry knowledge. The line is crossed when the expert shares specific non-public facts about an employer or client.

Financial institutions build compliance systems around these risks. Firms maintain watch lists for companies presenting potential information concerns and restricted lists for securities in which trading is prohibited because the firm may hold MNPI. They often impose cooling-off periods after material news becomes public, usually twenty-four to forty-eight hours, to give the market time to absorb it. These controls show how professional firms separate legitimate research from prohibited activity in daily practice.

The law ultimately distinguishes between process and privilege. Sharp analysis of public records helps markets work. Access to confidential corporate information does not. That line protects both fair markets and the legitimacy of serious investigative research.

Material Non-Public Information (MNPI) Risks

A fund-of-funds manager receives a quarterly update from a limited partner. Buried in it is a reference to a portfolio company being in exclusive negotiations to take a public technology firm private. The manager now has material non-public information about that public target. Trading on it would be illegal insider trading, even though the information arrived through an otherwise legitimate business relationship. That is how MNPI exposure often happens: not through an obviously illicit tip, but through ordinary professional channels.

MNPI creates two related risks. The first is legal. The second is reputational. The legal risk comes from insider-trading law. Under the Insider Trading and Securities Fraud Enforcement Act, trading on MNPI is unlawful when the information was obtained through theft, deception, breach of confidentiality, or misuse of a duty. Liability can attach even when a trader chooses not to ask where the information came from or ignores obvious warning signs. The penalties are severe: fines up to five million dollars for individuals and twenty-five million for firms, along with prison terms that can reach twenty years.

Materiality is judged under the substantial likelihood standard. Information is material if a reasonable investor would think it significantly alters the total mix of information available about a security. Regulators do not apply this test mechanically. They look at the full context. Common examples include unreleased sales results, earnings guidance, dividend changes, strategic plans, new product discoveries, senior personnel changes, acquisitions, divestitures, and financing arrangements. Market-moving order flow or large institutional portfolio shifts can also qualify.

One of the most misunderstood issues is timing. Many people assume that once information appears in a press release or an SEC filing, it instantly becomes public for legal purposes. In practice, the standard is broader than formal disclosure. Information is not fully public until it has been widely disseminated through channels available to ordinary investors and the market has had time to absorb it. That creates a gray area. A trade made soon after formal disclosure may still draw scrutiny if the evidence suggests the market had not yet fully processed the news.

Regulation FD speaks directly to selective disclosure. A company cannot intentionally give MNPI to analysts or institutional investors before giving it to the public. If the disclosure is accidental, the company must quickly correct it through a public announcement. At the same time, the rule leaves room for mosaic-style research by allowing companies to discuss non-material public information without automatically triggering broader disclosure obligations.

Private market participants often underestimate how exposed they are. Some assume insider-trading risk is largely a public-market problem. It is not. Limited partner updates, portfolio company communications, and dense industry networks create constant opportunities for accidental MNPI exposure. A venture capital firm that learns the likely timing of a portfolio company's IPO now has material non-public information about that company. Passing that information to other investors or portfolio companies can create liability further down the chain. In private markets, the line between legitimate intelligence and prohibited information can narrow very quickly.

Managing the risk requires structure. Firms use watch lists and restricted lists to block trading when employees may possess MNPI. They impose cooling-off periods after public disclosure. They document where information came from and how it was handled. Independent researchers need the same habits, even if the formal systems are simpler. Source documentation and clear boundaries between research activities are not bureaucratic extras. They are essential safeguards.

The real danger often lies in the chain of custody. Information that originates in a breach of duty can create liability for everyone who handles it, not just the first person to leak it. A trader who gets a tip from a friend who heard it from a corporate lawyer may face the same legal risk as the lawyer. The law cares less about proximity to the source than about whether the information entered the market through wrongful means.

Public vs. Non-Public Information Distinctions

A bank analyst working on a syndicated loan receives detailed financial projections from the borrower. That analyst is on the private side of the firm and is restricted from taking part in certain public-market activities because of that access. Another analyst at the same bank, assigned to the public side, has no access to those projections and can continue working on public issuances. This split shows how firms manage the boundary between public and non-public information in practice: through structure, not just legal definitions.

For information to qualify as material non-public information, both elements must be present. It must be material, meaning it is reasonably likely to affect a security's price or an investor's decision, and it must be non-public, meaning investors cannot lawfully access it through normal channels. Information that has been released but not yet absorbed by the market may still retain a non-public character for practical purposes. Mere early awareness is not enough by itself. A trader who hears about a possible asset sale does not necessarily have MNPI unless wider knowledge of that sale would likely move the company's traded securities.

Information ceases to be non-public only through real dissemination. SEC filings, widely distributed press releases, and public investor calls can all satisfy that requirement, but only if ordinary investors have practical access and enough time to process what has been released. That is why many firms impose internal waiting periods even after formal disclosure. They recognize that publication is not always the same as absorption.

Credit and loan markets use their own language to handle these distinctions. In syndicated lending, lenders often classify themselves as private-side or public-side participants. Private-side lenders accept that they may receive MNPI and agree to trading restrictions. Public-side lenders operate with less information but retain the ability to participate in public markets. Direct lending often uses even stricter categories, such as Borrower Confidential Information, reflecting the closer relationship between lender and borrower and the greater sensitivity of the data.

It also matters to separate material non-public information from non-public personal information. These are different regulatory categories. MNPI governs securities trading and insider-trading risk. Non-public personal information belongs to privacy law and concerns personally identifiable financial data not lawfully available to the public. Financial intelligence work usually focuses on the former, though privacy rules may still shape how individual-level records can be collected and handled.

Private company information adds another layer of difficulty. Private firms do not file with the SEC and often disclose little about their financial condition. Intelligence on them tends to come from secondary channels: news reports, competitor analysis, subscription databases, supplier comments, or litigation records. Much of that information is incomplete, speculative, or wrong. Verification becomes even more important because the absence of official disclosure makes rumor easier to confuse with fact.

Organizations that operate across several business lines need especially strong controls. A firm with both private equity and private credit operations, for example, must prevent one unit from passing sensitive borrower information into another unit that should not have it. Even where the information seems relevant to the business, the firm has to preserve separation or risk creating MNPI exposure across the organization. This is as much an operational problem as a legal one.

Materiality itself is always contextual. Some information may be non-public but too minor to matter. A small operational change may not meet the threshold even if it has not been disclosed. On the other hand, once important information is widely known, its materiality no longer matters for insider-trading purposes because it is no longer non-public. These judgments cannot be reduced to a simple checklist. They require continual assessment.

For practical research, the public/non-public boundary is not experienced as a clean binary. Information moves along a spectrum as it is disclosed, distributed, and absorbed. Enforcement may depend on bright-line distinctions, but day-to-day intelligence work depends on understanding where a particular fact sits along that continuum. Without that judgment, researchers either become so cautious that they paralyze legitimate work or so careless that they drift into prohibited territory.

Ethical Standards for Financial Investigators

A forensic accountant reviewing a company's books for signs of fraud comes under pressure from management to soften the conclusions. The legal rules may define what can and cannot be done. Ethics decides whether the work remains credible. Integrity requires that findings stay free of personal bias, commercial pressure, or fear of consequence. In practice, that means analysis that can survive scrutiny in court, in regulation, and in the market.

Objectivity is one of the core principles. Financial investigators must remain impartial and avoid conflicts that could distort judgment. That obligation goes beyond direct financial interest. It includes personal relationships, internal politics, and pressure from clients or superiors. Regulators are increasingly treating these issues as central rather than incidental. The UK Financial Conduct Authority, for example, has moved toward treating bullying and harassment as misconduct under its conduct rules, reflecting a broader view of fitness and propriety.

Confidentiality is another basic duty. Investigators routinely handle sensitive business information and must protect it except where disclosure is legally required. In the United States, these obligations intersect with SEC Rule 204A-1, which requires supervised persons to avoid using insider information for personal benefit or passing it along for gain. The ethical duty is broader than the legal minimum. It asks the investigator to protect sensitive information even where a disclosure might appear harmless or defensible in a narrow technical sense.

Competence and diligence are just as essential. Professional work has to be thorough, methodical, and honest. SEC-registered investment advisers must take account of a client's objectives and financial condition when giving advice, reflecting fiduciary duties of care and loyalty. In the investigative setting, the parallel obligation is to use methods that are reliable, transparent, and capable of independent verification. An analysis that cannot withstand challenge is not professionally competent, even if it is legally unobjectionable.

Regulatory frameworks give these duties operational form. SEC Rule 204A-1 requires registered investment advisers to adopt codes of ethics addressing standards of conduct, securities-law compliance, personal reporting for access persons, procedures for reporting violations, and distribution of the code itself. In practice, these codes often also deal with relationships involving directors, officers, employees, customers, and suppliers, as well as conflicts implicated by laws such as the Federal Bank Bribery statute.

Whistleblower situations test these standards. An investigator may discover misconduct involving colleagues, clients, or people with whom there are personal ties. Reporting it may be necessary, but so is protecting the whistleblower from retaliation. Professional organizations can help with guidance, but no external code can substitute for a practitioner's willingness to carry ethical obligations into difficult situations.

At the institutional level, ethics has to be made visible. Firms need an environment in which concerns can be raised without fear. Boards and senior managers have to signal clearly that integrity is not optional and that some conflicts or practices are unacceptable regardless of their short-term commercial value. Training helps, but only when it is paired with real accountability and regular reinforcement.

Professional certification bodies take the same view. The CFP Board, for instance, requires practitioners to disclose circumstances in which personal or firm interests may affect recommendations. But disclosure alone is not enough. Conflicts must also be managed appropriately, and serious violations must lead to discipline. That is what gives ethical standards practical force.

Regulators increasingly expect more than box-checking. The FCA's updated conduct code, which will apply to non-banks from September 2026, pushes firms to revise policies, provide role-specific training, and build stronger reporting cultures. Hong Kong's Market Sounding Guidelines reject passive compliance and require active enforcement of ethical standards. Across jurisdictions, the direction is the same. Ethical conduct is being treated less as an administrative burden and more as part of financial stability itself.

Financial intelligence professionals need to understand that ethical standards evolve with regulation and with market practice. The gap between the legal minimum and the ethical best practice is where professional judgment operates. It is also where reputations are built or lost. In that margin, credibility depends not on occasional declarations of principle, but on consistent conduct across difficult cases.

Key Takeaways

- ☐ The legal boundary is material non-public information (MNPI). The legality of your research depends entirely on the source and nature of the information, not on the sophistication of your analysis or the accuracy of your conclusions. Mosaic theory protects the synthesis of public fragments into material insights.
- ☐ Regulation FD prohibits companies from selectively disclosing material information to favored parties. But it explicitly protects legitimate research — companies may share non-material public information without triggering disclosure requirements, even if an analyst later assembles those fragments into something valuable.
- ☐ MNPI exposure often occurs through ordinary channels: LP updates, industry conferences, professional networks. The risk is not limited to dramatic scenarios involving corporate insiders passing tips. Recognizing these everyday exposure points is a practical compliance skill.

Fieldwork

- ☐ Review the compliance section of your own brokerage account agreement. Identify what restrictions, if any, apply to trading based on information you encounter through professional relationships. If you work in finance, confirm whether your firm maintains watch lists or restricted lists.
- ☐ The next time you receive an investment idea from a colleague, friend, or online source, trace the information back to its origin. Can you identify a public source — an SEC filing, a press release, a regulatory database — that independently supports the claim? If you cannot, the information may be closer to the MNPI boundary than it appears.

Apply This

When in doubt about a piece of information, apply two tests. First: Can I point to a public document where this information is available? Second: Did I learn this through lawful aggregation of public sources, or did someone with a duty of confidentiality share it with me? If both answers are clear, proceed. If either is ambiguous, stop and verify before acting.

CHAPTER 4

Public Information Sources and Reliability

Financial intelligence starts with raw information, but the quality of the analysis depends entirely on the quality of the inputs. The task is not just to collect public information. It is to judge it: to weigh reliability, bias, timeliness, and the incentives that shaped it. Government datasets, regulated corporate disclosures, media reporting, and alternative data all belong to the public-information landscape, but they do not deserve the same level of trust or serve the same analytical purpose.

Some sources are foundational. Government statistics and regulatory filings provide formal, structured disclosures produced under legal obligations. Others are indirect. Satellite images of oil-storage facilities can verify supply conditions months before official reports. Geolocation data can show changes in retail foot traffic before a company reports quarterly results. Web scraping and sentiment analysis can surface shifts in market psychology before they appear in price action. These newer sources can add real value, but they have to be judged by different standards.

Good financial intelligence comes from layering sources rather than leaning on one. Professional analysts assess data through practical attributes such as attribution, accuracy, freshness, coverage, and interoperability. They also conduct due diligence on the source itself: who produced the data, under what constraints, and with what incentives. The most durable investment theses come from convergence across the hierarchy, when government statistics, corporate disclosures, and alternative signals point in the same direction despite being produced for different reasons. That kind of layered verification is what separates robust analysis from narratives built on a single point of failure.

Primary Public Data Source Categories

A trader researching a pharmaceutical company can quickly drown in information. The problem is rarely scarcity. It is choosing which sources are likely to produce signal rather than noise. Public data falls into several broad categories, each defined by where it comes from, how reliable it is, and what kind of question it can answer.

Government and economic data provide the base layer for macro analysis. Sources such as Data.gov and Data.gov.uk publish official statistics covering everything from crime and climate to industrial production and employment. The World Bank and the IMF add cross-border economic and financial data, including trade flows, reserves, and growth indicators. These sources are useful because they establish context. They help explain the environment in which a company or sector is operating. Their weakness is often practical rather than conceptual: the data may arrive in clumsy formats and require considerable processing before it becomes analytically useful.

Financial market data serves a different function. It captures prices, volumes, and market behavior rather than underlying economic conditions. Institutional users may rely on platforms such as Bloomberg, but public tools such as Google Finance still provide basic quotes and headline information. The SEC's EDGAR system adds a more important layer by making corporate financial disclosures accessible in structured form. These sources are central to understanding what the market is doing, but by themselves they do not explain why it is doing it.

Specialized financial databases sit somewhere between official data and market feeds. Services such as CEIC compile long historical series across economic, industrial, and financial variables, including deep coverage of countries that are otherwise difficult to analyze. The National Bureau of Economic Research provides another set of economic and industry data with strong historical depth. These databases are especially useful for trend analysis and historical comparison. Their limitation is that they are often slower-moving than markets. Some important series update only annually or with long lags.

Academic and research collections serve another purpose entirely. They are less useful for current positioning than for understanding precedent. Case repositories such as SAGE Business Cases, along with university data guides and financial-resource indexes, help researchers study how similar situations unfolded in the past. They offer frameworks, historical analogies, and context rather than tradable data.

The most effective research does not confuse these categories. It uses them together. Government data defines the macro setting. Market data shows current pricing. Specialized databases reveal patterns over time. Academic resources provide analogs and structure. A trader studying a pharmaceutical company might begin with government drug-approval databases, move into SEC filings to assess the company's financial condition, use specialized databases to understand clinical-trial patterns, and then consult historical case studies of comparable drug launches. That is how a large and disorderly universe of information becomes a usable intelligence picture.

Reliability Hierarchy of Financial Information

Trevor Milton tweets that Nikola has a fully functioning hydrogen truck. Company press releases describe breakthrough technology. SEC filings and independent investigations tell a different story: an inoperable prototype rolled downhill for a promotional video. Three source types, three versions of reality. That pattern is not unusual. Corporate communications can conflict with regulatory disclosures. Alternative data can undermine management guidance. Social media can amplify claims that no primary source supports. The challenge is not gathering information. It is resolving contradiction in a disciplined way.

The basic discipline is triangulation. No material claim should be accepted on the strength of a single source. A company issues a press release announcing record quarterly sales. That is one source. The next step is to check the relevant 10-Q or 10-K and confirm that the revenue appears there in consistent form. Then a third source is needed: shipping data, foot-traffic data, satellite imagery, payment-processor information, or an independent industry report. If all three point in the same direction, confidence rises. If they diverge, the gap itself becomes the story.

RS Metrics used satellite imagery to track Walmart parking-lot traffic from 2011 through 2017. When parking-lot fill rates rose year over year and Walmart's filings showed matching same-store sales growth, the data supported management's account. When parking-lot traffic was flat but the company's public messaging remained upbeat, the mismatch raised a different possibility: that the narrative was stronger than the underlying demand.

Timing is part of source evaluation. Information moves through the system at different speeds. SEC filings appear on regulated schedules. Annual reports on Form 10-K arrive within sixty to ninety days of fiscal year-end, depending on company size. Quarterly reports on Form 10-Q arrive within forty to forty-five days. Material events on Form 8-K are generally due within four business days. Press releases often come out the same day. Social media and news aggregation move instantly, but also with the least built-in verification.

That timing creates a practical workflow. A company posts preliminary revenue guidance on social media. The natural question is whether the same numbers appear in an 8-K within the required window. If they do not, the market has a claim without formal disclosure behind it. Elon Musk's 2018 tweets about taking Tesla private at $420 with "funding secured" are the obvious example. The tweet arrived before any filing. No 8-K followed, because no actual transaction existed in the form the market was led to believe. The SEC's fraud case rested on that gap between social-media claim and regulatory reality.

Each source type also has its own warning signs. In SEC filings, restatements, unexplained auditor changes, going-concern warnings, and growing legal-contingency disclosures all deserve close attention. Nikola's 2020 10-K showed zero revenue despite public demonstrations of supposedly operational vehicles. That discrepancy mattered more than the promotional material. In press releases, warning signs include vague claims without specific metrics, selective presentation of favorable numbers, and suspicious timing, such as dumping bad news late on a Friday or before a holiday. Alternative data has its own failure modes: opaque methodology, undisclosed sampling bias, stale datasets, or commercial ties between the provider and the companies being tracked.

A disciplined workflow uses source-specific checklists. For filings, that may mean examining footnotes, checking whether MD&A language matches the financial statements, and reviewing related-party disclosures. For company communications, it may mean measuring quantitative specificity, comparing new guidance with prior guidance, and watching for changes in tone. For third-party datasets, it means understanding methodology, freshness, independence, and incentives.

Cross-referencing turns isolated facts into intelligence. A retailer claims record holiday sales in a press release. The analyst checks whether the same figure appears in the 10-K or fourth-quarter 10-Q. Then the cash-flow statement: did receivables rise sharply, suggesting the revenue may not be as clean as it appears? Then alternative data: parking-lot traffic, credit-card transaction data, geolocation metrics. Then independent analyst work. When several unrelated sources converge, the story becomes harder to dismiss. When they do not, the pattern of disagreement often shows where the weakness lies. Revenue in a press release but not in the filing may suggest premature recognition. Revenue in the filing but no sign of corresponding real-world activity may point to a more serious problem.

When sources conflict, a ranking system is necessary. Two questions help resolve the conflict: how independent is the source, and how much regulatory accountability attaches to it? SEC filings generally carry the most weight. They are audited, certified by management under Sarbanes-Oxley, and subject to legal liability for material misstatements. Alternative data comes next when the methodology is transparent and the provider is independent. Satellite imagery shows whether parking lots are full regardless of what management says. Credit-card data reflects actual spending patterns, not narrative. Press releases and prepared earnings-call remarks rank lower because they are selective by design and usually unverified by outside parties at the moment they are delivered.

That does not mean filings should be accepted blindly. They should be trusted, but verified. Analysts should look for changes in revenue-recognition policy, shifts in auditor language, unusual related-party transactions, and inconsistencies between narrative sections and the numbers. Corporate communications should be checked against the company's own reporting history. Does management routinely meet its projections, or miss them? Are press-release claims repeated faithfully in later filings, or quietly revised? Alternative data needs its own due diligence. Does the provider explain the sample? Can the collection process be understood? Does the provider have a commercial interest in validating a particular thesis?

The pharmaceutical sector shows why this is important. A biotech company issues a press release touting positive Phase III trial results. The analyst should not stop there. The next steps are to compare the claims with later risk-factor language in SEC filings, check trial-registration data in public FDA databases, and review conference presentations to see whether management introduces caveats outside the headline announcement. The issue is never whether the claim sounds plausible. The issue is whether it survives the trip across source boundaries.

False narratives often spread by replication. One weakly sourced claim appears in an analyst note, a conference remark, or a social post. News aggregators repeat it without independent verification. Social media circulates the headlines. Soon the claim appears to be confirmed by many outlets, when in fact everything traces back to the same original assertion. The only defense is backward tracing. Find the first disclosure. Was there an 8-K with an actual contract attached? Was the claim made only in a conference comment later repeated elsewhere? The Nikola story was a classic cascade. Management claims spread through media coverage and were then treated as though the coverage itself amounted to corroboration.

Professional workflows avoid dependence on any one type of source. They build a portfolio of sources: primary materials such as SEC filings and exhibits, secondary materials such as analyst research and industry reports, and tertiary materials such as media aggregation and sentiment tracking. That mix creates an important diagnostic benefit. If primary sources show weakening fundamentals while secondary and tertiary sources stay upbeat, management may still be controlling the narrative. If the reverse happens, the market may be overreacting or misunderstanding a temporary issue.

Cadence is a factor as well. 10-Qs and 10-Ks are worth checking on their normal schedule. 8-Ks need more frequent monitoring. Alternative data may be reviewed monthly or in line with the underlying business cycle. Social sentiment can be watched more closely, not because it is trustworthy on its own, but because sudden changes in narrative can signal where investigation should begin. This kind of portfolio approach helped identify Wirecard's problems long before its collapse. Press coverage and analyst commentary stayed positive. The filings, cash disclosures, and outside verification did not.

Institutional behavior adds another layer. Form 13F filings show the quarterly holdings of large investment managers. If several sophisticated investors reduce exposure at the same time while public messaging remains positive, that pattern deserves attention. It may reflect better analysis, closer management access, or both. Form 4 filings do something similar for insider activity. When executives sell stock soon after issuing bullish guidance, the behavior may not prove misconduct, but it does test the credibility of the message.

The point of all this is operational. Reliability is not an abstract concept. It is a workflow. Encounter a claim, identify the source type, apply the right verification protocol, cross-reference against independent evidence, resolve conflicts through a ranking system, and only then decide whether the claim belongs in the thesis. No source is perfectly reliable. But several independent sources pointing in the same direction can get close enough.

Government vs. Corporate vs. Media Sources

A Federal Reserve statement moves bonds. A company earnings release lifts a stock. A financial-news story amplifies both. Those three categories of source may all be public, but they are not alike. Each operates under different incentives, different constraints, and different reliability standards. The analyst's job is to understand those differences before assigning weight to any of them.

Government sources are usually the foundation. Agencies such as the SEC and the Federal Reserve produce data and disclosures under legal and procedural rules that require at least some methodological transparency. That gives them an important advantage: the analyst can usually see how the number was produced, what it measures, and what its limitations are. Government data is not infallible, but it is structured, attributable, and governed by formal process.

It is also vulnerable in ways that can be overlooked. Administrative transitions, funding disputes, and political pressure can disrupt access. Federal databases have, at times, reduced indexed content or gone partially dark during periods of transition, only to be restored later by court order or internal review. The SEC's EDGAR system is one of the most important public repositories in finance, but no analyst should assume uninterrupted availability as a matter of course. Critical indicators should always have backup paths for verification.

Corporate sources are more complicated because the category contains very different things. SEC filings are the strongest corporate sources because they are made under legal obligation, often audited, and expose management to liability for misstatement. Investor presentations, conference remarks, and earnings calls are weaker. They can be highly useful, especially for understanding management's framing, but they are selective by nature and are not independently verified in the same way.

Corporate-owned media adds another wrinkle. Many major outlets now sit inside larger multinational companies whose incentives are shaped by profitability, consolidation, and audience demand. That does not make their reporting false. It does mean the analyst has to consider ownership, business model, and editorial incentives as part of source evaluation. Local coverage can become thinner after consolidation. The distinction between editorial judgment and commercial pressure can weaken.

Media sources also reflect audience segmentation. In the United States, media consumption has become sharply polarized, and that affects how financial and economic events are framed. Democratic-leaning audiences tend to consume a broader mix of outlets. Republican-leaning audiences rely more heavily on a narrower cluster of sources, especially Fox News and related properties. Only a small share of outlets enjoy broad trust across both groups. Financial publications such as the *Wall Street Journal*, the *Financial Times*, and *Forbes* tend to perform better than most because their audience is often more cross-pressured and professionally motivated. But even there, framing varies.

That makes bias classification useful. Analysts should know whether a source is broadly ideological, overtly partisan, institutionally centrist, or primarily commercial. Liberal-coded outlets, conservative-coded outlets, and sensationalist outlets all treat the same event differently. Some add more heat than light. For intelligence work, the relevant question is not whether an outlet is biased in a moral sense. It is whether the analyst understands what kind of bias is likely to shape the presentation.

The most useful approach is to assign different roles to each category. Government data establishes a factual baseline. Corporate disclosures provide the company's regulated financial record along with its strategic narrative. Media reporting filters both through editorial judgment, commercial incentives, and audience expectations. Good analysis does not confuse those roles. It triangulates across them. The strongest theses usually appear where official statistics, regulated filings, and several independent media sources all point to the same conclusion despite very different originating incentives.

SEC Filing Types Overview

A company announces a major acquisition in a press release. The regulatory filing describing the same event contains additional financial terms, risk disclosures, and legal detail that never appeared in the public summary. The filing is the version that matters most. SEC filings are the authoritative public record for U.S. public companies, and each form exists for a specific purpose.

Three periodic filings form the core of the reporting system. Form 10-K is the annual report. It provides audited financial statements, management discussion, risk factors, and a broad description of the business. It is usually the single most important document in the company's reporting cycle. Form 10-Q is the quarterly update. It contains unaudited financials, operating commentary, and changes that matter between annual reports. Form 8-K is the immediate event filing. It is used for material developments such as leadership changes, acquisitions, significant agreements, or financial restatements, and is generally due within four business days.

Registration statements sit under a different part of the regime. The Securities Act of 1933 governs securities offerings, which is why forms beginning with "S" are central when companies sell securities to the public. Form S-1 is the standard registration statement for an initial public offering. It lays out the business, the financial condition, the use of proceeds, dilution, and the risks. Form S-3 is a shorter form available only to issuers that meet certain eligibility standards, usually including reporting history and market-float requirements. Form S-4 is used for mergers and acquisitions. Form S-11 is tailored to real estate investment trusts. Foreign private issuers use parallel "F" series forms.

Insider ownership filings serve a different function. Form 3 records the initial holdings of officers, directors, and large shareholders when they become subject to reporting requirements. Form 4 records later transactions in the company's securities. These forms are essential for tracking insider purchases and sales, changes in ownership, and behavior that may support or contradict management messaging.

Other forms handle transitions and administrative issues. Form 10 is used by companies registering under the Securities Exchange Act of 1934 to become reporting companies. Form 12b-25 is the notice of late filing. It gives a company a short extension for a delayed 10-K or 10-Q, provided the company explains the delay and gives an expected filing date. The DEF 14A proxy statement deals with matters submitted to shareholders, including director elections, executive compensation, and other issues raised at the annual meeting.

A common mistake is to treat the glossy annual report sent to shareholders as equivalent to the 10-K. It is not. Companies often produce annual reports that are visually polished and selective in emphasis. The 10-K is the binding disclosure document. Another mistake is to assume that every company uses the same forms in the same way. Eligibility rules apply. A seasoned issuer that qualifies for S-3 has a different filing path than a newly public company. Form choice often signals something about the issuer's status and flexibility.

All of these filings are submitted electronically through EDGAR, the SEC's Electronic Data Gathering, Analysis, and Retrieval system. For practical purposes, it helps to think of the filing system by function. Some forms govern securities registration under the 1933 Act. Others govern ongoing reporting under the 1934 Act. Others reveal insider behavior or handle operational transitions. That functional map makes it easier to find the right document quickly.

The 10-K remains the richest single filing, but no serious analyst stops there. A full understanding of a company comes from knowing how different forms fit together and what each one contributes to the larger corporate record.

International Regulatory Sources

A bank in Singapore tightens its capital position after new guidance influenced by the Basel Committee. A European insurer expands climate-risk disclosure because regional authorities now require it. These are local actions, but the logic behind them is often international. Financial intelligence across borders depends on understanding not just national regulation, but the institutions that shape it upstream.

Global standard setters create the broad rules that domestic regulators later adapt and enforce. The Financial Stability Board coordinates post-crisis financial-stability policy across major jurisdictions. The Bank for International Settlements hosts the Basel Committee, whose capital and supervision standards shape banking regulation around the world. These bodies do not usually enforce rules themselves. Their influence comes from setting the template that national authorities then implement.

Other organizations focus on particular sectors. The International Organization of Securities Commissions sets principles for securities regulation and cross-border supervisory cooperation. The Financial Action Task Force develops anti-money-laundering and counter-terrorist-financing standards that later appear in domestic compliance rules. These bodies produce recommendations, not statutes, but the practical effect can still be significant once those recommendations are adopted into national law or supervisory guidance.

Regional authorities are of consequence because they often turn broad principles into binding technical standards. In the European Union, the European Banking Authority, the European Securities and Markets Authority, and the European Insurance and Occupational Pensions Authority all play that role. Their decisions affect disclosure, conduct, trading rules, prudential requirements, and consumer protection across the bloc. For any company operating in Europe, these are not background institutions. They shape the economics of the business directly.

National regulators then apply international standards through local legal systems, often with important variation. The Australian Prudential Regulation Authority has a reputation for conservatism in supervising banks and insurers. The Monetary Authority of Singapore oversees one of Asia's key financial centers with particular attention to wealth management and fintech. The Hong Kong Monetary Authority operates in a market that remains central to flows between mainland China and global capital. Those local differences are important to note because uneven implementation creates uneven cost, risk, and competitive advantage.

International datasets add another layer. The IMF's World Economic Outlook provides growth forecasts and policy analysis. Its reserves data sheds light on currency composition and balance-sheet trends across central banks. The World Bank's financial-development databases provide long historical series across countries and sectors. These sources are especially useful when the research question is not just about a company, but about the macro and policy environment in which that company operates.

Climate regulation is increasingly part of this picture. Networks such as the Network for Greening the Financial System have brought central banks and supervisors into closer coordination around climate-related financial risk. Databases tracking climate-policy adoption across dozens of countries make it possible to monitor how disclosure rules and supervisory expectations are evolving over time. For analysts covering energy, insurance, banking, or carbon-intensive sectors, this is no longer peripheral.

A common misunderstanding is to treat international regulatory bodies as though they directly impose rules on companies. Usually they do not. Their role is standard setting. The enforcement power sits with national or regional authorities that translate guidance into law, rulemaking, or supervision. But for intelligence work, the upstream bodies still matter because they often signal future regulatory change before it appears in company filings. Watching them closely can reveal compliance costs, strategic pressure, or competitive asymmetry well before the market prices them fully.

Alternative Data Source Introduction

Satellite images of Walmart parking lots showed weakening occupancy before disappointing quarterly sales were reported. Mobile-device location data showed falling Starbucks visits before the slowdown became visible in the financials. This is the promise of alternative data: information generated outside traditional disclosures and market feeds that captures business activity before management reports it formally.

One major category is geolocation and foot-traffic data. Aggregated mobile-device signals can show how consumers move through stores, restaurants, and entertainment venues. That kind of data can reveal market-share shifts or changes in consumer behavior months before earnings calls explain them. Used well, it is a leading indicator. Used badly, it becomes noise. Seasonal effects, regional differences, panel bias, and holiday distortions all have to be normalized before the signals mean much.

Transaction and spending data provides another window. Aggregated credit-card records or point-of-sale data can show changes in consumer spending in near real time. Payment-processor data has been used to estimate restaurant volume, retailer momentum, and same-store sales ahead of company disclosures. Email-receipt scraping has served a similar function in some sectors. These datasets can be powerful, but only when privacy is protected and the sampling methodology is understood.

Then there is what might be called digital exhaust: operational byproducts from devices, platforms, and connected systems. Sensors on oil rigs generate data about drilling activity and equipment use. Container trackers show freight flows across major ports and shipping lanes. App-download data and web-traffic analytics can capture bursts of user interest, as in the dramatic rise in Robinhood downloads during the meme-stock episode. None of this is a financial statement. All of it can become financially relevant once processed properly.

Satellite and geospatial imagery remains one of the clearest examples of alternative data producing hard signals. Imagery firms have tracked production ramps at Tesla's Shanghai factory, monitored parking lots to estimate retail demand, and watched traffic through the Suez Canal to gauge supply-chain pressure. The attraction is obvious: the camera records physical reality whether management wants it seen or not. But interpretation still plays a role. Images are objective; conclusions drawn from them are not always.

Web scraping and sentiment analysis address a different part of the problem. Automated collection of online reviews, job postings, forums, and social-media content can reveal shifts in customer experience, hiring activity, or public mood. Declining sentiment around Boeing's 737 MAX appeared in online discourse before regulatory consequences were fully visible. Social-media monitoring flagged coordinated attention around GameStop before the short squeeze took shape. News analytics turns unstructured text into measurable patterns that can be tracked over time.

It is a mistake to think alternative data belongs only to large quantitative funds. Many useful alternative signals begin in public records that independent researchers can access for little or no cost. Building permits for Amazon warehouses, airline prices scraped from travel sites, vessel movement data, court dockets, procurement notices, and local zoning records can all function as alternative data. The barrier is often not access. It is method.

The alternative-data industry has also expanded rapidly. Commercial vendors now process and license large datasets derived from transactions, geolocation, imagery, and online behavior. Investors who ignore those sources may miss meaningful signals. But that does not make every alternative dataset useful. The analyst still has to ask the same questions as with any other source: Where does the data come from? How is it sampled? How fresh is it? What are the blind spots? What incentives shaped its presentation?

Alternative data works best when it is integrated with traditional analysis rather than treated as a substitute for it. Satellite imagery can support or challenge inventory disclosures buried in a footnote. Payment data can help test the credibility of revenue guidance. Geolocation data can add a real-world check on a management narrative. In that role, alternative data is not exotic. It is simply another layer in the mosaic, one that can turn scattered observation into early, usable intelligence.

Key Takeaways

☐ Not all public sources carry equal weight. The reliability hierarchy runs from primary regulatory filings (highest) through audited financial statements, management commentary, established financial media, down to social media and anonymous sources (lowest). Weighting your evidence by source quality prevents low-reliability data from driving high-stakes conclusions.

☐ Government databases, corporate registries, and regulatory filings form the evidentiary core. Alternative data — satellite imagery, job postings, web traffic — provides supplementary signals that are most valuable when they confirm or contradict what primary sources report.

☐ Source access is not guaranteed. Government databases have experienced access restrictions during political transitions, and corporate registries vary widely in completeness across jurisdictions. Maintaining alternative verification paths for critical data is an operational requirement, not a contingency plan.

Fieldwork

☐ Build a personal source reliability matrix. List every information source you used for your most recent investment decision. Rate each on a 1–5 scale for reliability (1 = anonymous social media, 5 = audited SEC filing). Calculate what percentage of your evidence came from sources rated 3 or below. If the answer is more than half, your thesis rests on a weak evidentiary foundation.

☐ Bookmark the five databases you will use most frequently from Appendix C. For each, spend fifteen minutes navigating the interface, running a test search, and noting any registration requirements or cost structures. Familiarity with these systems before you need them under time pressure is the difference between reactive scrambling and efficient collection.

Apply This

For every factual claim that enters your analysis, note the source tier. When two sources conflict, default to the higher-reliability source unless you have specific reason to believe it is compromised. When a thesis depends primarily on Tier 4 or Tier 5 sources, treat it as a hypothesis requiring confirmation rather than an actionable conclusion.

Part 2

Core Public Data Sources and Regulatory Basics

The SEC filing system is the richest single primary source of corporate intelligence in the world, and most investors never really read it. They read summaries, analyst notes, and earnings recaps—second-order accounts of documents that are freely available and, to anyone who knows how to navigate them, far more revealing than the commentary built on top of them. This section treats the filing system as a primary source: how the major documents are structured, where the real analytical value tends to sit, and what it actually means to read between the lines.

The chapters move from the routine to the unusually revealing: from annual and quarterly reports that establish the baseline, to proxy statements that expose governance and incentives, to beneficial ownership filings that show who actually controls the company, to the IPO registration statement, where companies are forced into a level of candor they will rarely match again. Mastery of these documents is not simply preparation for what follows. It is the evidentiary foundation against which everything else in the public record has to be tested.

CHAPTER 5

SEC Filing Types and Their Importance

The SEC filing system creates a structured, time-stamped record of corporate reality. For financial intelligence work, these documents are the primary source layer. The 10-K provides the full annual view, the 10-Q tracks quarterly movement, the 8-K captures unscheduled material events, and the proxy statement exposes governance, incentives, and internal power. Each serves a different monitoring role inside a continuous stream of disclosure.

Professional analysis does not treat these filings as isolated compliance exercises. It treats them as connected parts of a corporate narrative. Their standardized formats make systematic comparison possible across companies and across time. Their mandatory nature creates a predictable flow of information. The real task is to extract operational intelligence from the structure of each form rather than merely reading for headlines.

10-K Annual Reports: The Comprehensive Picture

A company's glossy annual report to shareholders is a polished narrative. The Form 10-K is the legal record. That distinction matters because the 10-K contains the audited financial statements and required disclosures that form the real foundation of investment analysis. Serious analysts do not skim it. They work through it as a structured dataset.

The document follows a standardized architecture. Part I covers the business, risk factors, and legal proceedings. Part II contains the financial statements and management's discussion. Part III lays out executive compensation and governance. Part IV includes exhibits and schedules. Each section serves a different purpose. Risk factors, for example, can run for dozens of pages in complex companies such as Tesla, covering everything from supply-chain pressure to regulatory exposure. The analytical task is to separate boilerplate language from vulnerabilities that are genuinely specific to the business.

Management's Discussion and Analysis is the center of gravity. This is where management explains the numbers in narrative form, tying financial results to the underlying business. When Microsoft's MD&A discussed Azure margin pressure tied to enterprise licensing deals, it added context that the income statement alone could not provide. The section explains revenue drivers, shifts in cost structure, liquidity pressure, and changes in working capital. It tells you why receivables rose faster than sales or why inventory moved in ways the headline numbers do not explain.

The footnotes are just as significant. They often determine how the headline numbers should be read. This is where companies disclose accounting policies, debt covenants, lease obligations, stock-based compensation, segment reporting, and other details that can materially change the picture. A company may report strong earnings while the notes reveal aggressive revenue recognition, restrictive debt terms, or off-balance-sheet obligations. Tesla's notes, for instance, have included details on warranty accruals and battery-development costs that bear directly on any assessment of profitability.

The textual sections of the 10-K are not decorative. They are often where the most useful signals sit. Analysts increasingly apply textual and sentiment analysis to these sections, looking for patterns in tone, ambiguity, and word choice. A term like "challenge" may read as neutral in ordinary language but carry a negative signal in business disclosure. Changes in language from one filing to the next can reveal shifts in strategic posture, competitive pressure, or management confidence. Research has shown that these linguistic patterns can carry predictive value when tied back to financial metrics.

The numbers alone rarely tell the whole story. More than eighty percent of a typical 10-K is text, and much of that text exists precisely because raw financial statements cannot explain the business on their own. Risk factors change over time. New threats appear. Old ones disappear. Legal proceedings disclose liabilities that may not yet be visible in the financials. Executive-compensation disclosures reveal incentive structures that shape decision-making long before the effects show up in operating results.

The best analysts read the 10-K with a set of concrete questions and cross-reference sections against each other. Does the confidence in the MD&A match the conservatism of the accounting in the notes? Do the risk disclosures fit the business description's account of competitive advantage? Are management's strategic claims consistent with the incentives embedded in compensation? Read that way, the 10-K stops being a compliance document and becomes the most comprehensive single source for judging corporate health.

10-Q Quarterly Reports: Tracking Performance

The 10-K gives the full annual picture. The 10-Q shows the movement between those annual snapshots. It is the form that tracks operating performance and financial condition through interim periods, offering a closer view of business momentum as it develops. The financial statements are unaudited, but the structure is standardized enough to allow consistent quarter-over-quarter comparison.

The filing begins with condensed financial statements: a balance sheet at quarter-end, along with income and cash-flow statements for both the current quarter and the year-to-date period. Amazon's third-quarter filing, for example, showed net sales of $143 billion, up thirteen percent from the prior year. The format places that result beside the comparable prior-year period, making changes in pace visible immediately. The question is never just whether the business grew. It is whether growth is accelerating, flattening, or beginning to break.

The MD&A remains the analytical core here too. In the quarterly filing, management explains what drove material changes in revenue and expense. That may mean higher volume, pricing changes, shifts in mix, increased labor cost, or a swing in marketing spend. Analysts use this section to test whether management's explanation fits the numbers and whether early signs of margin pressure or liquidity strain are beginning to emerge.

The 10-Q also includes sections on market risk and internal controls. The market-risk discussion addresses outside forces such as inflation, competitive conditions, and macroeconomic pressure. The controls-and-procedures section speaks to whether management believes the company still has adequate processes for financial reporting and asset protection. These disclosures help show how management understands the company's vulnerabilities between annual audits.

The 10-Q is not just a shorter 10-K. That is a common mistake. It has a different function. It does not repeat the full business description, the full governance record, or a three-year financial history. Its value lies in incremental change. Another common misunderstanding is that it provides only a point-in-time quarterly figure. In fact, it always presents both the quarter itself and the cumulative year-to-date results, with prior-year comparisons. That dual view makes it possible to track both immediate movement and broader trend.

Professional analysts read sequential 10-Qs as a running stream rather than as individual documents. They track line items over time, watching for receivables rising faster than revenue, inventory building ahead of slowing demand, or margin erosion that management tries to frame as temporary. They also compare narrative against prior narrative. A subtle change in tone, a new emphasis, or the quiet removal of a once-prominent theme can matter as much as the numbers.

There is also a limit to how much assurance the filing provides. Quarterly statements are reviewed under PCAOB standards, but they do not receive the same level of audit scrutiny as annual financials. That means the 10-Q has to be used with some caution. The framework ensures a minimum level of quality, but it does not eliminate the need for corroboration. If the MD&A remains upbeat while cash flow weakens and working-capital strain grows, that tension deserves further investigation.

The best use of 10-Qs is cumulative. Analysts build spreadsheets tracking gross margin, operating cash flow, working-capital ratios, and similar metrics across successive quarters. They annotate management's explanation for each major change, building a chronology of the company's own account of its performance. Over time, that record makes it easier to distinguish a temporary disruption from structural deterioration. The real value of the 10-Q is not in any single filing. It is in the trajectory that appears when several of them are read together.

8-K Current Reports: Material Events

The 10-K and 10-Q provide periodic disclosure. The Form 8-K is what captures the unexpected. It is the SEC's real-time event filing, used to report material developments as they occur. In most cases, companies have four business days from the triggering event, or from the point at which they determine materiality, to file. That deadline makes the 8-K the market's formal alert system for developments that may affect the investment case immediately.

The form is organized around specific reportable events. Item 1.01 covers entry into a material definitive agreement outside the ordinary course of business. A major credit facility, a transformational partnership, or a long-term headquarters lease may fall here. Routine contracts generally do not. The value of the filing is that the underlying agreement is often attached as an exhibit, which means the analyst can see terms and conditions that would never appear in a press release.

Item 2.02 covers public announcements of financial results. These are technically furnished rather than filed, a distinction that matters for certain liability questions. Item 2.06 requires disclosure when the board or a committee concludes that a material impairment charge is necessary. If a company determines that goodwill, securities, or other assets must be written down, that conclusion belongs here unless it will be disclosed in a timely upcoming periodic report.

A newer disclosure item, 1.05, addresses material cybersecurity incidents. The filing clock begins not when the breach is discovered, but when the company determines that the incident is material. The company must describe the likely impact on finances, operations, competition, or legal exposure. Because the full scope of a breach is often unclear at first, initial filings are frequently followed by amendments.

Item 5.02 captures changes involving directors and executive officers, along with material compensatory plans for senior management. A change in CEO, the adoption of a new bonus arrangement, or a revised severance agreement may appear here. These are not minor governance details. They often reveal shifts in control, strategy, or internal stress that will not show up in the numbers until later.

The 8-K reaches far beyond earnings announcements. It covers any development material to operations or financial condition. Some analysts assume cybersecurity incidents are disclosed the moment they are discovered. That is not how the rule works. The trigger is the materiality determination, and that often comes later. Timing applies, and understanding the filing mechanics matters just as much if the goal is to interpret what the filing means.

Subsidiary events can add another layer. If a development at a subsidiary is material to the parent registrant, it can trigger an 8-K even if the parent itself was not directly involved in the underlying transaction. A major contract signed by a foreign subsidiary, for example, may have to be disclosed because of its significance to the consolidated entity.

Analysts use 8-Ks as an early-warning system. A sequence of filings involving executive departures, auditor turnover, impairments, or financing changes often points to trouble before a quarterly report makes it obvious. The exhibits can be especially valuable. Loan agreements, acquisition contracts, and partnership terms often contain the exact financial commitments and operating constraints that corporate press releases gloss over or omit.

The filing deadline also creates a rhythm analysts can exploit. If a company is known to be in negotiations over an acquisition, financing, or litigation settlement, the market expects a filing within the required window if a material event has occurred. If the filing never comes, that absence becomes meaningful. It may suggest the event was not material after all, that negotiations collapsed, or that management has not yet concluded the situation is reportable.

Good 8-K analysis is always comparative. A new credit facility should be read against the latest balance sheet. An impairment should be checked against prior management commentary about the asset's value. A leadership change should be placed against prior performance and compensation disclosures. The 8-K is the record of discontinuity, the point where the company's planned path is interrupted by something the market needs to know now.

Proxy Statements (DEF 14A) and Governance

A company sends shareholders notice of its annual meeting and asks for their vote. The proxy statement, Form DEF 14A, contains the information needed to cast that vote intelligently. It reveals the internal power structure of the company, the incentives paid to management, and the governance arrangements that shape strategic decision-making. It is the formal public record of how the company is governed.

There are two versions. A preliminary proxy, PRE 14A, is often filed first when the matter is contested, as in a merger vote or an activist campaign. That gives the

SEC staff time to review the solicitation materials. The definitive proxy, DEF 14A, is the final version sent to shareholders before the meeting. It is required whenever the company solicits proxies for a shareholder vote, not only for the annual meeting.

Director disclosure is one of the core sections. The proxy lists each nominee's name, age, principal occupation, committee assignments, and qualifications. It also describes whether directors are considered independent under applicable standards. Read closely, this section shows whether the board has real operating expertise, whether it is overly tied to management, and where there may be obvious gaps in competence.

Executive compensation is laid out in much greater detail than most casual readers realize. The Compensation Discussion and Analysis explains the board's rationale for pay, and the summary compensation tables break out salary, bonus, stock awards, option awards, and incentive compensation for the named executive officers. Performance targets tied to compensation are often disclosed as well. These details are noteworthy because compensation systems tell you what management is being paid to optimize.

The proxy also includes the say-on-pay vote, a non-binding advisory vote on executive compensation required under Dodd-Frank. A poor result does not force an immediate change, but it does reveal shareholder dissatisfaction, and boards often respond when opposition is significant. The filing will usually explain how the board has handled any prior say-on-pay result that drew serious resistance.

Shareholder proposals appear here too under Rule 14a-8. Eligible shareholders can submit proposals for inclusion in the company's proxy materials, at the company's expense, so long as the proposal meets the rule's procedural and substantive requirements. Companies can try to exclude proposals by seeking a no-action letter from the SEC. These proposals often address climate risk, political spending, governance reform, or other environmental, social, and governance questions.

Proxy access and universal proxy rules have changed the landscape further. Proxy access allows qualifying shareholders to nominate directors for inclusion in the company's own materials. The universal proxy rule requires all director nominees in a contested election to appear on a single ballot. That has changed the mechanics of proxy fights by making it easier for shareholders to split their vote between management and dissident slates.

Activist campaigns make the proxy statement especially rich. Elliott Management's challenge to Southwest Airlines, for example, used the proxy process to present an alternative slate and argue that the existing board lacked the operational expertise needed to fix performance problems. In these fights, the proxy becomes not just a disclosure document but a direct argument about governance, strategy, and management failure. Even in a contested setting, though, it still includes the ordinary machinery of corporate voting: auditor ratification, say-on-pay, committee oversight, and routine shareholder business.

The proxy is not limited to annual meetings. It is required for any shareholder meeting involving proxy solicitation, including special meetings for mergers or other major corporate actions. Some assume DEF 14A filings are always instantly public in full. In practice, companies can request confidential treatment for certain information, though they must certify that the redacted material is being withheld only for SEC staff review.

The governance sections repay close reading. They describe the board's committee structure, including audit, compensation, and nominating committees, and explain what each is supposed to oversee. They often report director attendance, which can reveal whether the board is actively engaged or merely formal. Related-party transactions are disclosed here as well, showing business dealings between the company and its executives, directors, or family members. If significant conflicts exist, this is often where they first become visible.

Director compensation appears separately, allowing comparison with peers and showing how the company values board service. Excessive pay, unusual equity grants, or weak attendance combined with generous compensation can all raise governance questions.

The most useful way to read proxy statements is comparatively, year over year. Changes in director biographies can signal changing strategic priorities. New compensation metrics show where the board now wants management focused. The disappearance or appearance of shareholder proposals reflects shifting investor pressure. These are developments that never show up cleanly in quarterly financial reports but often tell you as much about a company's future as the financial statements do.

The proxy statement is, in the end, a document about power. It shows how authority is distributed between management and shareholders, how oversight is organized, and whether investors are being given the information they need to vote intelligently. Governance quality, viewed through this lens, is not peripheral. Over time, it is tightly linked to risk management, capital allocation, and corporate performance.

Key Takeaways

- ☐ Four filing types form the backbone of U.S. public-company intelligence: the 10-K (annual, audited, comprehensive), the 10-Q (quarterly, unaudited, incremental), the 8-K (event-driven, real-time), and the DEF 14A proxy statement (governance, compensation, voting).
- ☐ The 10-K's value lives primarily in its text, not its tables. More than 80% of a typical 10-K is narrative — risk factors, MD&A, footnotes, legal proceedings — and that narrative is where management's actual concerns, accounting choices, and strategic shifts become visible.
- ☐ The 8-K is the closest thing to a real-time intelligence feed in the regulatory system. It covers material events — mergers, executive departures, cybersecurity incidents — filed within four business days. The trigger is materiality, not discovery, which means the filing date and the event date are often not the same.

Fieldwork

- ☐ Pull the most recent 10-K for a company you follow. Before reading, write down three questions you want answered. Then read only the sections relevant to those questions: MD&A for operational context, risk factors for threats, footnotes for accounting detail. Time yourself. The goal is targeted extraction, not cover-to-cover reading.
- ☐ Set up EDGAR email alerts for one company using its CIK number. Monitor for two weeks. Note which filing types arrive and how quickly you can assess whether each requires immediate attention or routine review.
- ☐ Compare the 8-K filing date and the event date for any recent material announcement by a company on your watchlist. The gap between the two tells you how quickly management disclosed the event — and whether the market had already reacted before the filing appeared.

Apply This

Signals to watch for in filings: changes in revenue recognition policy between consecutive 10-Ks, new risk factors that did not exist in the prior year's filing, going-concern language in the auditor's report, and 8-K filings for executive departures that cite vague reasons like "to pursue other opportunities" without naming a successor.

CHAPTER 6

IPO Registration Statement Analysis

A company files its initial registration statement on a Tuesday afternoon. By Wednesday morning, anyone with an internet connection can read what the business has avoided saying publicly for years: which customers it depends on, how much debt it carries, how management has been paid, and which risks the company itself believes could damage or destroy the enterprise.

No later filing is usually this candid. After the company has traded through a few quarterly cycles, the sharpest disclosures begin to soften. The most uncomfortable details migrate into boilerplate, and the unusual precision of the S-1 starts to fade.

Most investors treat IPO documents as sales material. That is a mistake. The registration statement is a legal filing prepared under Section 11 liability, which means material misstatements or omissions create civil exposure for the company, its officers, and its underwriters.

That liability changes the document. Management cannot omit inconvenient facts as casually as it can on an earnings call. The Securities Act of 1933 imposes a level of disclosure discipline that the periodic reporting system under the 1934 Act, once the company is public, rarely replicates in quite the same way.

That is the central analytical point. The S-1 is the most constrained disclosure a company will ever make, and if it is read with the right questions, promotional language gives way to usable intelligence.

This chapter maps the structure of the registration statement, identifies the sections where the real intelligence tends to concentrate, and lays out a repeatable workflow for extracting it. It covers the filing sequence from the initial S-1 through later amendments and the final 424B4 prospectus, the red flags that have repeatedly appeared ahead of post-IPO disappointments, and the monitoring routine that links pre-IPO work to post-listing position management.

The Registration Statement Family

The Securities Act separates the registration of securities from the ongoing reporting regime that follows a public listing. A company that wants to raise capital from the public must first register those securities, and the forms used for that process are different from the 10-K and 10-Q system that governs disclosure after trading begins.

Form S-1 is the standard registration statement for domestic issuers. It applies to companies that do not qualify for shorter forms and remains the primary vehicle for most initial public offerings. Foreign private issuers use Form F-1, which follows the same basic structure but allows financial statements prepared under International Financial Reporting Standards rather than U.S. GAAP.

From an analytical standpoint, the difference matters less than it may appear. The accounting conventions may vary, but the reading method does not. The same sections carry the same kinds of intelligence.

SPACs also file on Form S-1, but the substance is different. A SPAC prospectus is not the registration statement of an operating business with revenue, products, and customers. It is the prospectus of a blank-check vehicle looking for a target, and it should not be read as the kind of IPO document this chapter addresses.

Amendments appear as S-1/A or F-1/A and are both routine and important. The first filing is rarely the last. Companies revise these documents to respond to SEC comment letters, update financial statements as time passes, and adjust offering terms as roadshow demand becomes clearer.

The price range usually first appears in an amendment filed roughly one to two weeks before pricing. That moment matters because it is the first formal indication of what the stock may actually cost. A company that cuts its price range or reduces the size of the offering late in the process is conveying something about demand that the original filing could not yet show.

The 424B4 is the final prospectus filed after pricing. It is the definitive record. It contains the actual offering price, the exact share count, the final net proceeds, and the final split between primary shares, which raise new capital for the company, and secondary shares, which allow existing holders to sell.

That final prospectus is the document against which later performance should be measured. All of these filings are submitted through EDGAR and become public the moment they are filed. The full sequence is visible to anyone willing to compare the documents line by line.

Mapping the Document's Architecture

A registration statement follows a standard structure, but the sections are not equally useful. Some exist mainly to satisfy formal disclosure requirements. Others are where the real intelligence is concentrated.

The Prospectus Summary opens the filing and is usually the most promotional part of the document. It contains the company's self-description, its selected metrics, and the growth narrative management wants investors to absorb first. It should be read, but not trusted on its own.

The better move is to treat the summary as a list of claims to be tested. If management highlights revenue growth, customer count, gross margin, or market opportunity here, those claims should be checked against the financials and note disclosures later in the filing. The first meaningful red flags often appear in the gap between the summary and the underlying numbers.

The Risk Factors section is where the document starts to become genuinely valuable. SEC rules require risks to be company-specific rather than generic, and that requirement often produces more candor than will appear in the company's first several earnings calls. If a company discloses that one customer accounts for forty percent of revenue, that is not background noise. It is a material dependency that may be hard to detect anywhere else.

The useful way to read risk factors is to sort them into three groups. Some are boilerplate and appear in every filing in the sector. Some are genuinely specific to the company. Others are structural risks built into the business model itself and unlikely to fade with time.

Those structural risks matter most. A platform with permanent customer concentration, a manufacturer dependent on one supplier, or a software company whose sales efficiency is tied to unusually high stock-based compensation is not describing a temporary problem. It is describing part of the underlying economics of the business.

The Use of Proceeds section deserves more attention than it usually gets. Companies often say proceeds will be used for "general corporate purposes and working capital," which is informative mainly in its vagueness. More specific disclosures—debt repayment, plant expansion, acquisitions, or technology investment—are easier to test.

The comparison to make is between the proposed use of proceeds and the capital history disclosed elsewhere in the filing. If management says the offering will finance a major manufacturing build-out but historical capex has been minimal, the question is no longer whether the plan sounds appealing. It is whether the company has shown any sign that it can execute the plan it is now funding.

The Dilution section is often dismissed as mechanical. It should not be. It shows book value per share before and after the offering and usually includes a table laying out shares by class, options, restricted stock units, warrants, and other claims on equity.

That table is, in effect, the pre-IPO cap table made public. It shows how much control founders, venture investors, management, and other holders will retain after the offering. A founder group retaining sixty percent of the equity creates one set of governance dynamics; a heavily distributed structure creates another.

The conversion of preferred stock into common at IPO can also create dilution patterns that are not obvious from the headline share count. A company may look less diluted than it really is if the analyst focuses only on currently outstanding common shares rather than on the full equity stack being converted.

Management's Discussion and Analysis covers the company's disclosed financial history, usually two or three fiscal years plus interim periods. This is where the real operating picture emerges. Revenue growth, gross-margin direction, operating-expense growth, cash burn, working-capital pressure, and whatever unit economics the company discloses can all be traced here.

Pre-IPO companies often rely heavily on non-GAAP measures such as adjusted EBITDA, contribution margin, customer acquisition cost, or lifetime value.

Some of these metrics are useful. Some are designed to produce the most favorable possible picture of the business.

The test is whether the non-GAAP story survives contact with the standard financial statements. The MD&A is the first place where that comparison becomes possible.

The Principal and Selling Shareholders section is one of the most important in the filing. It shows exactly who is selling into the offering and in what quantity. Some selling by early investors or employees is normal. Heavy selling by senior management, especially the CEO or CFO, deserves a different level of attention.

Pre-IPO Financial Analysis

The financial history in a registration statement is often the first time the market gets to see the business as a set of actual operating numbers rather than as a venture-capital story. Two or three years of audited statements are usually enough to establish whether the trend is improving, deteriorating, or simply not as strong as the summary implies.

Revenue growth is the most visible number, but it is not the most informative on its own. The better question is whether growth is becoming more efficient as the company scales. One useful test compares revenue growth to the growth in total operating expense.

A company growing revenue at fifty percent while operating expense rises seventy percent may still be gaining share. But it is doing so with worsening leverage, and that raises doubts about how quickly, or whether, profitability can emerge.

Gross-margin history is equally important because it reveals the economics of the core product. If gross margin is declining before the stock has even begun trading, the business may be more competitive, more capital-intensive, or less scalable than the prospectus narrative suggests. That is often visible well before management will ever describe it that way.

Robinhood's S-1 is a useful example of this principle. The filing made clear that payment for order flow was the dominant revenue source, which clarified the business model in a way the company's branding had consistently softened. That is the standard to apply to all pre-IPO financials: do the disclosed economics support the narrative, or do they quietly contradict it?

Cash burn and cash runway are existential measures for companies that are not yet profitable. The analyst can calculate both directly from the balance sheet and cash flow statement. The question is not simply whether the company is losing money, but how long it can continue doing so under its current trajectory.

If the numbers suggest the company will need another capital raise within twelve to eighteen months, the IPO is not solving the financing problem. It is postponing it. The current offering is then better understood as one step in an ongoing dilution cycle rather than as the capital event that gets the business to sustainability.

Related-party transactions require their own pass. Pre-public companies often do business with entities tied to founders, directors, or major investors. Many of those arrangements are ordinary and temporary. Some are not.

The key question is whether the same deal could plausibly have been done with an unrelated counterparty on similar terms. If the answer is clearly no, then the public market is inheriting a structure that transfers value to insiders in a way that may not persist under full market scrutiny.

Amendment Monitoring and Price Discovery

The registration statement changes between the initial filing and pricing, and those changes carry intelligence about how the process is unfolding. The S-1 should be read as a sequence, not as a single static document.

Early amendments usually respond to SEC staff comments. Those comment letters are not public during the live offering process, but they typically appear on EDGAR about twenty business days after the review process ends. That often means the first round of SEC questions becomes visible within weeks of the company's listing.

Those comment letters are worth reading. They reveal which parts of the filing the SEC found unclear, incomplete, or potentially misleading. In effect, they show where the regulator itself applied pressure to the company's story.

Later amendments reveal something different: demand. A company that initially indicates a price range of twenty-four to twenty-six dollars, later cuts it to twenty-two to twenty-four, and then prices at twenty-two is describing investor appetite with unusual precision. That information is fully recoverable from EDGAR just by comparing the amendment sequence.

A company that raises its range late in the process is showing strength. A company that lowers its range, cuts its share count, or adjusts terms defensively is showing the opposite. The language of the prospectus may remain upbeat, but the amendment trail is often more honest than the prose.

The secondary component should also be tracked from version to version. If selling shareholders reduce the number of shares they plan to sell late in the process, one possible reading is that they are responding to investor discomfort with insider liquidity. Another is that the market would not absorb the original level of selling without penalizing the deal.

Either way, the message is not reassuring. The insider selling pressure has not disappeared. It has simply been pushed forward, often toward the lock-up expiration.

The 424B4: The Final Record

The final prospectus is the document against which the company's first year as a public company should be judged. It contains the exact offering price, the definitive share count, the final use-of-proceeds figures, and the real allocation between new money for the company and secondary selling by existing holders.

It also states the lock-up terms precisely. Lock-up agreements prohibit insiders from selling for a fixed period after the IPO, usually ninety to one hundred eighty days. That makes the expiration date a known future catalyst from the moment the stock is priced.

If insiders hold large stakes and the stock has traded above the offering price, lock-up expiration creates a predictable window of possible selling pressure. That date can be calendared immediately from the 424B4, and it should be. The analyst does not need to guess when the market may face insider supply. The prospectus provides the date.

Some investors treat lock-up expiration as an automatic short. That is too mechanical. Many management teams do not sell the first day they are allowed to, even when the stock is well above the IPO price.

The better approach is to compare the expectation set by the prospectus with the behavior revealed later in Form 4 filings. Who sold, how much, and how quickly after the restriction lifted? Taken together with the company's first few quarters as a public issuer, that behavior starts to show whether the IPO story rested on something durable.

Red Flags in Registration Statements

The S-1 is the fullest disclosure most companies will ever make, but the warning signs are not always easy to read at first glance. Certain patterns recur ahead of post-IPO underperformance, and they tend to appear in the same places.

Heavy insider selling at IPO is one of the clearest. Founders and venture investors do sell for legitimate reasons, including diversification and fund-life pressure. But when senior management is selling a large fraction of personal holdings while simultaneously marketing the stock as a long-term compounder, the behavior and the message do not sit comfortably together.

Aggressive revenue recognition deserves attention in any filing where top-line growth is the central selling point. The accounting policy note will explain how revenue is recognized, and some policies create much more room for judgment than others. Percentage-of-completion accounting, milestone recognition, and complex bundled arrangements all widen management discretion.

When rapid growth is paired with complicated revenue recognition, the next step is to test the story against receivables growth, cash collection, and the relationship between bookings and recognized revenue, where bookings are disclosed. The more complex the recognition policy, the more corroboration is needed elsewhere.

Non-GAAP metrics are common in IPO filings, especially for companies that are still unprofitable. Some are analytically useful and help describe the economics of the business at scale. Others are signs of a presentation problem.

The red flags are familiar. Adjustments that grow over time as a share of total expense are one. Stock-based compensation presented as though it were incidental, when it is clearly recurrent and operational, is another. A path to GAAP profitability that depends on assumptions the disclosed operating history does not support is a third.

Customer concentration often appears more clearly in risk factors than in the tabular revenue disclosures. A company that admits one customer accounts for twenty-two percent of revenue and says the relationship is under renegotiation is telling investors that more than a fifth of the revenue base is exposed. The fact that the customer may not be named does not make the signal any weaker.

Related-party revenue should always be reviewed when a meaningful share of revenue comes from entities tied to insiders, directors, or major investors. Palantir's S-1, for example, disclosed an equity investment program involving certain customers, which created a relationship in which investment and revenue were intertwined. The structure was disclosed, but the revenue quality was harder to assess cleanly because of it.

The broader lesson is that related-party arrangements often require a slower read than the rest of the filing. They are easy to overlook and rarely look alarming in isolation. Once they are mapped systematically, they can change the entire quality assessment of the revenue base.

Connecting the S-1 to Post-IPO Research

The registration statement is not the end of the analysis. It is the baseline against which the next phase of the company's public life should be measured.

The first Form 10-K after the IPO usually contains the same financial history as the S-1, updated through the first full year of public operation. Comparing that filing directly to the assumptions and narrative in the registration statement reveals whether the company is tracking against the story it sold to the market. Growth, margin, concentration, and capital use all become testable in a way they were not at pricing.

Form 4 filings start accumulating as soon as officers and directors become reporting persons. Building a Form 4 timeline from the IPO date through the lock-up expiration creates a clear view of insider behavior. A CEO who exercises and holds is sending a different signal from one who immediately liquidates into strength.

Those signals are significant because they test the alignment implied by the prospectus. Investor-relations language rarely acknowledges what insider behavior makes plain. The forms do.

The first quarterly earnings call is also a research event. By then, management knows whether the business has tracked the assumptions embedded in the offering narrative. Comparing what is said about customer growth, margin direction, and revenue trajectory with what was emphasized in the S-1 can be more revealing than the reported numbers alone.

Omission carries weight here. If the S-1 highlighted bookings growth as a core performance measure and the first earnings call avoids bookings entirely, that is not a stylistic choice. It is information.

A workable monitoring plan for any IPO position should include a calendar alert for lock-up expiration, EDGAR alerts for Form 4 filings by key insiders, a comparison of the first two quarterly reports against the S-1 baseline, and a review of the SEC comment letter once it appears on EDGAR. Setting that up takes little time at the beginning and turns a one-time document review into a continuing intelligence process.

Key Takeaways

- ☐ The registration statement is the most constrained disclosure a company will ever make. Section 11 of the Securities Act creates civil liability for material misstatements and omissions, which forces a level of candor that routine periodic filings do not require. The S-1 often contains the most operationally specific risk disclosures the company will ever publish — read them before the offering narrative.
- ☐ The three sections that carry the most intelligence are the Risk Factors (genuine operational risk, not boilerplate), the Principal and Selling Shareholders table (insider selling behavior at the IPO price), and the footnotes to the financial statements (accounting policy, revenue recognition, related-party transactions). Most market participants read the Prospectus Summary and skip the rest. That is where the edge lives.
- ☐ Amendments tell the roadshow story in real time. A price range reduction, a shrinking offering size, or a reduction in secondary shares mid-process all communicate institutional demand signals that the company will never state directly. Those signals are recoverable in full from EDGAR by comparing amendment filings chronologically.
- ☐ The registration statement is a baseline, not a conclusion. Its value compounds when the first one to two years of post-IPO filings, Form 4 activity, and earnings-call language are read against the original S-1 claims. The gap between what management promised before listing and what the company delivered is where the most durable IPO research insight lives.

Fieldwork

- ☐ Pull the S-1 or F-1 for any company that has had its IPO in the past eighteen months. Read the Prospectus Summary and list every quantitative claim management makes about its business. Then locate each claim in the financial statements or footnotes. Note how many are verifiable, how many are vague, and how many cannot be found in the audited numbers at all. That gap is your first analytical output.

- ☐ Using EDGAR's full-text search system (efts.sec.gov), retrieve all amendments filed after the initial S-1 and track the price range across each one. Then find the 424B4 and compare the final offering price to the original range. Research the company's stock performance in the six months following the IPO. Ask whether the price discovery process across the amendments predicted anything about the post-listing trajectory.
- ☐ For any IPO company you are analyzing, calculate the lock-up expiration date from the 424B4 and set a calendar reminder. On the day after expiration, pull all Form 4 filings by insiders for the subsequent thirty days. Compare the pattern of selling to the stock's performance over the same window and to management's most recent public commentary about the business.

Apply This

When beginning any IPO analysis, read the Risk Factors section before the Prospectus Summary. The risk factors were written under legal obligation. The summary was written for marketing. Once you have identified the three most material company-specific risks from that section, ask: are these risks quantified anywhere in the financial statements? If they are, how does the financial history suggest the company is managing them? If they are not quantified, your first research task is to find an independent source that can put a number on the exposure. An IPO thesis built on the summary and not tested against the risk factors is a narrative, not an analysis.

CHAPTER 7

Regulatory Disclosure Workflows

A trader notices unusual volume in a mid-cap industrial stock. The price rises five percent on no apparent news. A check of recent SEC filings turns up nothing. The trader can dismiss the move as noise or begin a disciplined search through regulatory disclosures that might explain it. That choice marks the line between casual market observation and professional financial intelligence.

Regulatory filings are the structured backbone of public-market information, but they become valuable only when used through systematic workflows. These documents contain mandatory disclosures about ownership changes, corporate actions, and financial performance. Most market participants treat them as compliance artifacts, not intelligence sources. A professional workflow turns filing databases into early-warning systems.

Three disclosure categories matter here, each illuminating a different part of market behavior. Each demands its own search methods and analytical discipline. The workflows connect separate filings into coherent narratives about ownership shifts, institutional positioning, and contests for corporate control. In markets where information asymmetry creates opportunity, command of these systems offers a structural edge.

EDGAR Navigation and Search Techniques

A financial analyst needs to track recent merger announcements across the technology sector. Typing "merger" into EDGAR's search bar produces thousands of irrelevant results stretching back decades. The problem is not the database. It is the search method. Effective use of the SEC's Electronic Data Gathering, Analysis, and Retrieval system begins when the analyst stops treating it as a keyword search engine and starts using structured queries to cut noise and isolate precise information.

The Central Index Key is the foundation. Every SEC filer receives a unique CIK number that remains constant even if the company changes its name or ticker symbol. A search for "Apple" may return filings from Apple Inc., Apple REIT, and Apple Bancorp. A search by CIK 320193 returns only filings from Apple Inc. That level of precision is important when a company has a common name or when the research requires following a business through acquisitions and spinoffs. The CIK appears in every filing header and remains the most reliable way to isolate a single entity's complete regulatory history.

Form-type filtering adds the next level of precision. Each SEC filing serves a distinct regulatory purpose, so a serious search targets specific forms rather than all documents at once. A search for "10-K" returns annual reports with audited financial statements. Adding "8-K" captures current reports for material events such as mergers or executive changes. The suffix "/A" marks an amendment, so "10-K/A" identifies corrected annual reports. Form filters are most useful when paired with date ranges, which let the analyst focus on a specific reporting period rather than a company's entire filing history. The SEC sets different filing deadlines by company size, with accelerated filers submitting 10-K reports within 75 days of fiscal year-end and smaller companies receiving up to 90 days.

Boolean operators turn a basic search into targeted collection. EDGAR's full-text search supports standard logical operators, though it uses an implied AND between terms by default. A search for "cybersecurity breach" finds documents containing both words somewhere in the text. OR broadens the search. NOT removes unwanted results. Parentheses control the order of evaluation in more complex queries. Proximity operators such as NEAR() locate terms within a specified word distance, which is useful when related concepts tend to appear together in particular sections of a filing. Quotation marks force exact-phrase searches and are essential when the analyst is looking for standardized disclosure language.

Field-specific searches target metadata in filing headers. These searches use colon notation to filter by attributes such as company name, state of incorporation, or Standard Industrial Classification code. A query like "STATE-OF-INCORPORATION=DE AND FORM-TYPE=S-4" returns merger registration statements filed by Delaware-incorporated companies. EDGAR's historical archives preserve these header fields even for filings that predate full-text search, which allows researchers to locate documents by metadata rather than by content alone.

Date filtering works on filing dates, not on the reporting periods covered by the documents. That distinction is consequential because companies often file quarterly reports weeks after a quarter has closed. A filter covering the first week after quarter-end captures the earliest filers and can reveal which companies report quickly and which need more time to prepare results. The SEC's real-time filing system accepts submissions until 5:30 p.m. Eastern Time on business days. Filings received after that deadline appear the following morning.

Experienced practitioners combine these tools into search strings built around a defined intelligence requirement. A query such as "formType:'8-K' AND item:2.02 AND filing-date:[20250101 TO 20250331]" returns first-quarter earnings announcements filed on Form 8-K. Adding "ticker:(AAPL, MSFT, GOOGL)" narrows the results to selected technology companies. A structured search like this replaces hours of manual review with minutes of targeted analysis.

The most common mistake is to treat EDGAR as a document warehouse instead of a structured database with searchable fields and logical operators. A professional workflow starts with collection planning: which forms matter, which dates matter, which companies matter. Only then does the analyst translate those requirements into search syntax designed to eliminate irrelevant results while capturing the disclosures that count.

13D and 13G Beneficial Ownership Filings

A hedge fund accumulates seven percent of a mid-cap technology company's shares. The market remains unaware until the fund files a regulatory document disclosing its position and intentions. That disclosure appears on Schedule 13D or the shorter Schedule 13G, depending on the investor's relationship to the company. These filings are the earliest public signal of major ownership changes and potential control contests. They are required under Section 13(d) of the Securities Exchange Act once any person or group acquires beneficial ownership of more than five percent of a class of equity securities registered under Section 12.

The line between 13D and 13G is drawn by intent, not ownership percentage alone. Schedule 13D applies when an investor acquires shares with the purpose or effect of influencing control of the issuer. That includes activist investors seeking board seats, strategic acquirers considering a deal, or shareholders planning major corporate changes. The filing requires detailed disclosure about the investor's background, source of funds, and plans for the company. Schedule 13G is the abbreviated alternative for passive investors who cross the five percent threshold without seeking to influence management. Qualified institutional investors, including banks, insurance companies, and registered investment advisers, usually file 13G unless their intentions become activist.

Beneficial ownership reaches beyond direct registration of shares. The concept turns on voting power or investment power, not formal legal title. An investor is a beneficial owner if it can vote the shares or direct their disposition, even when another entity holds the shares of record. That includes shares held through derivatives such as total return swaps, options exercisable within sixty days, or securities convertible into common stock. Recent regulatory amendments also require 13D filers to disclose all security-based swaps and other derivatives that reference the issuer's equity securities. The definition is designed to capture economic exposure as well as formal ownership and to prevent investors from concealing influence through more complicated instruments.

Filing deadlines create real information advantages for anyone watching regulatory feeds closely. Under current rules, Schedule 13D must be filed within five business days after an investor crosses the five percent threshold. Amendments are due within two business days after any material change in the facts disclosed in the original filing. Schedule 13G follows a different timetable depending on the filer. Qualified institutional investors must file within forty-five days after the calendar quarter in which they exceed five percent ownership. If their ownership rises above ten percent, they must file within five business days after month-end. Because of these staggered deadlines, market-moving ownership changes can remain hidden for weeks.

A shift from passive to active status triggers immediate disclosure obligations. An investor already filing Schedule 13G must switch to Schedule 13D within five business days once its intent changes from passive to activist. The same switch becomes mandatory if passive ownership reaches twenty percent, regardless of stated intent. That conversion signals a meaningful change in shareholder posture and often appears before proxy contests, takeover efforts, or major governance fights. Watching for these switches can provide early warning of corporate action before it surfaces elsewhere.

Several mistakes recur around these filings. Some investors assume they need not file if the shares are held in street name by a broker. They are wrong. In that arrangement, a brokerage firm or nominee such as Cede & Co. appears as the legal owner on the company's books, while the investor retains the economic rights. That does not remove the reporting obligation. The beneficial ownership test applies regardless of record ownership. Others wrongly assume that preexisting shareholders escape filing duties when a company completes its initial public offering. Pre-IPO shareholders who owned more than five percent before registration typically file Schedule 13G within forty-five days after the IPO, not Schedule 13D, unless they acquired additional shares after the company became subject to Section 12 reporting requirements.

The intelligence value lies largely in the purpose section of Schedule 13D. That narrative disclosure sets out the investor's plans, which may range from generic language about monitoring the investment to explicit proposals involving mergers, asset sales, or dividend changes. Changes in wording from one filing to the next often matter as much as the original filing itself. An investor who first says the shares are held for investment purposes and later adds language about strategic alternatives has materially altered its posture. When those disclosures are cross-referenced with insider trading reports and options activity, they can reveal coordinated movement before a major corporate announcement.

Recent rule changes have standardized filing formats to make them easier to read by machine. Both 13D and 13G filings now include structured data elements that allow automated systems to monitor ownership changes across thousands of companies at once. That reduces the burden of manual review and speeds the delivery of ownership intelligence to decision-makers. The standardized format also supports historical analysis of the ownership patterns that precede specific corporate events, making it possible to build predictive models based on filing characteristics rather than ownership percentages alone.

The most advanced use of these filings goes further than tracking individual positions. It looks for ownership clusters across multiple filers. When several investment firms accumulate positions in the same company at roughly the same time, their combined ownership may trigger group filing obligations if they appear to be acting together. Such coordinated accumulation often comes before activist campaigns, even when each firm remains below the reporting threshold on its own. Mapping the relationships among filing entities—through shared investment managers, overlapping board seats, or prior patterns of collaboration—can expose informal alliances that shape control battles long before any formal proxy materials are filed.

13F Institutional Holdings Reports

A hedge fund manager wants to understand why a competitor outperformed the market by fifteen percent in the last quarter. The manager cannot see the competitor's private trading records. What is available is the competitor's quarterly Form 13F filing, which shows a concentrated position in semiconductor stocks established three months earlier. The disclosure is delayed, but authoritative. It offers a public window into institutional positioning across U.S. equity markets. Form 13F is the mandatory quarterly report filed by institutional investment managers that exercise discretion over at least one hundred million dollars in Section 13(f) securities.

The filing threshold acts as a natural screen for significant market participants. Institutional investment managers include registered investment advisers, banks, insurance companies, broker-dealers, pension funds, and corporations managing their own accounts. Natural persons also qualify if they exercise investment discretion over accounts they do not own. The one-hundred-million-dollar threshold is measured by the aggregate fair market value of Section 13(f) securities on the last trading day of any month. Once a manager crosses it, the filing obligation applies for that quarter and continues in subsequent quarters until the manager falls back below the threshold.

Section 13(f) securities are a defined subset of publicly traded instruments. They include exchange-listed equities, certain equity options and warrants, shares of closed-end investment companies, and some convertible debt securities. They do not include open-end mutual funds, unlisted foreign securities, or securities of issuers controlled by the filing manager. That limitation is important to keep in mind. Form 13F captures only part of an institution's portfolio, focused on U.S.-listed equities where the regulatory system demands transparency.

Each filing is a quarter-end snapshot. It identifies the manager and, for each reported holding, lists the issuer name, security class, CUSIP number, number of shares or principal amount, and fair market value at quarter-end. Securities are listed alphabetically by issuer, which creates a standardized format for comparing managers. The filing is due forty-five days after the end of each calendar quarter, which leaves a substantial lag between the portfolio snapshot and the moment the market can see it.

The analytical value comes from patterns across multiple filings, not from isolated reactions to one report. A professional framework moves beyond simple holdings comparison and tries to identify conviction, crowding, and thematic change. One method estimates portfolio turnover by comparing quarter-over-quarter changes in positions. Another measures active share, showing how far a portfolio departs from its benchmark. These metrics help distinguish performance driven by real differentiation from performance that mostly reflects market exposure.

Convergence analysis strengthens the signal when 13F data is paired with faster-moving indicators. If several well-regarded institutions establish new positions in the same sector during the same quarter, the pattern carries more weight than any single filing on its own. Cross-referencing those positions with insider trading reports, options activity, and management commentary creates a broader picture of conviction. The method is especially useful when the institutions involved have long time horizons and low turnover but are making concentrated bets.

Crowding detection is one of the most important risk-management uses of 13F data. By aggregating holdings across hundreds of institutional managers, analysts can identify stocks where concentrated ownership creates systemic vulnerability. A security held by an unusually high percentage of reporting institutions is more exposed to sharp moves during periods of stress. Historical analysis shows that when more than thirty percent of reporting institutions hold the same security, the crowded trade often suffers steep drawdowns during coordinated unwinds.

The meme-stock episodes offer a recent example of how 13F data interacts with retail-driven price action. In those cases, social-media amplification helped drive extreme volatility in heavily shorted names, and institutional investors often appeared in the subsequent filings. Comparing 13F disclosures with spikes in social sentiment can help distinguish durable institutional conviction from temporary retail euphoria that may reverse once filings reveal profit-taking.

Tax-sensitive investor classification adds another analytical layer. Research divides institutional investors by how their trading behavior responds to tax considerations. Tax-sensitive investors tend to rebalance differently during market declines and often cut holdings more aggressively than tax-insensitive peers. This classification system identifies managers that seek to minimize taxable events through lower turnover, which helps analysts anticipate flows that may pressure particular securities during quarter-end rebalancing.

The most advanced applications rely on parsing structured data from thousands of filings at once. Automated systems download, parse, and compile 13F reports from EDGAR to build historical datasets for backtesting investment strategies. They apply quality controls to screen out erroneous filings, including those with implausible price deviations or formatting errors. Clean datasets of that kind allow researchers to test for institutional herding, momentum effects, and the persistence of manager skill.

A persistent mistake is to treat 13F filings as real-time trading intelligence. The forty-five-day lag makes them poorly suited to short-term timing. Their value is strategic. They reveal multi-quarter trends in institutional positioning that often continue after the reporting date. Another mistake is to assume the filings show full portfolio exposure. They do not. Because short positions, derivatives, and non-qualifying assets are excluded, 13F reports disclose only long equity holdings and omit exposures that may materially offset the apparent bullish view.

A practical workflow starts with a curated list of institutional managers that have distinctive strategies and a demonstrated record of predictive value. Rather than trying to follow every filing, the analyst focuses on managers whose decisions have historically mattered for future price movements. The emphasis falls on new positions established during periods of market stress, concentrated bets that represent meaningful portfolio weight, and coordinated moves by managers in the same philosophical camp. Used that way, regulatory compliance data becomes something more useful: a map of institutional conviction across market cycles.

Key Takeaways

- ☐ EDGAR is a structured database, not a search engine. Effective use requires CIK numbers for entity precision, Boolean operators for targeted queries, and full-text search (efts.sec.gov) for cross-company investigation. Treating it as a keyword search tool wastes time and produces noise.
- ☐ A 13D filing is the earliest public signal that an activist investor has crossed the 5% ownership threshold with the intent to influence corporate direction. The "purpose" section of the 13D describes what the investor wants. A 13G indicates passive ownership without activist intent. The switch from 13G to 13D signals a change in posture.
- ☐ 13F institutional holdings reports show what large managers owned at the end of each quarter, with a 45-day reporting lag. They reveal multi-quarter positioning trends and institutional consensus, but they exclude short positions, derivatives, and non-equity assets.

Fieldwork

- ☐ Go to efts.sec.gov and search for the name of a CEO or board member from your watchlist in quotes. Filter to the past three years. Review every filing that appears — across every company — where that person is mentioned. You will likely find affiliations the proxy statement omits.
- ☐ Pull the three most recent 13F filings from one institutional manager you respect. Track which positions were added, increased, reduced, or eliminated across the three quarters. The pattern of change is more significant than any single snapshot.
- ☐ Search EDGAR for all 13D filings by a single activist investor (try Elliott Management, Starboard Value, or Third Point). Read the "purpose" sections. Note how the stated objectives compare to the actual corporate outcomes over the following 12 months.

Apply This

When a company on your watchlist appears in a new 13D filing, read the "purpose" section before reading the market reaction. The stated intent — board seats, strategic review, asset sale, management change — frames the catalyst calendar for that position. When a 13G converts to a 13D, the passive investor has become active. That conversion is itself a signal.

CHAPTER 8

Reading Between the Lines in Filings

Financial statements present a curated reality. The numbers look precise, the categories fixed, the conclusions almost unavoidable. That surface clarity hides the harder truth: the most important information about a company's health, risks, and prospects often sits in the narrative and explanatory sections wrapped around the numbers. Most market participants treat those sections as compliance debris—footnotes, risk factors, management commentary—something to skim or ignore. That habit creates a durable information gap.

The gap exists because financial reporting works on two levels. One is the standardized accounting output: the balance sheet, income statement, and cash flow statement. Those statements provide a consistent, comparable snapshot. The other is the layer of qualitative explanation, forward-looking assessment, and context that explains why the numbers look the way they do and what they may become. Professional analysts bridge that divide methodically. They do not treat the explanatory sections as supplemental. They treat them as the main source for understanding accounting choices, operating pressure, and management's real concerns.

What makes a difference is not simply collecting disclosures, but interpreting the signals embedded in them. Footnotes, risk factors, and management commentary all carry patterns that can point to financial stress, strategic change, or vulnerabilities that have not yet been stated plainly. The signal rarely comes from reading one filing in isolation. It comes from tracking how language, emphasis, and disclosure habits change over time. That is the difference between surface-level financial review and an evidence-based reading of corporate reality.

Footnote Analysis and Hidden Details

A company's balance sheet shows $7.7 billion in long-term debt. A footnote on "other long-term liabilities" discloses another $16.4 billion, including $6.9 billion in capital lease obligations. That gap is why footnote work separates professional research from casual financial review. Footnotes contain the disclosures that explain, qualify, and sometimes undercut the headline numbers in the statements.

Google's proxy statement offers a clear example. The main ownership table shows co-founders Larry Page and Sergey Brin holding only modest amounts of Class A shares, the publicly traded common stock with ordinary voting rights. Footnote 1 explains that Class B shares carry ten votes each, against one vote for Class A. Those super-voting shares are often held by founders and insiders to preserve control. Page and Brin control 83.6 percent of the Class B shares, which gives them 51.1 percent of the company's total voting power despite a relatively small economic stake. Investors who focus only on share percentages miss the governance risk built into that structure.

Facebook's 2012 amended prospectus contained a footnote disclosing a new four-year contract for COO Sheryl Sandberg that granted her stock awards designed to maintain parity with other senior executives. That footnote undercut earlier claims of lower compensation and exposed an agreement made the prior month that had not appeared in the original filing. Timing mismatches of that kind often point to gaps in transparency.

Footnotes regularly disclose information that does not appear clearly anywhere else. Related-party transactions may reveal below-market rents paid to owners' relatives or favorable terms granted to entities controlled by management. These arrangements can make profitability look stronger than it really is. Contingent liabilities disclose off-balance-sheet exposures—lawsuits, warranty claims, environmental remediation costs—that may not hit the statements until later. A footnote may disclose a $180,000 accounts receivable write-off after a customer bankruptcy even though the income statement does not call attention to it.

Going-concern issues often surface in footnotes when companies discuss funding plans against a backdrop of continuing losses or negative cash flow. Pension assumptions appear there as well, including the discount rates used to value future obligations. Small changes in those assumptions can materially alter reported liabilities. Footnotes also disclose management's expected returns on pension assets, which may be optimistic enough to obscure funding gaps. Those shifts can change the economics meaningfully even when the main liability line on the balance sheet barely moves.

The scale of footnote disclosure has grown sharply. A modern 10-K may contain more than 250 pages of footnotes, against roughly twenty pages in the 1990s. Part of that reflects regulation. Part reflects the greater complexity of modern companies. Serious analysts treat footnotes as the main source for understanding accounting policy, risk exposure, and the economic substance behind reported figures. Read over time, they also reveal strategic changes in research and development spending, inventory accounting, and revenue recognition that point to changing business conditions.

The cost of ignoring footnotes is not theoretical. Companies have faced SEC enforcement actions for inadequate disclosure of investment loss reserves and inventory valuation methods. Those cases can lead to fines, restatements, and trading suspensions, all of which can damage shareholder value. Footnotes exist because accounting rules require disclosure of material information needed to interpret the statements properly. In practice, that means they often contain the very information management would rather investors not examine too closely.

Auditor Changes and Going-Concern Flags

A company announces that its auditor has resigned. The press release thanks the outgoing firm for its years of service and warmly welcomes the replacement. The SEC filing that reports the change—Form 8-K, Item 4.01—can tell a very different story. It may reveal that the prior auditor's report included a going-concern modification, a formal statement that substantial doubt existed about the company's ability to continue operating for the next twelve months. The distance between the press release and the filing is exactly why auditor changes deserve forensic attention.

Going-concern opinions are the modification most often cited in auditor-change filings. They are not casual remarks. An auditor issues that warning after assessing whether the company can meet its obligations without liquidating assets or restructuring debt. Once that flag appears, deeper financial trouble often follows. Companies dealing with restatements or material weaknesses in internal control are almost three times as likely to change auditors within a year as the broader market. Auditor turnover often follows serious problems rather than anticipating them.

The mechanism is part market pressure, part strategic response. After a restatement, companies sometimes replace auditors to signal a commitment to better audit quality and to rebuild damaged credibility. Research suggests the market can react positively when the underlying restatement was severe, reading the change as corrective action. That link between restatements and auditor turnover is stronger when corporate governance is relatively robust, which suggests boards use auditor changes as visible proof of accountability.

A new audit firm can also uncover issues the old one missed or tolerated. That fresh-eyes effect means a restatement discovered after an auditor change does not automatically prove the former auditor failed. The underlying errors may have arisen only after the new engagement began. Timing alone proves little without a close look at the accounting issues involved. Companies that change auditors also file late more often than their peers. Some hire a new firm only weeks before a reporting deadline, which predictably delays completion of the financial statements.

SEC rules require a company reporting an auditor change to disclose whether either of the prior two annual audit reports contained modifications. If that disclosure is absent or vague, investors immediately lose a layer of accountability. Analysts should cross-check the auditor-change filing against the audit opinions in the two prior 10-Ks rather than relying on management's summary. Sarbanes-Oxley created a separate rhythm—mandatory audit partner rotation every five years—and that should not be confused with a full change of audit firm, which carries much more signaling value. The law imposed stricter independence rules after a wave of corporate scandals, but partner rotation is routine. Firm turnover is not.

Treat every auditor change as a potential warning sign. The work begins with the prior two years of audit opinions and expands to any simultaneous restatements or disclosures of material weakness.

Accounting Red Flags in Financial Statements

A company reports revenue growth of fifteen percent. Its accounts receivable rise forty percent over the same period. That mismatch between reported sales and actual cash collection is a classic accounting red flag. Professional analysts do not dismiss these gaps as quirks. They treat them as potential evidence of deeper manipulation. When revenue rises much faster than cash collection, the problem is often aggressive recognition, including channel stuffing—pushing excess inventory onto distributors to inflate quarterly sales.

Revenue recognition creates many such warning signs. Bill-and-hold transactions allow revenue to be booked before products are shipped. Barter deals can inflate both revenue and expense at the same time. Membership businesses that recognize annual dues immediately instead of over the service period overstate current earnings. These practices produce lumpy revenue patterns with no seasonal logic, often showing up as unexplained fourth-quarter surges.

Receivables growing faster than sales point either to slower collections or to more aggressive booking of revenue. The receivables turnover ratio measures how quickly a company gets paid. When that ratio deteriorates relative to peers, it may mean customers are delaying payment or that the company is extending credit to weak buyers. Lucent Technologies showed this pattern when it recognized $700 million in revenue on products not yet sold or accepted by customers.

Expense manipulation takes a different form. A company may capitalize costs that should be expensed immediately, turning operating expense into a long-term asset. WorldCom's capitalization of billions in line costs remains the best-known example. Ordinary expenses were moved onto the balance sheet, inflating net income in the process. Delaying depreciation on aging equipment or failing to write down obsolete inventory produces the same kind of distortion. The gain is temporary. The risk is deferred.

The balance sheet carries its own warnings. More current liabilities than current assets can signal a liquidity problem. A debt-to-equity ratio above one hundred percent indicates heavy leverage. Some companies carry more total debt than cash and equivalents by such a wide margin that the balance sheet is effectively upside down. Comcast once reported $6 billion in cash against $98 billion in total debt. That structure is not always fatal, but it leaves little room for operational trouble.

Cash-flow irregularities often expose what accrual accounting can hide. A business funding operations out of cash reserves may have a profitability problem that earnings do not yet show. Cash-flow patterns that do not line up with revenue cycles can suggest timing manipulation. A buildup of cash with no matching growth in operations may point instead to undisclosed liabilities or looming capital needs.

Late reporting is another process warning. Companies that miss filing deadlines often have weak record-keeping or accounting problems they have not yet disclosed. Auditor remarks about revenue adjustments or non-GAAP compliance deserve close attention. An overly elaborate chart of accounts, with layers of granular categories, can also function less as clarification than as camouflage.

Related-party transactions with thin disclosure often sit near the center of financial manipulation. Deals between connected entities at above-market or below-market terms move value without transparent pricing. Enron's use of special purpose entities to hide large debts remains the most familiar case. Aggressive asset valuations and earnings estimates that repeatedly overshoot reality create their own pattern of predictable disappointment.

Luckin Coffee fabricated more than $300 million in retail sales through fake transactions, a reminder that fictitious revenue can persist until someone checks it against external evidence. Forensic accountants use tools like Benford's Law to identify unnatural digit patterns in financial data, while ratio analysis compares core metrics against industry norms. Formal audits detect only about a third of occupational frauds. That makes independent analysis of the statements indispensable as an early-warning tool. These schemes often involve employees or executives using company resources for personal gain through theft, corruption, or manipulation of the accounts.

Related-Party Transaction Detection

A company's accounts payable ledger shows a $350,000 payment to a vendor called Strategic Consulting Partners. The transaction description is vague. Cross-checking the vendor against board minutes reveals that Strategic Consulting Partners is owned by the CEO's spouse. What looked like an ordinary expense is now a related-party transaction that should have been specifically disclosed and approved. Discoveries like this usually come from process, not luck.

Auditors use structured methods to find these relationships. They run electronic keyword searches through transaction records using the names of known related parties. They combine data from investment statements, accounts payable ledgers, and director questionnaires. Round-dollar payments outside the ordinary course attract attention. The $350,000 figure stands out not only because it is exact, but because consulting work usually produces variable billing tied to hours or deliverables.

Management may conceal problematic transactions, but subordinate staff often know more than executives assume. Auditors therefore speak not only with senior management, but also with supervisors in cash receipts and accounts payable. Those employees see transactions every day and recognize patterns that do not fit. An approval that bypasses ordinary channels or a vendor address that matches a director's home address should trigger immediate scrutiny. The inquiry process specifically asks about unusual transactions during the year and after period close.

The regulatory framework makes this a mandatory line of inquiry, not an optional one. PCAOB Auditing Standard No. 18 requires auditors to understand related-party relationships during risk assessment. The standard reflects the view that companies may fail to identify all such transactions on their own. International rules focus on the same core areas: undisclosed relationships, significant transactions outside the normal course, and claims that the terms were at arm's length.

That framework requires more than accepting management's representations at face value. Arm's-length pricing means terms equivalent to those unrelated parties would negotiate in an ordinary commercial setting. Auditors have to determine whether the transaction reflects those terms or whether preferential pricing is being used to transfer value improperly.

Decentralized organizations are especially vulnerable. Controllers at a subsidiary may have no visibility into relationships elsewhere in the group. Quarterly certification processes therefore require designated personnel to confirm that they have performed enough work to identify related-party transactions. ERP master-data controls can also flag possible relationships when new vendors or customers are set up in the system.

Those controls generate periodic reports for review by finance and legal teams. Small transactions matter here because they accumulate. A series of low-value payments can cross a materiality threshold even if each payment looks harmless in isolation. CONSOB, the Italian securities regulator, uses a value-based significance measure that compares transaction value to shareholders' equity. Thresholds of that kind determine when disclosure and board approval become mandatory.

Materiality is not just a technical threshold. It shapes what gets noticed. Several small payments to a director's family business may individually seem immaterial, but together they can amount to a meaningful transfer of value. Detection is only the first step. Auditors then have to determine whether the terms match those available from unrelated parties, whether the documentation is complete, and whether the transaction has a real commercial purpose. Deals that lack ordinary business justification deserve more scrutiny.

Good detection systems also deter misconduct. Companies with strong monitoring disclose fewer related-party transactions after the fact. When management knows electronic searches will flag particular names and relationships, it has a stronger incentive to disclose them properly at the outset. The result is a repeatable process for gathering financial intelligence, not investigative guesswork.

Management Discussion and Analysis (MD&A) Insights

The Management Discussion and Analysis section appears in every 10-K and 10-Q, usually fifteen to thirty pages between the financial statements and the footnotes. Most investors skip it. They assume it is boilerplate. That assumption leaves an opening. MD&A contains management's required explanation of what happened, why it happened, and what management expects next. Just as important, its wording, emphasis, and omissions often signal trouble before the statements do. The SEC requires this disclosure under Item 303 of Regulation S-K, covering liquidity, capital resources, results of operations, and known trends or uncertainties. The signal rarely comes from one MD&A alone. It comes from comparing one quarter against the next.

The most useful technique is side-by-side comparison of the same section across consecutive quarters. Open the current 10-Q and the prior one. Start with Results of Operations. Which segments receive more space this quarter than last? When a previously minor business suddenly gets much more discussion, management is signaling heightened attention, whether the problem is unexpected growth or emerging weakness. A retail company that gave two paragraphs to e-commerce last quarter but six this quarter is telling the reader something before it states it directly. The extra space is itself information.

Management language also softens in predictable ways when conditions worsen. "Strong demand trends" becomes "evolving market conditions." "Industry-leading margins" becomes "a competitive margin environment." These downgrades often appear quarters before the damage shows up fully in reported results. A simple comparison table—Q4 language, Q1 language, interpretation—can make the pattern visible. A software company that describes customer retention as "exceeding historical averages" in Q4 and then as "within expected ranges" in Q1 is not saying the same thing twice. The change signals deterioration, even if each phrase sounds neutral by itself.

Companies under strain also tend to rotate their explanations. One quarter a manufacturer blames margin pressure on temporary supply-chain disruption. The next quarter it points to industry-wide input-cost inflation. The quarter after that it cites competitive pricing. That migration of excuses often means management either does not understand the core problem or does not want to describe it honestly. When the issue is genuinely temporary, the explanation usually stays consistent and comes with a timeline that management later meets.

The Known Trends and Uncertainties section is where management's forward-looking claims are most exposed. Those statements should be tracked against what happens next. A useful spreadsheet includes the quarter, the specific statement, the metric involved, the eventual outcome, and the variance. A pharmaceutical company says in Q1 that it expects regulatory approval in Q3. Q3 arrives. There is no approval and no explanation for the delay. The omission is itself a signal. Systematic tracking prevents management from relying on investor forgetfulness.

The Liquidity and Capital Resources section often reveals management's real priorities more clearly than public presentations do. Compare the capital allocation described there with the emphasis management uses on earnings calls. If executives spend five minutes talking up international expansion on the call, but MD&A shows international capital expenditures falling while domestic spending rises, the mismatch matters. It may mean the strategy is faltering, or that management is managing perception more aggressively than reality. The statement of cash flows provides the check on whether the spending narrative is true.

Uncertainty language can also be measured. Count the hedging words: may, could, potential, might, anticipate, believe, expect. Then calculate their share of the total words in the forward-looking sections. A rising hedge ratio across quarters often signals waning confidence even when the overall tone remains upbeat. A company may still describe growth prospects as robust while the hedge ratio moves from three percent to seven percent. The positive adjective says one thing. The language pattern says another.

Another useful comparison is the share of MD&A devoted to each segment against that segment's share of revenue. A segment producing 40 percent of revenue but receiving only 15 percent of the discussion may be getting downplayed, perhaps because it is weakening. The reverse pattern—a small segment attracting disproportionate attention—can mean either fast-growing importance or mounting operational trouble. Cross-checking that allocation against segment operating income can sharpen the conclusion. Segments with declining margins often receive more narrative attention as management works to explain away the deterioration.

The treatment of non-GAAP metrics provides another clue. Companies tend to highlight adjusted EBITDA, free cash flow, or similar measures when those figures look better than GAAP results. What changes over time is important to note. A company that once led with revenue growth but now leads with adjusted earnings is often telling the reader that revenue growth has become less flattering. A shift toward metrics that strip out stock compensation or restructuring costs often precedes quarters when GAAP results miss badly. The MD&A starts preparing investors to look somewhere else before the full deterioration becomes impossible to miss.

MD&A also shows how management wants investors to interpret the quarter without challenge. Earnings call transcripts show whether that interpretation survives contact with analysts. Read the MD&A first, then the call. Notice what management drops from the written filing when it has to speak extemporaneously, and notice where analysts push against the narrative. If MD&A stresses operational efficiency but analysts keep asking about falling volume, the market is rejecting management's chosen frame. That dissonance usually means the filing is doing strategic positioning rather than candid explanation. Some of the best intelligence comes from the topics management declines to repeat when given the chance.

Certain patterns recur when MD&A is designed to obscure rather than clarify. Vague discussion with no concrete metrics often signals that management is avoiding something measurable. Sudden changes in segment reporting can make quarter-to-quarter comparison difficult, sometimes by design. Heavy technical jargon in the sections describing problems, paired with plain language in the sections describing success, often reveals discomfort with the disclosure itself. The most reliable approach is systematic: keep comparison files covering at least the last eight quarters, log specific wording changes, calculate hedge ratios, and compare each forward-looking statement with what happened next. Done that way, MD&A stops being a compliance document and becomes a quarterly readout on management credibility and business direction.

Risk Factor Analysis and Trend Monitoring

A pharmaceutical company lists clinical trial failure as a risk factor. The language stays unchanged across three annual reports. Then the company announces a failed Phase 3 trial and the stock falls forty percent. The risk was always there, but the static disclosure gave no signal that the probability was rising as the trial advanced. That is why risk-factor analysis depends on monitoring change, not merely reading the list. SEC rules require disclosure of material risks that make an investment speculative, but the real value comes from watching how those disclosures evolve.

Serious analysts treat risk factors as a time series, not a checklist. Each risk has to be judged across three dimensions: probability, magnitude, and mitigation. A retailer exposed to economic downturns has to be evaluated differently depending on whether it sells luxury goods or discount merchandise. The same risk category may imply very different sales sensitivity, recovery prospects, and defensive options.

Cybersecurity disclosures follow a recognizable arc. Early filings usually describe broad technology risk. Later filings begin naming ransomware, data breaches, or other specific threats. The most important change comes when the company moves from hypothetical language—an incident could occur—to language that implies an event has already happened. The SEC's enforcement action against SolarWinds turned in part on that distinction: generic cyber-risk language remained in place while known vulnerabilities were already being exploited. The difference between hypothetical and actual is not semantic. It has legal consequences.

Risk-factor monitoring also shows what management is starting to worry about. New categories appear as the environment changes. Recent filings have added artificial-intelligence risk, climate exposure, and geopolitical tension. The order of presentation can carry meaning as well. SEC guidance only suggests listing risks by significance, but a company that moves supply-chain disruption from the middle of the section to the top is signaling a shift in internal priority.

The analysis gets stronger when risk factors are checked against the rest of the filing. A company warning about customer concentration should show corresponding revenue concentration in the financial statements. If it highlights foreign-exchange volatility as a major threat while international revenue is minimal, the disclosure may be boilerplate rather than tailored. The presence of a risk matters less than whether the rest of the filing supports the claim.

Language changes matter more than risk labels. Companies use words like could and may for hypothetical scenarios, but they move toward the past tense once events have occurred. That shift often appears before the market fully understands the significance. If risk factors remain frozen while the business environment changes materially, either the company is unusually stable or its disclosure process has gone stale.

The useful output is a timeline. Each filing adds evidence about which risks management believes are increasing, fading, or newly emerging. That historical profile gives context when a long-disclosed risk suddenly becomes real. The intelligence lies not in spotting risks that everyone can read, but in tracking the path management appears to believe those risks are taking.

Key Takeaways

- ☐ Footnotes contain the legally required disclosures that explain, qualify, and sometimes contradict the headline numbers. Off-balance-sheet liabilities, related-party transactions, revenue recognition policy changes, and contingent liabilities all live in footnotes. Most investors skip them. That creates an exploitable information gap.
- ☐ MD&A analysis works best as a time series. The technique is side-by-side comparison of the same MD&A section across consecutive quarters, tracking language changes, segment emphasis shifts, excuse migration, and rising hedge ratios. A single filing tells you what management wants you to think. The comparison across filings tells you what changed.
- ☐ Auditor changes, going-concern flags, and Beneish M-Score components above -1.78 are specific, quantifiable red flags that warrant immediate investigation — not because they prove fraud, but because they signal conditions under which fraud is statistically more likely.

Fieldwork

- ☐ Pull the two most recent 10-Ks for a company you follow. Open the risk factor sections side by side. Note every risk that was added, removed, or reordered. For any new risk factor, ask: what changed in the business that required this disclosure?
- ☐ In the same 10-K pair, locate the footnote on revenue recognition. Compare the language word by word. Any change in recognition policy, measurement method, or judgment disclosure between the two filings is a red flag worth tracing through the income statement.
- ☐ Calculate a rough hedge ratio for the MD&A's forward-looking section: count hedging words (may, could, might, potential, anticipate, believe, expect) and divide by total words in that section. Do this for two consecutive quarters. A rising ratio signals declining management confidence even when the qualitative tone remains positive.

Apply This

Signals to watch for: footnote liabilities that exceed on-balance-sheet debt, revenue growing faster than operating cash flow for two or more quarters, depreciation rates slowing without operational justification, a new auditor in a non-routine year, and the disappearance of previously discussed operational metrics from the MD&A.

CHAPTER 9

Investor Relations and Earnings Intelligence

Financial statements present a curated reality. The numbers offer a standardized snapshot, but the explanatory sections carry the intelligence that explains why those numbers exist and where they may be headed. That gap separates surface-level financial review from an evidence-based reading of corporate reality. Professional analysts close it by treating narrative disclosure as primary material, not as an appendix to the numbers.

The focus here shifts from static documents to live corporate communication. Between quarterly filings, companies shape market perception through a steady stream of official messaging: investor relations pages, earnings calls, and management commentary. These channels carry structured signals about operating confidence, strategic priorities, and emerging risk.

The value does not come from reading them once. It comes from tracking them over time. Language, disclosure habits, and communication strategy change as business conditions change. The work is to turn ordinary corporate communication into an organized stream of intelligence by watching what companies say, how they say it, and what they choose not to say.

IR Page Monitoring and Guidance Tracking

A company's investor relations page contains the official version of events management wants shareholders to accept. The guidance posted there is not just a forecast. It is a set of forward-looking commitments that can move the stock when they are met, revised, or broken. Monitoring that page properly means more than checking it from time to time. It requires a disciplined process that distinguishes routine updates from meaningful changes in corporate messaging.

What used to require manual checking is now often automated. Specialized investor relations platforms such as Irwin and Nasdaq IR Insight monitor shareholder changes, track sentiment, and issue alerts when guidance or messaging shifts. These systems scan a company's own IR site, peer-company pages, and market data at the same time. They can detect odd investor behavior before those patterns become visible in quarterly filings. A mid-cap biotech company, for example, avoided regulatory trouble after an automated disclosure-tracking system flagged inconsistencies between public guidance and internal communication.

The work extends beyond the IR page itself. Shareholder surveillance tracks movement among institutional, retail, and non-reporting holders through regulatory filings and NOBO data. Non-objecting beneficial owner data does not identify retail holders by name, but it gives a clearer picture of the true ownership base. That information flows into investor CRMs that log every interaction, from emails to meetings. Over time, those records begin to reveal behavioral patterns that can help anticipate future action.

Guidance tracking also goes beyond headline revenue forecasts. A serious system monitors company-specific key performance indicators and checks them against outside evidence. If management guides to fifteen percent revenue growth, analysts compare that claim with supply-chain activity, hiring trends, and market-share data. Guidance becomes a benchmark. Quarter by quarter, performance gets measured against it. Breaks in the pattern often appear before formal revisions are announced.

The practical value is well established. Venture investors use tools like Investory to monitor startup KPIs and guidance across portfolio companies. European banks have improved investor targeting by using predictive analytics to estimate how guidance changes will affect investor behavior. AI-based extraction tools now process guidance documents and catch subtle wording changes that a human reader may overlook.

Several habits weaken this kind of monitoring. One is the view that IR tools only concern public-company investor relations teams. In practice, private equity and venture firms increasingly use them to oversee their portfolios. Another is the belief that manual checking is good enough. It usually is not. Automated systems catch sentiment changes and guidance drift when they happen, not weeks later. Generic CRMs also tend to fail at tasks specific to investor relations, such as integrating ownership data and managing compliance-sensitive communication.

The most effective systems create a feedback loop linking guidance, market reaction, and follow-on communication. When a company misses guidance, the explanation often begins to appear on the IR page before the formal earnings release. Monitoring tools capture those interim adjustments and expose how management is trying to reset the narrative before the wider market has fully absorbed the miss.

Professional investors do not treat guidance as prediction. They treat it as commitment. Breaking guidance changes how the market judges management and often affects valuation multiples. A strong monitoring process tracks not only the guidance itself, but the conditions under which management tends to revise it. Over time, that reveals patterns in confidence that correlate with the underlying condition of the business.

Earnings Call Preparation and Calendar Management

A company reports quarterly results after the market closes. The stock moves five percent in after-hours trading. The conference call the next morning may either reinforce that move or unwind it. Serious preparation for earnings starts well before the call. The earnings calendar is not a reminder list. It is a strategic tool.

Investor relations teams work from preparation schedules that reveal what matters to them. A typical five-week timeline assigns clear tasks in sequence. Five weeks before the announcement, the team sets the calendar and fixes the deadlines. Four weeks out, management holds a one-hour discussion to identify three or four main themes for the quarter. Two weeks before earnings, draft versions of the press release, prepared remarks, and internal Q&A begin circulating. In the final week, management reads through the script and runs mock Q&A sessions. The point is message discipline across every channel.

Calendar management involves much more than recording a date. A useful system distinguishes between confirmed and estimated earnings dates and notes whether a company usually reports before market open, after market close, or at an unspecified time. Traders shorten before-market-open releases to BMO. These reports, usually issued between 7:00 and 9:00 a.m. Eastern Time, create a specific kind of pre-market volatility and require their own preparation.

The same applies to AMC releases—after-market-close announcements that set up after-hours trading and frame the next morning's call. Some planning systems also mark earnings as TNS, or Thursday next week, when the exact date is not fixed but falls within a known window. Labels like these help researchers organize preparation across several companies reporting around the same time.

Earnings calendars also become more useful when treated as historical data rather than as a schedule alone. Companies that routinely beat estimates by narrow margins often keep doing so until something fundamental changes. Companies with erratic earnings histories tend to produce larger stock reactions when results surprise. Stocks that beat estimates often rise two to five percent. Those that miss often fall three to seven percent. Inline results usually move less. These are not trading rules, but they help shape position sizing and risk management ahead of the report.

Preparation starts two or three weeks before the announcement. Analysts compare expected results with both management's prior guidance and consensus estimates. They develop likely Q&A topics from industry developments, recent disclosures, and previous call transcripts. This gives them a framework for interpreting management's answers on the actual call. Did management address the concerns raised last quarter? Has its language changed around the metrics that matter most?

One week before earnings, the work shifts toward final materials. Investor relations teams refine the script, edit Q&A bullet points, and handle exchange notifications and website updates. Last-minute changes at this stage can be revealing. A company that materially revises its prepared remarks late in the process may be reacting to unexpectedly weak internal data or to an issue it had not planned to discuss.

The day before the call is typically reserved for final review and competitive context. Strong teams study calls from direct competitors that reported earlier in the season. They look for recurring themes and for points of divergence. That comparison helps determine whether the company's results reflect firm-specific execution or broader industry conditions. By the time the call begins, the analyst should already have a working view of the sector backdrop.

An earnings calendar does not predict direction. It provides timing and structure, not a buy or sell signal. Its value lies in forcing preparation and discipline. Another common mistake is to treat a published date as fixed. Companies often move reporting dates because of audit timing or unexpected events. A system that distinguishes confirmed dates from estimates is less likely to miss the event.

The best routines make earnings preparation continuous. Morning reviews check for announcements from portfolio names and watchlist companies. Pre-market trade plans account for scheduled reports. Each surprise, and the stock's reaction to it, gets logged for future reference. That turns earnings season from a scramble into a structured research cycle.

The best-prepared analysts enter an earnings call with most of the important questions already answered by their own work. They are not listening for novelty. They are listening for confirmation, contradiction, and stress in the narrative. That is what allows them to react quickly when management departs from the prepared script in a way that matters.

Transcript Analysis and Management Commentary

Earnings call transcripts are the only place in a company's public record where management is questioned in real time, without advance preparation for every exchange. That asymmetry — scripted prepared remarks followed by unscripted analyst questions — is where the most useful signals live. The prepared remarks show you what management wants you to think. The Q&A shows you what they're actually worried about.

Working a transcript effectively requires preparation before the call, discipline during it, and a comparison framework after it. All three stages produce different intelligence.

Before the Call: Build Your Checklist

Pull the transcript from the prior two quarters before the current call begins. Read the Q&A sections specifically and note:

- Which analyst questions were answered with specifics, and which received vague or deflecting responses?

- Which operational metrics — margins by segment, unit economics, inventory turns, customer acquisition costs — did management discuss in detail previously but may omit this quarter?
- What guidance language did management use last quarter? ("We expect," "we are confident," "we anticipate") — note the exact phrasing so you can compare it verbatim to this quarter's language.
- Were any topics introduced by analysts that management seemed unprepared for?

This pre-call checklist converts you from a passive listener into an active analyst tracking specific threads. The absence of a previously discussed metric is often more informative than the presence of new ones.

During the Call: Structure and What to Track

A standard earnings call has three components: the CEO's prepared remarks, the CFO's financial review, and the analyst Q&A. Each carries different evidentiary weight.

The **CEO's prepared remarks** are the most scripted element — reviewed by legal, IR, and often external counsel before delivery. Treat them as the official narrative. Note what topics receive the most time and what topics are conspicuously brief or absent.

The **CFO's financial review** bridges the narrative to the numbers. Watch for any divergence between the metrics the CFO emphasizes and the metrics that appear in the actual 10-Q filing. If the CFO spends four minutes on adjusted EBITDA and thirty seconds on free cash flow, ask why the metric with the most editorial control is receiving the most attention.

The **analyst Q&A** is where the call's real value sits. Track:

- Which analysts asked tough questions and whether they received substantive answers or redirection to "follow up offline"
- Whether management's language becomes more hedged or more definitive when pressed on specific topics

- How much time management spends defending the past versus discussing the future — a rising ratio of backward-looking defense to forward guidance is a directional signal
- Whether the CEO or CFO is speaking more in the Q&A than in prior quarters — executives who typically let the CFO handle questions but suddenly step in may be signaling that the financials need narrative management

After the Call: The Comparison Protocol

The most analytically valuable work happens after the call. Open three documents side by side: the current quarter's transcript, the prior quarter's transcript, and the current 10-Q filing.

Run these checks in sequence:

1. **Guidance consistency**: Does the numerical guidance in the prepared remarks match what appears in the 10-Q's forward-looking statements section? Discrepancies — even small ones — can indicate last-minute revisions to one document without updating the other.
2. **Q&A deflection tracking**: For every analyst question that received a deflecting answer this quarter, check whether the same topic appeared in a prior quarter and received a more direct response. A topic moving from "answered" to "deflected" across quarters is a degradation signal.
3. **Prepared vs. unscripted language**: Compare the CEO's phrasing in the prepared remarks to their phrasing on the same topic in a Q&A answer. When the unscripted version is noticeably more qualified than the scripted one, the script is carrying more confidence than management actually has.
4. **Metric migration**: Did any metric that appeared in prior prepared remarks disappear from this quarter's? If gross margin by segment was discussed for six consecutive quarters and is absent this quarter, that's a PIR — pull the 10-Q to see whether the underlying number deteriorated.

NLP Tools for Scale

For analysts tracking multiple companies simultaneously, natural language processing tools can automate parts of this workflow. FinBERT — a model trained specifically on SEC filings and earnings transcripts — classifies sentence-level sentiment as positive, negative, or neutral with higher accuracy than general-purpose tools, because it understands financial context ("revenue declined slightly" reads differently in a financial context than in general English).

Practical applications:

- Run FinBERT on the full transcript and compare the aggregate sentiment score to the prior quarter. A significant decline in the score — even if the prepared remarks still sound positive — indicates that the Q&A dragged overall sentiment down, which is often where management is most honest.
- Use speaker-separated sentiment analysis to compare CEO vs. CFO language. Divergence between the two — optimistic CEO, cautious CFO — is a flag worth investigating in the financial statements.
- Track sentence-level sentiment in the risk factors section of the 10-Q alongside the earnings call transcript. Risk factor language that deteriorates the same quarter that call sentiment improves suggests the official disclosure is telling a different story than management's oral presentation.

None of this replaces reading the transcript yourself for the companies you have high-conviction positions in. It extends your capacity to flag anomalies across a larger watchlist than manual review allows.

Identifying Tone Shifts and Hedging Language

Transcript analysis tells you *how* to work the document. This section tells you *what* to look for once you're in it — the specific linguistic patterns that consistently precede negative developments before they appear in financial results.

The core insight is that language changes before numbers change. Management rarely lies outright. Instead, they hedge — substituting confident assertions with qualified projections, replacing specific metrics with vague generalizations, and gradually increasing the density of conditional language as problems develop.

Learning to read these shifts systematically gives you a leading indicator that financial statement analysis alone cannot provide.

The Hedge Ratio

The hedge ratio measures the density of conditional language in management communications. Count the frequency of hedge words — *may, could, might, potential, anticipate, believe, expect, subject to, dependent on, if conditions allow* — as a proportion of total forward-looking words in a section of text.

The absolute value of a single quarter's hedge ratio matters less than the trajectory across quarters. A hedge ratio that has increased in three consecutive quarters, even while the absolute language still sounds positive, indicates declining internal confidence. The MDA analysis techniques in Chapter 8 cover this calculation in detail for written filings; the same method applies directly to earnings call transcripts.

Apply the hedge ratio specifically to forward-looking statements: guidance language, outlook commentary, and responses to analyst questions about future performance. Avoid applying it to descriptions of past results, where hedging is less informative. A rising hedge ratio in the Q&A section — specifically in responses to questions about future quarters — is the most predictive variant.

Excuse Migration

Excuse migration tracks how management attributes underperformance across consecutive calls. When a company misses a target, management offers an explanation. The pattern of those explanations over time reveals whether problems are being solved or reframed.

Isolated excuse: A single-quarter explanation ("supply chain disruption in Q3") that disappears in Q4 when results recover suggests the explanation was accurate.

Repeating excuse: The same explanation appearing in consecutive quarters ("ongoing supply chain pressures," then "continued supply chain headwinds," then "persistent supply chain challenges") without corresponding improvement in the underlying metric suggests the excuse has become a narrative shield rather than an operational description.

Migrating excuse: The explanation shifts topic across quarters — supply chain in Q2, labor costs in Q3, macroeconomic conditions in Q4 — while the same metric continues to disappoint. Migration without recovery is a strong signal that management doesn't have a clear picture of the root cause, or that the root cause is something they're not prepared to disclose.

Build an excuse log for any company you're tracking through a period of underperformance. A simple table with quarter, missed metric, stated explanation, and outcome the following quarter creates a visible pattern that would otherwise stay hidden across the volume of text in consecutive transcripts.

Attribution Shifts

Attribution analysis asks a different question than hedge ratio: not *how confident* management sounds, but *who gets credit and who gets blame*.

When management attributes positive outcomes to their own decisions and actions, they're claiming operational control. When they attribute negative outcomes to external factors — macro conditions, competitor behavior, currency headwinds, regulatory changes — they're deflecting responsibility. Neither pattern is automatically meaningful. The signal is in the *change* from one quarter to the next.

Watch specifically for:

- **Credit internalization, blame externalization**: Management takes credit for good results ("our execution was strong," "our pricing strategy delivered") while attributing every negative result to external conditions. This pattern, sustained across three or more calls, indicates a management team that isn't being honest about where operational control lies.
- **Reversal**: A management team that previously took ownership of problems ("we made mistakes in our inventory planning") and then shifts to external attribution ("unprecedented demand volatility made planning impossible") in a subsequent quarter. The reversal often signals that the internal problem is still present and no longer politically safe to acknowledge.

- **Analyst-triggered shifts**: Compare how management discusses a topic in prepared remarks vs. when pressed on the same topic by an analyst. If the prepared remarks attribute strong margin performance to "disciplined cost management" but the analyst's follow-up question about specific cost buckets produces a pivot to "favorable commodity tailwinds," the script carried more credit-taking than the facts warranted.

Non-GAAP Framing Drift

As covered in the MDA section (Chapter 8), the ratio of non-GAAP to GAAP discussion is itself a signal. In transcript analysis, apply this specifically to the call's time allocation: how many minutes does management spend presenting and defending non-GAAP metrics versus discussing GAAP results?

Track this ratio across consecutive calls. A company that spends 20% of prepared remarks on non-GAAP metrics in Q1 and 45% in Q4 — while GAAP results deteriorate — is signaling that the gap between reported and adjusted performance is widening and becoming politically important to manage. This framing drift often precedes a quarter where the non-GAAP adjustments themselves become controversial.

Calibrating Against the Baseline

All of these techniques require a baseline. A management team that has always spoken with heavy hedging isn't signaling deterioration when they continue to hedge. A CEO who has always attributed problems to external factors isn't newly deflecting when they do it again. The signal is deviation from that company's established pattern, not deviation from some universal standard.

Spend 30 minutes before initiating serious research on a new company listening to or reading two to three prior quarters of transcripts — not to extract specific information, but to calibrate the baseline. What does normal sound like for this team? What's their characteristic vocabulary? How direct are they typically in Q&A?

Once you have that baseline, every subsequent transcript is being compared to it rather than to abstract norms, and the deviations — when they come — will be immediately visible.

Omissions and What Management Doesn't Say

A company's quarterly earnings call runs forty-five minutes. Management talks about revenue growth, market expansion, and product innovation. Analysts ask about supply-chain pressure and competitive threats. No one mentions that a key executive left suddenly three weeks earlier. That omission is more revealing than most of what was said. The absence of expected information often carries more weight than the presence of routine disclosure.

Corporate filings sit inside regulatory frameworks that require some disclosures and leave others optional. The Management Discussion and Analysis section must address known trends and uncertainties reasonably likely to affect financial performance. Companies can satisfy that requirement with generic language while leaving out specific operating detail. Valeant Pharmaceuticals did not disclose its relationship with the pharmacy network Philidor, even though that network drove significant revenue through questionable channels. The omission distorted the picture of where sales were coming from. Once regulators focused on it, that narrative collapsed.

Social media and public records often expose gaps that filings leave untouched. An executive living far beyond reported compensation raises an immediate question. Property records, yacht registrations, and social-media posts showing luxury assets can all point to a mismatch between visible wealth and declared income. That does not prove misconduct. It does, however, create a priority intelligence requirement. The gap between observable lifestyle and disclosed compensation is a measurable risk signal.

E-commerce platforms create a newer version of the same problem. Amazon sellers may report little income on tax filings while their seller dashboards indicate millions in revenue. Advertising activity, review volume, and other digital traces produce alternative data streams that can contradict formal disclosures. Construction firms promoting luxury projects online while reporting minimal revenue to tax authorities present the same kind of discrepancy. These digital exhaust trails give the analyst something to compare against the official record.

Network mapping exposes another class of omission. LinkedIn profiles sometimes show directors serving on the boards of competing companies even though those connections do not appear in SEC filings. The missing link may indicate a conflict of interest. Corporate registries in offshore jurisdictions can reveal subsidiary structures that the parent company describes only vaguely in its own filings. The Panama Papers showed how shell-company networks could facilitate transactions that never appeared clearly in annual reports.

Earnings calls produce their own omission patterns. Management teams rehearse answers to expected questions. When an analyst raises something unplanned, hesitation, deflection, or a retreat to prepared talking points can say more than a direct answer. Transcripts often show executives circling back to script language instead of addressing a specific operating concern. That kind of avoidance usually marks an area where the official narrative is thin, unsupported, or concealing weakness.

The law draws distinctions among omissions. A pure omission is complete silence where disclosure is required. A half-truth arises when a statement becomes misleading because essential context has been left out. The distinction matters in enforcement. Analytically, both matter for the same reason: they reveal management's judgment about what investors should not be told.

Experienced analysts build industry-specific checklists of what a company should normally disclose. A pharmaceutical company should discuss clinical-trial timelines. A retailer should address inventory levels and same-store sales. A technology company should explain research and development spending. When those standard disclosures vanish from a quarterly report, the absence deserves attention. Often the missing discussion comes before the underlying operational problem becomes visible.

The best omission work comes from cross-referencing. Compare SEC filings with press releases and the narrative often shifts. Match executive compensation against property records and lifestyle gaps may appear. Compare supplier references on earnings calls with shipping data and supply-chain problems may emerge. Every source has blind spots. The advantage comes from using one source to expose what another leaves out.

Omission analysis begins with a baseline. Before an analyst can recognize what is missing, the analyst has to know what should be there. That requires industry knowledge and a record of the company's own past disclosure habits. A management team that once discussed specific metrics in detail but now retreats into vague generalities is signaling a change in priorities, or in confidence. What goes unsaid often reveals more about corporate reality than the language prepared for public release.

KEY TAKEAWAYS

- ☐ Earnings call preparation begins weeks before the call, not when the transcript drops. The highest-value pre-call work involves reviewing the prior quarter's transcript to identify which analyst questions were deflected or left unanswered, then building a checklist of operational metrics management previously discussed but may now omit.
- ☐ Tone shifts are measurable. Track specific phrases across quarters: "strong demand trends" becoming "evolving market conditions" is a signal, not a stylistic choice. The same applies to excuse migration — when management offers a different explanation for the same underperformance each quarter, they likely do not understand the problem or are unwilling to disclose it.
- ☐ What management does not say often matters more than what it does. The absence of expected disclosures — a key executive departure not mentioned on the call, a previously emphasized metric quietly dropped — creates a more revealing signal than anything in the prepared remarks.

FIELDWORK

- ☐ Before the next earnings call for a company you follow, read the prior quarter's transcript. Write down three questions that analysts asked but management did not fully answer. During the new call, track whether those questions resurface and whether the answers improve.
- ☐ After the call, compare the prepared remarks against the Q&A section. Note which topics from the prepared script management avoided elaborating on when pressed by analysts. That avoidance pattern identifies the areas where the official narrative may be weakest.
- ☐ Build an industry-specific disclosure checklist for one sector you follow. Pharmaceutical companies should discuss clinical trial timelines. Retailers should address same-store sales. Technology firms should detail R&D spending. When a standard disclosure disappears from a quarterly filing, its absence warrants investigation.

Apply This

Signals to watch for: a shift from specific guidance to vague qualitative language, management spending more time explaining past results than discussing forward outlook, recurring analyst questions about the same risk across multiple calls without a substantive response, and sudden emphasis on non-GAAP metrics after a period of leading with GAAP figures.

Part 3

Advanced Data Collection and Analysis Techniques

A company's regulatory filings provide the authoritative record of what it has chosen, or been required, to report. They do not provide a complete picture of what is happening in real time. Short sellers are building positions that will not be visible in the filing system until later. Options markets are pricing outcomes management has not discussed. Insiders are selling under prearranged plans. A federal court has docketed a complaint against a major subsidiary, and no 8-K has been triggered yet. This section covers that second ring of the public-information landscape: sources that operate on different schedules, through different institutions, and often with greater immediacy than the filing system, while remaining fully public and accessible.

The chapters examine market-structure signals, government economic data, insider trading patterns, activist and short-seller research, court records, and central-bank communications. Each source has to be read on its own terms. Each is shaped by the institutional setting that produces it. The edge comes not just from knowing where the data lives, but from understanding what kind of document it is, why it exists, and what interpretive mistakes it most often invites.

CHAPTER 10

Market Signals and Government Data

The workflow established in earlier chapters—collecting raw data, verifying sources, and structuring information—meets its first real test here. Markets do not react to the world as it is. They react to the world as it is reported, interpreted, and expected. The data streams in this chapter shape those perceptions in real time.

Scheduled government releases provide the official account of economic conditions, but their force depends on how they compare with what the market already expects. Financial media amplifies that account and sometimes distorts it, which makes verification essential before any headline enters an investment thesis. Short-interest data adds another layer by showing where professional capital has been placed against specific companies, offering a direct measure of bearish conviction that quarterly reports rarely capture.

The difficulty is not simply monitoring these channels. It is separating durable signals from passing noise. That requires an understanding of the mechanics behind data releases, the credibility hierarchy of information sources, and the statistical tools that distinguish real trends from random variation. It also requires close attention to the institutions that respond to the data. Central-bank language can move markets as powerfully as the rate decisions themselves.

Government Data and Macro Release Monitoring

A trader watches the Bureau of Labor Statistics website at 8:30 a.m. Eastern. The Consumer Price Index comes in hotter than consensus. Within seconds, Treasury yields jump and stock futures fall. That reaction shows the force of scheduled government releases. Macro monitoring turns these events from background noise into structured intelligence inputs.

Professional analysts treat the economic calendar as an operating document, not a checklist. The White House Office of Management and Budget publishes an annual schedule of principal federal economic indicators, coordinating release dates across agencies such as the Bureau of Economic Analysis, the Census Bureau, and the Federal Reserve. Each release follows a timing protocol. Major reports usually arrive at 8:30 a.m. Eastern, creating what traders call the "8:30 dump," a predictable liquidity event in which institutional order flow hits the market at once.

Holiday adjustments are also consequential. A Wednesday holiday can push a Friday release to 10:30 a.m.; a Thursday holiday can move it to Wednesday at noon. These details are administrative, but they shape when information reaches the market and how it is absorbed.

The useful signal lies not in the number itself, but in the gap between the number and expectation. Analysts track economist surveys and consensus forecasts, then compare the release against that benchmark. A GDP print showing 4.3 percent growth may look strong on its face. If the market expected 5.0 percent, the reaction is likely to be negative. That is the basis of what traders call surprise trades: positioning around the deviation from consensus rather than the absolute figure.

Two mistakes distort this process. The first is the belief that government releases directly cause market moves. Markets often price in expectations well before the data appears. The volatility comes from the surprise, not from the release alone. The second is the assumption that all economic data carries the same analytical weight. Initial GDP estimates are often revised by 0.5 to 1.0 percentage points in the following months. The advance number may matter for the immediate market reaction, but revised data tends to matter more for fundamental analysis.

A serious monitoring system also accounts for disruption. Government shutdowns create holes in the official data stream and force analysts to rely on substitutes. During one recent shutdown, analysts used State Street's PriceStats as a stand-in for official CPI data. That high-frequency measure showed goods inflation flattening before the government series resumed. Good workflows include contingencies of this kind. They do not depend on a single official source.

Some of the best signals appear only in combination. In one recent stretch, the Leading Economic Index declined for five straight months even as GDP remained strong. Analysts tracking both saw the divergence as an early warning and shifted toward more defensive positioning before the broader market caught up. The advantage came from integrating conflicting indicators rather than reacting to one release at a time.

Economic calendars help organize this work. Services such as TradingEconomics present releases in a table showing the actual number, the consensus forecast, and the historical comparison. The Bureau of Labor Statistics publishes its own release schedule. These tools help analysts decide what matters for a particular thesis. A fixed-income trader cares most about inflation and employment. An analyst following consumer stocks may care more about retail sales and personal income.

Timing also creates recognizable trading patterns. Liquidity often thins just before a major release as participants wait for the number. The first burst of volatility often reverses within minutes as algorithms react and human traders begin to interpret the full context. Experienced analysts do not confuse that first move with the final meaning of the data. They wait for the market to settle before making larger decisions.

Shutdowns are especially instructive because they expose the fragility of the release calendar. One recent shutdown forced the Bureau of Economic Analysis to combine October and November personal income data into a single January release. Quarterly GDP reports were delayed by weeks because source data was incomplete. Analysts who tracked those delays understood that catch-up releases would produce unusual volatility as multiple data points hit the market at once.

Federal Reserve policy expectations are tied directly to this release cycle. Each CPI report influences interest-rate expectations through the Fed's projected policy path, often summarized in the so-called dot plot. Analysts map the historical relationship between particular releases and changes in policy expectations, then use that history to anticipate how the Fed may respond to the current data. The result is a feedback loop: data changes policy expectations, policy expectations reprice markets, and that repricing conditions the response to the next release.

Alternative data adds another layer. Satellite images of Walmart parking lots showed declining traffic weeks before weak sales became visible in official reports. Mobile-device data revealed falling visits to Starbucks before the pandemic's effects appeared clearly in financial statements. These sources do not replace government data. They complement it, giving analysts an earlier read on trends the official releases will later confirm or contradict.

The options market offers its own secondary signal around scheduled releases. Participants often position for volatility by buying straddles ahead of major reports, owning both calls and puts in expectation of a sharp move either way. Unusual options activity before a scheduled release can therefore reveal institutional expectations about the likelihood of a surprise. The market for the data begins moving before the data itself appears.

Economic indicators also differ in their place in the cycle. The Conference Board's Leading Economic Index, for example, combines ten components, including building permits and stock prices, and often turns before GDP growth does. Analysts use such leading indicators as early warning tools, then confirm with lagging indicators such as unemployment. This creates a temporal framework rather than a flat stream of information.

Government agencies also explain how their own data should be read. The Bureau of Economic Analysis publishes methodological notes describing the effect of seasonal adjustment on GDP. The Census Bureau explains sampling error in retail-sales surveys. Analysts who study these notes understand what each indicator can and cannot do. They do not assume that all official data is equally precise or immediately actionable.

Global portfolios add another complication. European Central Bank announcements follow different schedules from Federal Reserve communications. Chinese releases operate under different standards of transparency from U.S. reports. Analysts following international markets need multiple calendars, multiple time zones, and standardized templates that preserve the context of each source while making the information operational.

A release is only one moment in a longer data life cycle. Preliminary estimates are revised as fuller information becomes available. Good analysts track the revision pattern itself. Some series tend to be revised upward, suggesting conservative first estimates. Others are revised downward, suggesting that the early number tends to overstate strength. Those biases make a difference. They improve forecasting beyond the headline print.

Market reactions change as the policy regime changes. Inflation reports once triggered predictable bond selloffs when central banks prioritized price stability above all else. In periods when labor-market weakness matters more, the same inflation data may provoke only a muted response. Analysts have to keep re-evaluating which data points count most in the current regime. Historical correlation alone is not enough.

Electronic markets now absorb data within milliseconds. In that environment, speed is a weak edge. Human analysts matter less because they are faster than machines and more because they can place new data in context—linking employment figures to consumer spending, or manufacturing weakness to supply-chain strain. Their advantage comes from synthesis, not reflex.

Scheduled government releases form the backbone of macro intelligence. Their value emerges only when they are integrated with corporate disclosures, market positioning, and alternative data rather than treated as isolated events.

Financial Media Verification and Source Weighting

A financial news outlet reports that a large pharmaceutical company has won FDA approval for a new drug. The stock jumps eight percent in pre-market trading. Another outlet repeats the story minutes later. Neither article links to the FDA's approval database or to the company's required Form 8-K. The approval turns out to involve a different drug with a similar name, and the stock gives back the entire move. That is why verification comes before source weighting.

The process starts before the article itself. The SIFT method offers a workable structure: stop and assess the reputation and purpose of the site; investigate the author's credentials and possible bias; find other coverage to see whether the claim is corroborated; and trace the claim back to an original source such as a regulatory filing or official announcement. A report based on unnamed people familiar with the matter deserves a different level of scrutiny from a report quoting directly from a Form 10-K. One is unattributed sourcing that may reflect an agenda. The other is evidence that can be checked.

Source weighting then assigns credibility according to origin. Regulatory filings sit at the top. Corporate communications come below them. Established financial media ranks below official filings but above social platforms. The hierarchy reflects incentives. A press release is written to cast the company in the best possible light. An SEC filing carries legal exposure if it omits a material fact. A news outlet balances accuracy against speed and audience engagement. Social media magnifies sentiment with almost no built-in verification.

Several frameworks help formalize the judgment. The CRAAP test—currency, relevance, authority, accuracy, and purpose—remains useful. Currency asks whether the information reflects present conditions, which is crucial in a fast market. Relevance asks whether the information actually answers the intelligence requirement at hand. Authority measures the expertise of the author and the standards of the publication. Accuracy looks for supporting evidence and obvious errors. Purpose forces the analyst to ask who benefits from the framing and whether advertising or ideology is shaping the presentation.

Financial media also shows recurring red flags. Promises of easy gains usually indicate promotional content rather than analysis. Sensational language often substitutes for evidence. Opaque methods and untraceable data sources reduce confidence. Undisclosed sponsorships and affiliations create hidden conflicts. More recently, regulatory warnings about deepfake fraud have highlighted another problem: manipulated identity documents, inconsistent IP-access patterns, and fabricated media assets can all be signs that the reporting itself is part of an effort to deceive.

Verification tools go well beyond financial terminals. Fact-checking organizations such as Snopes and PolitiFact track false claims that migrate into financial conversation. Reverse-image searches can expose stolen or altered photos. Metadata analysis can show when a supposedly original document has been modified. Academic databases such as JSTOR provide peer-reviewed context for economic claims that media reports flatten or exaggerate. These tools are crucial because financial misinformation is often sophisticated enough to mimic legitimate reporting.

Cross-referencing remains the most reliable method. A social-media rumor about a retailer's inventory problems becomes more credible when supply-chain data shows unusual shipping patterns and SEC filings mention distribution strain. The more independent channels that confirm the same factual claim, the higher the confidence. When sources diverge, the analyst has to decide whether the story is still developing or whether one of the sources is simply wrong.

Published material is not accurate by default. Even respected databases contain human-created content and therefore human error. Editorial process improves quality; it does not eliminate mistakes. Nor is one credible source always enough. A stronger base comes from multiple reputable sources arriving at the same fact through separate reporting or separate evidence.

The vocabulary of the process is important for professional analysts. Cross-verification means checking claims from one channel, often social media, against more established reporting or primary documents. Due diligence means increasing scrutiny when the claim is unusual or the source appears suspicious. Primary evidence means the original filing, order, transcript, or database entry, not a summary of it. Vested interest means the source may have a financial or reputational reason to slant the information.

Good verification changes the way analysts read the news. They open the source documents alongside the article. They compare how different outlets describe the same filing and notice which emphasize risk and which emphasize upside. They also keep track of reporters and outlets whose past accuracy earns them more weight over time. Media consumption becomes less passive and more forensic.

The goal is not a simple true-or-false label. It is a confidence score built from source credibility, evidence quality, and corroboration. High-confidence reports can enter analysis with little adjustment. Medium-confidence reports need more checking. Low-confidence reports are either excluded or investigated separately. That scoring system filters the flow of information before it contaminates the thesis.

Verification failures tend to cluster around breaking news, where speed pressures reduce standards. Even reputable outlets sometimes repeat claims from weaker sources during a competitive rush. Analysts who track these failures learn which outlets correct errors openly and which quietly revise stories without acknowledgment. That record becomes part of the weighting system itself, improving future judgment.

Short Interest Data and Borrow Market Intelligence

A stock's short interest rises from five percent of float to twenty percent across three reporting periods. The number of shares sold short climbs from two million to eight million. That fourfold increase signals a major shift in professional sentiment, one that ordinary earnings reports may not reveal. Short-interest data measures bearish conviction directly. It shows where capital has been committed against a company's prospects.

The mechanics of collection are important because they define both the usefulness and the limits of the data. Brokers report short interest twice each month under FINRA and exchange rules. The figures capture open short positions as of specific settlement dates. They are then published with a lag of roughly one to two weeks. That makes the series valuable as context, but not as a real-time map of current positioning.

A crucial distinction separates short interest from short-sale volume. Short interest is the stock of open positions at a point in time. Short-sale volume is the flow of shares sold short during a trading day. That flow can be large even when no meaningful position remains open by the end of the period. A trader who shorts intraday and covers before the close affects volume but not short interest. A position held for weeks appears in short interest continuously but affects short-sale volume only when it is first established. That is why a stock can show heavy short interest while daily short-selling activity looks modest.

Analysts standardize the raw numbers to make them comparable. Short float is the percentage of tradable float that has been sold short. A figure below two percent usually signals low bearish conviction. Two to five percent suggests moderate skepticism. Five to ten percent is elevated. Above twenty percent is extreme. Days to cover adds another dimension by dividing short interest by average daily volume. It estimates how long it would take for all shorts to buy back their positions at a normal trading pace. Above five days, squeeze risk becomes meaningful. Above ten, the vulnerability is severe.

Historical cases show how these metrics can foreshadow major events. GameStop reached short interest of roughly 140 percent of float before the 2021 squeeze, a condition made possible by synthetic exposures layered on top of ordinary borrowing. Those exposures included options structures and swap-based positions that reproduced the economics of a short without requiring a simple borrow. Volkswagen's 2008 squeeze followed Porsche's disclosure of a large stake, trapping shorts in a stock with very limited float. Tesla's rally in 2020 forced a slower but persistent unwind of a large short base. In each case, extreme short interest mattered because a catalyst forced buying into a constrained market.

Borrow-market intelligence adds information the regulatory figures cannot. The fee required to borrow shares reflects supply and demand in the securities-lending market. When borrow costs rise sharply, the stock is becoming hard to borrow and short demand is increasing relative to available supply. Daily loan fees can jump from single digits to annualized triple digits when shares become scarce. Data providers that track these fees in real time give analysts a more current picture of stress in the short base. A stock with rising borrow costs, limited availability, and elevated short interest can become dangerous for shorts even before a formal squeeze begins.

The most useful signals often come from divergence. Rising short interest alongside insider buying creates a clear conflict between external pessimism and internal confidence. A stock whose short base keeps growing while the price remains stable or rises suggests that shorts are entering at progressively worse levels, building potential fuel for a future move higher if they are forced to cover. The opposite pattern can also be revealing. Falling short interest during a decline may mean bears are taking profits rather than pressing the position.

The biggest analytical mistake is to treat high short interest as a prediction by itself. It is not. Plenty of heavily shorted companies continue to fall because the bearish thesis is correct. The data becomes actionable only in combination with catalyst analysis, liquidity, and market structure. A company with forty percent short interest and high days to cover becomes dangerous when positive news or a supply squeeze forces shorts to compete for limited stock.

Good monitoring systems therefore track the rate of change as much as the level. A five-percent move in short interest may be routine. A twenty-five-percent jump in one reporting period is a sentiment event and deserves investigation. Analysts also compare the stock with peers. A retailer showing twenty percent short interest while competitors average five percent is probably facing company-specific skepticism rather than a sector-wide headwind.

The final step is integration. Regulatory filings may show worsening fundamentals that justify the short base. Options data may reveal hedging around those positions. Retail sentiment may show the potential for a crowded challenge to professional shorts. Taken together, these sources turn a raw short-interest number into a broader reading of positioning, concentration, and the conditions under which sentiment might reverse violently.

Separating Signal from Noise in Market Data

A trading model processes thousands of price changes across global markets every second. Most of those moves are noise. A small fraction contains useful information about future direction. The difficulty is not collecting more data. It is telling the difference between the two. Signal extraction is the work of isolating persistent trends from transitory randomness.

Inflation analysis provides a clear example. Economists often decompose the Consumer Price Index into a persistent component and a transitory component. The persistent part behaves like a random walk and reflects the underlying inflation trend that matters for monetary policy. The transitory part captures temporary shocks—seasonal distortions, supply disruptions, one-off price spikes. The decomposition improves forecasts because it separates the part of inflation that matters for longer-term decisions from the part that will fade. The same logic applies to company analysis. A revenue increase driven by genuine demand is not the same as a revenue increase caused by seasonal timing or a one-time accounting adjustment.

The signal-to-noise ratio determines how useful the data is. A high ratio means the meaningful information dominates the random variation. Core inflation is one attempt to improve that ratio by excluding volatile food and energy prices. A low ratio creates the conditions in which machine-learning systems find patterns that disappear out of sample because the model has fit noise rather than structure. That is one reason quantitative firms spend so much effort on data quality before they ever build a model.

In practice, signal separation often begins with a version of the 80/20 rule. A small number of clean indicators usually carries most of the predictive value. One company consolidated thirty data sources and found that customer purchase history and verified transaction records accounted for almost all of the forecasting power. Survey responses and incomplete records mostly added noise. The important dimensions here are familiar: accuracy, completeness, and consistency. Standardized regulatory data usually carries a stronger signal than conflicting media summaries.

Demand modeling shows how signal can sometimes be preserved by getting more granular rather than more abstract. Analysts may break sales data down to the level of item, order line, and ship-to location, then layer in seasonality, promotion effects, and other market information. This approach does not try to erase all variation. It accepts that some noise is part of the system and focuses instead on preserving the underlying demand signal.

More data is not automatically better. Large datasets often contain as much noise as signal, and they can hide sampling bias under a veneer of scale. Analysts become overconfident when they mistake broad correlation for causation. The corrective is a balance between theory and data discipline. A strong causal framework matters as much as the volume of inputs. Newer causal AI approaches try to produce regime-specific, nonlinear predictions while also showing which variables actually drive the output.

Trend-following offers another example. Diversifying across more uncorrelated markets can improve the strategy because true trends show up across different asset classes while random noise tends to cancel out. That logic does not apply everywhere. In stock picking, adding more names can dilute the quality of research. Sentiment analysis shows a similar distinction. Direct measures of sentiment around a single stock often outperform broader proxies such as put-call ratios, which may reflect hedging rather than simple directional conviction.

The final analytical test is to distinguish coincidence from causation. A stock rising alongside an increase in social-media mentions may reflect real retail demand, or it may reflect organized manipulation. Cross-checking the move against options activity helps clarify the picture. Heavy volume in options relative to open interest may show institutional positioning ahead of the move. Multi-source verification allows each signal to be weighted by reliability rather than treated equally.

That is how raw market data becomes usable intelligence. The goal is not to eliminate all noise. It is to remove enough of it that the remaining signal is durable, interpretable, and connected to something real.

Fed Communications and Central Bank Watching

The Federal Reserve publishes more text about its intentions than almost any institution in the world. The challenge isn't access — it's knowing which documents carry which kind of signal, whose words move markets, and when to expect meaningful communication versus noise. Working the Fed's communications stack systematically is a distinct analytical skill, separate from macroeconomic forecasting, that pays consistent dividends across asset classes.

The Fed Communications Taxonomy

The Fed communicates through seven distinct channels, each with different authority, timeliness, and signal value (see table).

The hierarchy is important to keep in mind. The FOMC Statement is the official output — the policy rate decision and any accompanying forward guidance language. But the Chair's press conference is often more market-moving than the statement itself, because it's the only moment in each cycle where a journalist or question can surface something management didn't prepare language for. Watch specifically for any divergence between the statement's written language and the Chair's oral elaboration on the same point.

Fed Communication Taxonomy Table

Document / Channel	Timing	Signal Type
FOMC Statement	Day of meeting (~2:00 PM ET)	Official policy decision + forward guidance language
Chair Press Conference	Day of meeting (~2:30 PM ET)	Unscripted elaboration; often more informative than statement
Summary of Economic Projections (SEP)	Quarterly (4 of 8 meetings)	GDP, inflation, unemployment forecasts + dot plot
FOMC Minutes	~3 weeks after meeting	Range of internal views; debate not visible in statement
FOMC Transcripts	5-year lag	Full verbatim record; useful for historical regime analysis
Governor/President Speeches	Ongoing, calendar-driven	Individual policy signals; weight depends on speaker role
Beige Book	~2 weeks before each meeting	Regional economic conditions; qualitative leading indicator

The Dot Plot: What It Shows and What It Doesn't

The Summary of Economic Projections — published four times per year at the March, June, September, and December meetings — contains the "dot plot": each

FOMC participant's projection of the appropriate federal funds rate at year-end for the current year, the next two years, and the "longer run."

The dot plot is frequently misread. Common errors:

Treating median dots as commitments. The dot plot is a snapshot of individual expectations, not a policy commitment. A participant whose dot shows two cuts this year may vote differently if data changes between now and December. The Fed has said explicitly that dots are not a forecast of the committee's collective intentions.

Ignoring the distribution. The median dot gets most coverage. The range of dots is often more informative — a wide dispersion signals genuine internal disagreement about the trajectory, which implies higher uncertainty about future policy and typically gets priced into rate volatility. A tight cluster signals rare consensus and reduces near-term policy surprise risk.

Comparing dots across meetings without adjusting for composition. Participants rotate on and off the voting roster. The median dot can shift between meetings even if no individual changed their view, simply because different participants are voting. Track which participants are voting in a given year and weight their dots accordingly.

Reading the "longer run" dot as a target. The longer-run dot represents each participant's estimate of the neutral rate — the rate consistent with stable inflation and full employment over time. This is a useful long-run benchmark but has limited tactical relevance for near-term positioning.

Speaker Hierarchy and Hawkish/Dovish Signal Weighting

Not all Fed speakers carry equal weight. A systematic hierarchy helps prioritize whose remarks warrant immediate attention versus a footnote review:

Tier 1 — High market impact:

- Fed Chair (currently Jerome Powell) — all speeches, testimonies, and press conference remarks
- Fed Vice Chair — statements on monetary policy and financial stability

- NY Fed President — permanent FOMC voter; closest to markets; oversees open market operations

Tier 2 — Meaningful signal:

- Remaining 4 regional bank presidents currently serving as voting members (rotate annually)
- Fed Vice Chair for Supervision — on bank regulation and financial stability topics specifically

Tier 3 — Background context:

- Non-voting regional bank presidents — express individual views but have no vote; useful for tracking the range of opinion, less useful as policy signals
- Board of Governors research staff publications — inform but don't determine policy

When a Tier 1 speaker uses language that diverges from the most recent FOMC statement — either more hawkish (emphasizing inflation risks, signaling fewer cuts) or more dovish (emphasizing growth risks, signaling more cuts) — that divergence is itself the signal. Map the exact phrasing against the statement language. Replace a single word like "patient" with "attentive" and the market will often price in a meaningful shift.

Maintain a rolling vocabulary log: a short list of the precise words and phrases that appeared in the most recent FOMC statement and press conference. New speeches that substitute or drop those words without explanation deserve scrutiny.

The Blackout Calendar

The Fed observes a communications blackout period beginning the Saturday before each FOMC meeting and ending the Thursday after the meeting decision. During these roughly ten-day windows, no FOMC participant makes public statements about monetary policy.

The practical implication: the last speeches before each blackout window carry disproportionate weight. Participants who want to signal a view — or float a trial balloon before a major decision — do so in the days immediately preceding the blackout. Mark these pre-blackout windows on your catalyst calendar and treat any policy-relevant speech in that window as a deliberate communication, not an incidental one.

The Fed's public calendar (federalreserve.gov/newsevents) publishes scheduled speeches, testimonies, and appearances. Set a basic alert — even a simple bookmark check on Sunday evenings — to identify which Tier 1 or Tier 2 speakers have events scheduled in the coming week and whether those events fall inside or outside the blackout window.

The Beige Book as a Leading Qualitative Indicator

The Beige Book — formally the "Summary of Commentary on Current Economic Conditions" — is published approximately two weeks before each FOMC meeting. Each of the twelve Federal Reserve districts contributes a section describing local economic conditions gathered from business contacts, surveys, and interviews. It is explicitly qualitative and explicitly anecdotal.

Its value lies precisely in that anecdotal character. The Beige Book surface-mines what company management teams are telling their bankers before those conditions show up in official data. Watch specifically for:

- Changes in language describing consumer spending, with attention to whether retail contacts are reporting trade-down behavior or demand softness
- Labor market descriptions — whether contacts are reporting easier hiring, wage pressure changes, or layoffs in sectors not yet visible in BLS data
- Credit availability language — whether small business contacts describe tightening lending standards before bank earnings confirm it

Compare the current Beige Book to the prior two editions, looking for directional shifts in the dominant tone. The New York Fed's regional section carries particular weight for financial sector conditions.

Monitoring Non-Fed Central Banks

For analysts with international exposure, three other central banks generate market-moving communications on regular schedules:

European Central Bank (ECB): The ECB Governing Council meets approximately every six weeks. The press conference following each meeting is the primary signal source — the structure mirrors the Fed's, with a prepared statement followed by unscripted questions. ECB watchers track the specific phrasing around "data-dependent" and "meeting-by-meeting" to gauge forward guidance commitment. Published communications are at ecb.europa.eu.

Bank of Japan (BOJ): The BOJ's communications require particular attention to policy framework language — the shift away from yield curve control in 2024 demonstrated how a single framework change can generate multi-standard-deviation moves in JGB yields and yen crosses. Policy statements are published at boj.or.jp; the Governor's post-meeting press conference is the primary unscripted signal source.

Bank of England (BOE): The Monetary Policy Committee (MPC) publishes a quarterly Monetary Policy Report alongside rate decisions, providing forecasts analogous to the Fed's SEP. The vote breakdown — which MPC members dissented and in which direction — is published immediately with the decision, making it more transparent than the Fed's minutes for tracking internal disagreement in real time.

For each central bank, apply the same taxonomy principle: identify the highest-authority communication channel, map it against the next scheduled event, and flag divergence from prior language as the primary signal rather than the absolute level of any policy statement.

The Risk Premium Channel

The mechanism connecting Fed communication to asset prices runs through risk premiums as much as through rate expectations. When the Fed explicitly acknowledges uncertainty about economic conditions and signals readiness to adjust policy quickly, it influences the compensation investors demand for holding risky assets — not just the rate path itself.

This means dovish communication doesn't automatically reduce risk premiums or trigger equity rallies if investors read the dovishness as a response to genuine deterioration. The market response depends on whether Fed communication signals vigilant monitoring (confidence-enhancing) or reactive catch-up (confidence-reducing). Reading which frame applies requires tracking the data the Fed was responding to — which makes the macro release monitoring in the preceding section the analytical prerequisite for interpreting central bank communications accurately.

Key Takeaways

- ☐ Scheduled government data releases move markets through the surprise element, not the data itself. Markets price in expectations before the release. The intelligence value lies in understanding what consensus expects and positioning for the gap between expectation and outcome.
- ☐ Source verification is not optional. Financial media verification requires a confidence score — incorporating source credibility, evidence quality, and corroboration level — not a binary true/false judgment. High-confidence reports enter analysis directly. Medium-confidence reports require additional verification. Low-confidence reports trigger deeper investigation or exclusion.
- ☐ The Fed communicates through seven distinct channels with different authority and timeliness. The Chair's press conference often moves markets more than the FOMC statement because it is the only unscripted moment in the cycle. The dot plot is a snapshot of individual expectations, not a policy commitment. Pre-blackout speeches carry disproportionate weight because participants who want to signal a view do so in the days immediately before the communications window closes.

Fieldwork

- ☐ Mark the next month's major economic release dates on your calendar: CPI, employment report, retail sales, and any scheduled Fed speeches. For each, note the consensus estimate before the release and the actual figure after. Track how the market reacted relative to the surprise, not the absolute number.
- ☐ Build a simple Fed speaker log. For the next FOMC cycle, note which Tier 1 and Tier 2 speakers have scheduled events, whether those events fall inside or outside the blackout window, and whether the language used diverges from the most recent FOMC statement. Compare specific phrases.
- ☐ Pull the two most recent Beige Book editions from federalreserve.gov. Compare the language describing consumer spending and labor market

conditions across the same Fed districts. Directional shifts in the dominant tone often foreshadow the data that follows.

Apply This

Signals to watch for: a Tier 1 Fed speaker substituting a single word in language that otherwise mirrors the FOMC statement, a wide dispersion of dots in the SEP indicating genuine internal disagreement, short interest rising above 20% while the company's stock price holds steady or climbs, and high-yield bond spreads widening while equity indices continue rising — credit markets often detect stress months before equities adjust.

CHAPTER 11

Activist Investor and Short-Seller Analysis

Market narratives do not always shift on their own. Often they are pushed. This chapter looks at organized campaigns in which capital and research are used to force corporate action or expose what the campaign believes to be fraud. The task is not simply to decide whether a position is bullish or bearish. It is to understand how influence is being applied, how strong the evidence is, and what regulatory structure governs the conflict.

Recent years have brought a sharp rise in activist short campaigns. In 2025 alone, 166 were launched globally, up fifty-five percent from the prior year. Technology companies, especially those tied to artificial intelligence, were the most frequent targets, accounting for fifty-five campaigns. The average short campaign generated returns of 7.2 percent within thirty days of launch (Diligent Market Intelligence, 2026). The point is not just that these campaigns are more common. It is that public confrontation has become an ordinary investment tactic rather than a marginal one.

Regulatory changes have also compressed the timeline. The SEC shortened the initial Schedule 13D deadline from ten calendar days to five business days after an investor crosses five percent ownership. Amendments now must be filed within two business days of a material change, replacing the older and looser "promptly" standard. The effect is to shorten the period of undisclosed accumulation and bring possible catalysts into public view sooner, while still preserving some element of surprise.

The harder problem is telling legitimate analysis from manipulation. Recent enforcement actions show what that distinction can look like in practice. The Department of Justice charged Andrew Left with securities fraud and market manipulation, alleging that misleading reports produced $20 million in illicit gains and triggered average stock swings of more than twelve percent. In another case, the SEC settled charges against a trader accused of a two-year spoofing scheme in thinly traded stocks, where fake orders were used to move the price before genuine trades were placed on the other side.

The analytical task is not to pick a team. It is to test the evidence chain supporting each side. Strong activist reports usually rest on primary-source material: internal emails, former employees who can supply names and dates, or forensic accounting that follows transactions through multiple layers of ownership. Weak reports tend to rely on circumstantial readings of public filings, stretched inferences, and aggressive framing. The company's answer is equally informative. A strong rebuttal addresses the allegations point by point and produces documents. A weak one falls back on broad denial, outrage, or attacks on the messenger.

The market's reaction often says something about credibility. A short thesis based on real structural weakness usually leads to a sustained decline as investors work through the evidence. A manipulative campaign more often produces a sharp drop followed by a quick recovery once the claims begin to fall apart. Options activity and short-interest data around publication can help show whether more sophisticated participants regard the thesis as credible or merely opportunistic.

The last step is scenario work. Could the allegations be partly true but not large enough to change valuation? Could the accounting be aggressive without being fraudulent? The useful insight often lies in the space between the opposing stories. That is where signal emerges from noise.

Reading Activist and Short-Seller Reports Critically

An activist short seller publishes a long report claiming that a company fabricated customer contracts and overstated revenue by forty percent. The stock falls twenty percent in a few hours. The company answers with a forceful denial, accusing the report of factual error and distortion. Both sides cite evidence. Both claim the facts are on their side. That kind of situation calls for a methodical framework, not intuition. The work begins before the first allegation is read and continues after publication, through the market's response.

The first question is simple: when did the activist establish the short position relative to publication? Legitimate activists usually disclose that they are short, and they generally build the position days or weeks before going public. That sequence aligns the financial incentive with the claim that the research is intended to correct a mispricing. The disclosure section matters. Hindenburg Research's January 2023 report on Adani stated plainly: "We have taken a short position in Adani Group Companies through U.S.-traded bonds and non-Indian-traded derivative instruments." Specificity matters. "May have positions" is weaker than a direct statement of exposure and timing.

The next step is to examine the activist's record and method before getting lost in the details of a single report. Firms such as Muddy Waters, Hindenburg, Citron, and Spruce Point have public histories that can be checked. Some of their campaigns led to regulatory action, auditor resignations, or confirmed fraud. Others led to litigation or rapid stock recovery, suggesting that the claims reached too far. Methodological transparency counts here. Muddy Waters, for example, describes the use of forensic accounting, channel checks, site visits, expert consultation, and document work. Anonymous reports or firms with no verifiable record deserve more skepticism. A basic scorecard helps: age of firm, number of campaigns, percentage that led to confirmed problems, litigation history, and the quality of the method disclosure.

The evidence itself then has to be sorted by strength. Not all evidence deserves equal weight. Primary evidence is the strongest: internal emails with verifiable headers, named former employees with dates and specifics, photographs of facilities, contracts attached as exhibits, or transaction tracing that links entities across layers. Hindenburg's Adani report, for example, named offshore entities, mapped flows through Mauritius and Caribbean jurisdictions, and tied shell companies to family members through registries and leaked databases. Secondary evidence is weaker but still useful: statistical patterns in public financials, peer comparisons, expert commentary, and inconsistencies across filings. Tertiary evidence is weakest: speculation, unnamed sources without details, and guilt by association. The easiest way to keep the distinctions straight is to build a table while reading—primary, secondary, tertiary—and force each major claim into one of the three buckets. High-quality reports lean heavily on the first bucket. Weak reports lean on the third.

Every serious allegation should then be treated as a hypothesis to be checked against primary documents. A claim about revenue inflation means pulling the latest 10-K and 10-Q from EDGAR and seeing whether the activist's calculations match the company's presentation. If the claim concerns offshore structures, the work moves to corporate registries, offshore-leak databases, and named directors. In the Adani case, for instance, verification required asking whether the cited entities appeared in company filings, whether the named directors actually had the claimed family ties, and whether the transaction figures reconciled to the footnotes. A spreadsheet helps keep the process honest: claim, page number, primary source checked, result, notes. Without that kind of structure, it is easy to verify only what fits the initial bias.

The company's rebuttal deserves the same treatment. A useful response answers the most serious allegations directly, supplies documents, and explains the specific discrepancies the activist identified. Adani's response to Hindenburg ran more than 400 pages and included appendices, analysis, and legal opinions, though critics argued that it still failed to deal squarely with certain offshore beneficial-ownership questions. Strong rebuttals provide auditor or legal support, document exhibits, quantitative reconciliation, and timeline evidence. Weak rebuttals fall back on general denials, personal attacks, vague promises of future review, or emotional appeals unrelated to the allegations. Tone is less reliable than substance. Aggression can be a substitute for proof.

The market's behavior after publication supplies another kind of evidence. The price path matters, but so do the reactions of institutions and gatekeepers. Short reports in 2022 produced an average immediate decline of 31.3 percent across 113 campaigns. The more important question is what happens over the next one to three months. A sustained decline suggests that investors are confirming the concerns for themselves. A quick recovery to pre-report levels suggests that the thesis is weak or overstated. Institutional exits visible later in 13F filings, or gatekeeper responses such as auditor resignations, credit downgrades, withdrawn financing, regulatory inquiries, or serious securities litigation, all carry weight. In the Adani case, the group lost roughly $150 billion in market value before recovering some ground as new investors stepped in. That pattern suggested that the market saw the governance concerns as real, but not every allegation as equally damaging.

There are also recurring green flags and red flags. Reports deserve more suspicion when they come from anonymous or newly formed entities, disclose positions vaguely or only after publication, rely mostly on circumstantial evidence, use sensational language, contain basic factual mistakes, offer no clear method, or come from actors with prior sanctions or defamation losses. They deserve more credit when they disclose the short explicitly, come from firms with real histories, supply primary-source exhibits, cite precise filing locations, maintain a measured tone, explain how the research was done, and build quantitative claims that can be reconciled to public statements. Hindenburg's Adani report scored well on several of those dimensions, though it still drew criticism for relying too heavily on circumstantial evidence in places.

The last step is probabilistic rather than binary. Fraud or exoneration is too crude a frame. A better approach is to build three scenarios. In the bear case, the activist is substantially right and the valuation damage is material. In the base case, the accounting may be aggressive and the governance weak, but the ultimate valuation effect is limited. In the bull case, the claims are mostly wrong and the selloff has created an overreaction. Each scenario should be tied to concrete evidence and assigned a rough probability. In the Adani situation, for example, one could have imagined a bear case built around concealed beneficial ownership and unsustainable leverage, a base case built around opacity and governance weakness without fatal fraud, and a bull case built around political and rhetorical overstatement. The probabilities would then move as auditor opinions, regulatory actions, and third-party diligence reports emerged. That framework makes position sizing more disciplined and reduces the temptation to become certain too early.

Used properly, this process turns activist analysis from side-taking into structured intelligence work. The sequence becomes familiar: verify position timing, assess the activist's record, sort the evidence by quality, check the major claims independently, test the rebuttal for substance, watch the market and the gatekeepers, identify the pattern of credibility, and then build scenarios with explicit triggers that would change the view. That discipline mattered in the Nikola case, where investors who focused on the primary evidence of nonfunctioning prototypes had a chance to get out before the stock collapsed. It also matters in the opposite direction, when a weak short report is met by strong documentation and the stock recovers. The edge comes from finishing the work before taking a side.

Identifying 13D Activist Filings and Catalysts

A hedge fund buys six percent of a mid-cap industrial company. For a time, the market does not know. Then a Schedule 13D appears on EDGAR, disclosing the position, the funding source, and a plan to nominate three directors. The stock jumps twelve percent before the open. That is the predictive value of the filing. It often appears before the broader public narrative has formed, and it lays out a strategy in plain sight for anyone who knows where to look.

The obligation begins when an investor acquires beneficial ownership of more than five percent of a voting class of equity securities. Beneficial ownership is broader than direct shareholding. It includes voting or investment power held through derivatives such as options and swaps. The decisive issue is intent. A holder with no plan to influence control generally files the short-form Schedule 13G. An investor with activist intent must file Schedule 13D, and the clock starts once that investor crosses the five percent threshold.

The filing window has shortened. What used to be ten calendar days is now five business days. That reduces the time in which an activist can build a position without public attention. The initial filing has to disclose the exact ownership percentage, the source of funds, recent transactions, and, most important, the purpose of the transaction. That section often functions as a public outline of the campaign.

The "Purpose of Transaction" section deserves close reading. Boilerplate stating that the investment is held for "investment purposes" points to passivity. Specific plans described in Item 4—board representation, mergers, asset sales, dividend changes, recapitalization—point to activism. The language often develops over time. A first filing may say only that the investor is evaluating strategic alternatives. An amendment filed weeks later may disclose meetings with management about a spin-off or sale process. That progression shows the campaign taking shape.

Amendments are significan because they provide live intelligence on momentum. Material changes in plans or stake size must now be reported within two business days. An increase of one percent in ownership often coincides with greater pressure. Amendments can also reveal the results of management meetings, revised proposals, or the existence of a group. Under securities law, casual discussion is not enough to form a group. There must be an agreement to act together with respect to acquiring, holding, or disposing of the securities. When a filing begins to show coalition-building, the pressure on management is changing.

A 13D does not mean that a company is about to sell itself or replace its board. Many campaigns drag on for months. The filing is an opening move. Another common mistake is to miss the significance of a shift from 13G to 13D. A passive holder that develops activist intent must switch forms. That shift also triggers a cooling-off period: the investor cannot vote the shares or take certain activist steps until ten days after filing the 13D. The rule is meant to prevent an investor from accumulating quietly and then acting immediately before the market has a chance to absorb the disclosure.

In practice, screening begins with EDGAR filters for "SC 13D" and "SC 13D/A." Daily alerts by sector or market capitalization can surface new campaigns as soon as they become public. Once a filing appears, the next step is to compare it with the filer's history. Some funds specialize in operational turnarounds. Others push balance-sheet changes or outright sales. Their past filings often reveal the playbook.

The real catalyst often comes in the response. The filing forces management into public reaction. Press releases, proxy materials, litigation, and additional SEC filings usually follow. Those responses expose management's level of preparation and vulnerability. A slow or defensive response can suggest weakness. A prompt rebuttal grounded in operational detail suggests the company was ready. Once the 13D appears, the campaign becomes a public sequence of pressure and counterpressure, documented in real time.

Distinguishing Legitimate Short Thesis from Manipulation

A research firm publishes a report claiming that a company's assets are overstated by forty percent. The stock drops hard. The company denies everything. The central question is whether the report represents legitimate analysis or manipulation. The difference turns less on the eventual stock move than on intent, method, and evidence. Legitimate short analysis tries to correct a mispricing by surfacing factual weaknesses. Manipulation tries to create an artificial price move through deception.

The law draws the line the same way. Legitimate short selling means taking a bearish view based on fundamentals—poor earnings, overleverage, weak governance, flawed accounting—and profiting if the price falls. Manipulation involves tactics designed to move the price without a real basis in value. That includes spoofing, layering, wash trading, and bear raids built on illegal or deceptive trading pressure rather than analysis.

The contrast becomes clearer when set against a pump-and-dump scheme. In that structure, an actor accumulates stock in an illiquid name, spreads false bullish claims through social media or fake releases, and then sells into the buying frenzy created by the deception. A legitimate short thesis does the opposite. It may be aggressive and self-interested, but it stands or falls on verifiable information, not fabrication.

Regulators look for manipulative intent through observable patterns. Surveillance systems monitor for conduct such as marking the close, where trades near the end of a session are used to influence the closing price, or spoofing, where orders are entered with no intention of execution in order to create a false impression of demand or supply. Those behaviors differ from ordinary short selling because the point is to distort the market, not to express a view on value.

Not all aggressive shorting is manipulation. Short selling serves a valid function in price discovery and liquidity provision. Only certain tactics cross the line. A related mistake is to assume that trades executed openly on the market cannot be manipulative. They can. Legal and academic work on open-market manipulation shows that real trades, placed at specific times and in specific sequences, can be used to force an artificial price if the trader's purpose is distortion rather than economic value.

For financial-intelligence purposes, the most reliable test is the quality of the thesis under independent review. Legitimate reports cite exact filings, page numbers, registries, contracts, or court records. Manipulative ones rely more heavily on vague accusation, emotional rhetoric, and claims that cannot be checked. Position disclosure also matters. Established research firms usually disclose that they are short and acknowledge their conflict. Manipulative actors tend to obscure the position or the identity of the speaker.

The publisher's own history matters as well. A firm with a documented record of accurate analysis deserves different treatment from an anonymous account or a newly created entity. That does not make the firm right. It does affect the burden of proof the analyst places on the claims. The same goes for disclosure. Complete and timely disclosure of the short position is a point in favor of legitimacy. Concealment cuts the other way.

The market's response is informative but not dispositive. A legitimate short thesis grounded in real weakness tends to result in a decline that persists as investors verify the claims. A manipulative attack often creates a steep drop followed by a rebound once the allegations fail to hold up. Options activity, short-interest changes, and the reaction of other informed participants can help show how seriously the market is taking the thesis.

The challenge is that enforcement usually requires proof of specific intent to deceive or create an artificial price. That is a high bar, which is why many cases remain ambiguous. For analytical purposes, that ambiguity is less important than the observable facts. The best question is not what was in the speaker's mind. It is whether the thesis survives disciplined verification against primary-source evidence. That is the most dependable dividing line.

Key Takeaways

- ☐ Evaluate activist and short-seller reports using an evidence classification system: primary evidence (internal documents, named sources, forensic accounting with transaction traces), secondary evidence (statistical analysis of public filings, expert commentary, peer comparisons), and tertiary evidence (speculation, unnamed sources, guilt by association). High-quality reports lean heavily on primary evidence. Weak reports lean on tertiary.
- ☐ The company's response is as informative as the report itself. Strong rebuttals address specific allegations point by point with counter-documents. Weak rebuttals rely on general denials, character attacks, or appeals to reputation without factual rebuttal. Score the response on the same evidence framework you applied to the report.
- ☐ Avoid binary fraud-or-vindication thinking. Construct three scenarios — bear case (allegations largely accurate), base case (aggressive but legal, governance concerns legitimate), bull case (claims mostly wrong, stock oversold) — with probability weights that shift as new evidence emerges.

Fieldwork

- ☐ Find a recent activist short report from a firm with a public track record (Hindenburg, Muddy Waters, Spruce Point, or Citron). Before reading the report, check: Did the firm disclose its short position? When was the position established relative to publication? Then read the report and classify every material claim as primary, secondary, or tertiary evidence using a three-column table.
- ☐ Read the target company's official response. Score it: Does it address the three most serious allegations specifically? Does it provide counter-documents? Does it cite independent third-party verification? A high-quality report paired with a low-scoring rebuttal is a stronger signal than either document alone.
- ☐ Track the stock price, institutional 13F changes, and gatekeeper reactions (auditor actions, credit rating changes, regulatory announcements) for 90

days after publication. These revealed preferences tell you more about credibility than either side's rhetoric.

Apply This

Red flags suggesting manipulation: anonymous or unknown firm with no track record, vague position disclosure, evidence heavily circumstantial, sensationalist language dominating over factual analysis, demonstrable factual errors in basic data. Green flags suggesting legitimate research: explicit position disclosure with timing, established firm with documented prior successes, primary source documentation with verifiable references, transparent methodology, measured tone focused on facts.

CHAPTER 12

Options and Credit Market Intelligence

A semiconductor stock trades flat for weeks, then suddenly sees a surge in out-of-the-money call volume. A high-yield bond spread begins widening while the equity index tied to it keeps rising. These are not random fluctuations. They are structured signals from market participants working with different priorities, different constraints, and different access to information. Equity prices reflect the market's collective judgment, but that judgment reaches the tape through different channels, each moving on its own timeline and reacting to different pressures.

Two of those channels matter here: the options market, where volatility expectations are priced, and the credit market, where default risk is assessed. The intelligence problem is to read the signals these markets produce, understand their limits, and fit them into a coherent view of corporate and sector health. The task is not to find a single predictive indicator. It is to recognize when different asset classes begin telling conflicting stories about the same underlying reality.

The discussion starts with unusual options flow as a real-time sign of professional positioning. It then turns to the delayed and incomplete disclosure of institutional derivatives exposure through regulatory filings. From there it moves into credit markets, where bond spreads and credit default swap spreads often serve as early warnings of equity stress. Debt sits above equity in the capital structure, and credit markets often react sooner when conditions begin to weaken.

Unusual Options Activity as a Signal

A trader notices a burst of out-of-the-money call buying in a semiconductor stock. Volume rises to ten times the daily average, with contracts trading at a strike price 20 percent above the current share price. The strike price is the fixed level at which the option can be exercised to buy or sell the underlying stock.

The pattern does not guarantee that the stock will rise. It does suggest that a sophisticated participant is placing a substantial directional bet with clearly defined risk. Unusual options activity is a category of market signal in which order flow departs from normal patterns in size, timing, or structure. Its value lies less in predicting direction than in showing where professional capital expects volatility.

The signal becomes unusual through a mix of quantitative thresholds and qualitative features. The simplest indicator is a volume spike, often defined as trading volume more than five times the daily average. A stronger signal appears when trading volume exceeds existing open interest.

If only 250 put contracts are open in a stock and 10,000 are bought in one session, the trade represents new exposure rather than a reshuffling among existing holders. In share terms, it is equivalent to a one million share short position. Notional size also helps separate serious positioning from background noise. Trades above $100,000 usually indicate meaningful capital commitment.

Execution details add another layer. Orders filled on the offer, where buyers pay the asking price, point to aggressive buying rather than passive limit-order activity.

Market structure can reveal intent. A sweep trade is a market order split across multiple exchanges to capture the best available prices. Exchanges tag these transactions, and they often point to algorithmic execution by an advanced investor or institution trying to limit market impact. A cluster of smaller, near-simultaneous trades across venues can conceal the full size of one large order.

Block trades work differently. They are large, privately negotiated orders executed off-exchange, typically involving more than 10,000 contracts. Institutions use them when they want secrecy or when size and price constraints make ordinary exchange execution impractical. Both sweep and block activity point more toward institutional participation than retail flow.

The strongest unusual-activity profile combines several features. The notional amount is large. The trade is executed on the offer. Volume materially exceeds open interest. The options are well out of the money, with strike prices far from the current stock price. Implied volatility is low enough that standard pricing models treat a move to the strike as unlikely.

When those conditions line up, the trade reflects a high-conviction, low-probability bet by someone willing to risk capital on a specific catalyst or price move.

Several mistakes weaken the value of this signal. One is to assume that unusual activity predicts stock direction with certainty. It does not. Large trades are directionally ambiguous in the sense that both buyer and seller are committed. The trade confirms heightened attention, not inevitable price movement.

Another error is to treat unusual options activity as presumptive insider trading. That can happen, but more often the flow reflects institutional hedging, positioning around earnings, or a response to anticipated news. Volume by itself is not enough. An analyst has to combine volume exceedance, trade side, distance from the money, and the apparent improbability implied by volatility pricing to separate genuine signals from ordinary noise.

In practice, unusual options activity belongs inside a broader intelligence cycle. It is a collection trigger, not a conclusion. The signal should prompt a deeper look at why sophisticated capital expects volatility. That investigation may lead to regulatory deadlines, patent expirations, supply-chain disruptions, or other catalysts.

The signal becomes more useful when checked against 13F filings for institutional equity exposure and insider transaction reports for executive behavior. It is one tile in a mosaic, not a trading system on its own. Often the best insight comes not from one stock but from clusters of similar activity across related companies or an entire sector. That is where institutional capital begins to reveal an expectation of systemic change rather than an isolated event.

13F Options Disclosures and Derivatives Positioning

An activist investor builds economic exposure to a retail company through total return swaps and call options. The quarterly Form 13F shows nothing. Six weeks later, a Schedule 13D discloses the activist's full economic stake, assembled through derivatives that bypassed 13F reporting.

The gap captures the central weakness of 13F options disclosure. The filing offers a partial and delayed snapshot of institutional derivatives positioning, not a full map of market exposure.

Form 13F requires institutional investment managers with more than $100 million in qualifying securities to report their long holdings each quarter. The SEC maintains an official list of Section 13(f) securities that includes U.S. exchange-traded stocks, ETFs, options, and warrants. Managers must report long put and call positions held at quarter-end, mark them with "COM" in the filing's second column, and list the underlying stock's CUSIP.

Written options are excluded entirely. A fund that sells covered calls against a stock position reports the long stock but not the short call that limits its upside.

The reporting thresholds create another blind spot. Managers may omit positions smaller than 10,000 shares and $200,000 in fair market value, but only if both conditions are met. A position of 9,800 shares worth $205,000 must be reported because it crosses the value threshold. A position of 10,500 shares worth $198,000 must also be reported because it crosses the share threshold.

The de minimis rule lets funds hide small option positions while disclosing larger ones, which adds noise to the data. Once a manager crosses the $100 million aggregate threshold, the filing requirement continues through the next calendar year even if holdings later fall below that level.

The quarter-end snapshot creates a large timing problem. A 13F reflects positions as they stood on the final day of the calendar quarter. Managers then have 45 days to file. If an activist starts building a derivatives position in early October, that exposure will not appear in any 13F until the December 31 quarter-end filing becomes public in mid-February.

That lag helps explain why 13D filings sometimes reveal positions that looked absent from recent 13Fs. The exposure was built during the reporting gap.

Broker-dealer masking is a more deliberate form of concealment. Hedge funds use swaps, over-the-counter options, and forward contracts with investment bank counterparties. In the 13F, the prime broker or investment bank appears as the holder of record. The activist's name disappears behind the counterparty.

That allows funds to build economic exposure without drawing public attention until they decide, or are forced, to file a 13D. The filing shows generic institutional ownership, not specific activist intent.

Confidential treatment requests add another layer of opacity. Managers engaged in risk arbitrage can ask for confidential treatment for positions they consider sensitive. They disclose those positions privately to the SEC while withholding them from the public 13F. The exception is meant to protect merger-arbitrage strategies, but in practice it also obscures significant derivatives exposure.

When options are absent from a public 13F, the absence may mean there is no position. It may also mean the position was filed confidentially.

For that reason, 13F options data should be treated as a starting point, not a definitive source. It shows what institutions were required to disclose, and willing to disclose, under narrow regulatory rules at a specific historical moment. It captures long options exposure in securities on the official list while leaving out the much larger universe of over-the-counter derivatives, futures, and short positions that shape modern institutional strategies.

Cross-checking 13F data against unusual options activity provides a more current signal. Monitoring 13D filings helps identify activist derivatives positions that bypass quarterly reporting. The clearest picture comes from combining those delayed disclosures with real-time market evidence, while recognizing that a great deal of institutional exposure sits in the spaces between reporting rules.

Credit and Bond Market Signals as Leading Indicators

A high-yield bond spread starts widening while the S&P 500 trades near cycle highs. Credit turns cautious while equities remain optimistic. The divergence is familiar, and often it appears before equity markets fully absorb the same information. Bondholders must be paid before shareholders receive anything. That seniority makes credit markets more sensitive to worsening fundamentals.

The spread between high-yield corporate bonds and Treasuries is among the more reliable leading indicators of equity-market corrections. When investors demand much higher yields to hold riskier corporate debt, they are signaling rising default risk before stock prices necessarily adjust. The spread is the additional return required to compensate for possible loss.

If it expands steadily while equities remain elevated, bond investors may be pricing trouble that stock investors have yet to acknowledge.

Investment-grade spreads offer a subtler, more sector-specific signal. Aggregate investment-grade spreads may look stable while weakness develops underneath. Energy and materials issuers often see spreads widen first in an economic slowdown. Technology and healthcare companies with stronger cash generation tend to hold tighter spreads for longer.

Watching divergence at the sector level inside the investment-grade universe can show where equity risk is likely to surface first.

Credit default swap spreads add another forward-looking measure. A CDS is insurance against default. When spreads rise, the market is paying more for protection against corporate failure. That can happen even when actual defaults remain low. The gap between low realized default rates and higher protection costs signals concern about future conditions rather than current ones.

The distance-to-default framework gives a related measure of corporate fragility, though it is derived from equity. It estimates how many standard deviations a company's asset value sits above its default point. Research on bank fragility found that distance-to-default measures can signal weakening six to eighteen months in advance. Subordinated bond spreads, by contrast, often begin to signal trouble only three to six months before default events.

In that setting, equity-based measures can provide earlier warnings than debt markets for the same institutions.

Yield-curve analysis offers the macro version of the same logic. The spread between ten-year Treasury yields and short-term rates has historically predicted recessions roughly twelve months ahead. When the curve inverts and that spread turns negative, economic contraction has often followed. The New York Fed maintains a recession-probability model based on movements in the term spread. The relationship persists because an inverted curve usually reflects tight monetary policy and weaker lending incentives.

Liquidity conditions in credit markets provide another early warning. As investors become more risk-averse, money moves out of corporate bonds and into Treasuries. That flight to quality drains liquidity from corporate credit markets. A flight to quality is the broad shift of capital away from risky assets and toward safer government securities in periods of stress.

Tighter credit conditions then weigh on business investment and growth. The result is a feedback loop: thinner liquidity widens spreads, and wider spreads reduce liquidity further.

Several common assumptions distort the picture. One is the belief that equity markets fully and immediately reflect all available risk information. Credit markets often identify stress months earlier. Another is the idea that all credit spreads carry the same predictive value. High-yield spreads are generally far more useful than investment-grade spreads in forecasting equity corrections.

A third mistake is to read narrow spreads as proof of continued health. Spreads can remain exceptionally tight during equity-market highs, then widen abruptly when sentiment turns.

Credit signals work best in combination. The Conference Board's Leading Economic Index includes six financial indicators with forward-looking value: swap spreads, LIBOR-Treasury spreads, margin balances, investor sentiment, loan officer surveys, and security repurchases. Combining credit spreads with measures like these produces a stronger warning system than any one indicator can provide.

The useful approach is not to rely on a single spread. It is to watch a set of credit indicators with different lead times and different sector exposures.

CDS Spreads and Credit Rating Actions

A credit default swap spread is the annual cost of insuring against a company's default. It is quoted in basis points on the contract's notional amount. A 100-basis-point spread on a $10 million notional contract requires quarterly premium payments of $25,000 from the protection buyer to the protection seller. The premium reflects the market's aggregate judgment about default probability and expected recovery.

The link between rating actions and CDS spreads shows how formal credit assessments become market prices.

Downgrades usually widen spreads, but the size of the move depends on whether the market was surprised. A downgrade that was not expected can produce an overnight jump as investors revise default probabilities. If spreads had already been drifting wider for weeks, the formal rating action may add little because the deterioration was already priced in.

The asymmetry runs one way. Research shows that negative credit events push spreads wider by roughly three times as much as positive events pull them tighter.

The mechanics of CDS valuation explain why. A CDS spread has two sides. The payment leg is the present value of the future premiums paid by the buyer. The protection leg is the expected payout if default occurs. A downgrade raises the perceived hazard rate, the probability of default conditional on survival to that point. That increases the expected value of the protection leg, so spreads have to widen to bring the two legs back into balance.

Recovery-rate assumptions create another channel. Rating agencies often revise expected recovery values when they reassess credit quality. If the expected recovery rate on defaulted debt falls, the protection seller faces a larger expected payout. Spreads then widen to compensate. The CDS formula depends on both default probability and expected recovery. Even if default probability is unchanged, a lower recovery assumption pushes spreads higher.

Bank CDS contracts add a complication that does not affect most non-financial issuers to the same degree: counterparty risk. A CDS written by Bank A on Bank B exposes the buyer to the possibility that both institutions fail. In systemic stress, that counterparty risk can actually lower the observed spread because the market discounts the value of protection that may never be paid.

That breaks the usual arbitrage relationship between bond yields and CDS spreads. For non-financial corporates, the distortion is typically less severe.

Volatility and jump risk explain a large share of spread movement that ratings alone cannot capture. Studies find that volatility measures by themselves explain roughly half of CDS spread variation. Jump-risk variables, which capture sudden discontinuities in price, explain another 19 percent. Together, volatility and jump metrics account for 54 percent of spread variation even before adding ratings, macro conditions, or balance-sheet variables.

Rating actions often arrive alongside rising volatility and negative jumps, which is why spread reactions can be so sharp.

Geopolitical events and broad market sentiment add noise around rating signals. A downgrade in a period of heightened market-wide risk aversion will usually produce a larger spread move than the same downgrade in calm conditions. To isolate the company-specific effect of the rating action, an analyst has to compare the issuer's spread move with sector peers and relevant credit indexes.

That comparison helps separate idiosyncratic deterioration from a market-wide repricing of risk.

Liquidity is a factor too. Less liquid CDS contracts usually trade with wider bid-ask spreads and can react more violently to rating changes. Standard fixed coupon conventions vary by credit quality. Investment-grade contracts typically use a 1 percent fixed annual rate, while high-yield contracts generally use 5 percent. The conventions make contracts easier to compare across credits, but they also create valuation complications when spreads move far away from those standard levels.

Watching CDS trends can provide early warning of future rating actions. Spreads often widen gradually for weeks or months before a formal downgrade. The market sometimes identifies deterioration before rating committees do. The same logic works in the other direction: spread tightening can signal improving credit quality ahead of an upgrade.

The most useful intelligence comes from comparing the path of CDS spreads with agency outlooks and watchlist status.

The relationship can break down entirely when markets stop trusting the rating agencies. During the financial crisis, CDS spreads on some financial institutions widened sharply while ratings remained investment grade. The divergence reflected a market view that the rating models had failed to capture systemic interconnectedness.

In those moments, CDS markets function as a corrective to formal ratings. A spread is the price of insurance, not a theoretical judgment.

Good analysis tracks both level and direction. A BBB-rated company trading at spreads more typical of BB-rated peers is often being priced for downgrade before any formal action occurs. The pace of the move plays as much of a role as the absolute level. A rapid widening usually signals new adverse information. A slow drift may reflect broader sector pressure rather than a company-specific shock.

Combining CDS intelligence with bond-yield analysis and equity-volatility measures produces a fuller credit assessment.

KEY TAKEAWAYS

- ☐ Unusual options activity is a collection trigger, not a conclusion. The strongest signal combines several features: notional amount is large, trade is executed on the offer, volume materially exceeds open interest, strike prices are far from the current stock price, and implied volatility is low enough that the move seems improbable by standard pricing.
- ☐ Credit markets often detect corporate stress months before equity markets adjust. High-yield spreads are significantly more reliable than investment-grade spreads for forecasting equity corrections. CDS spread widening for a specific company while its equity price holds steady is a divergence worth investigating immediately.
- ☐ 13F filings disclose institutional options positions but with severe limitations: 45-day lag, no distinction between directional bets and hedges, and no information about position timing or strategic intent. Treat 13F options data as context for other signals, not as standalone intelligence.

FIELDWORK

- ☐ Identify one stock on your watchlist that recently showed a volume spike in options trading. Check whether the volume exceeded open interest for that strike and expiration. Cross-reference the timing against the company's catalyst calendar — was there an earnings date, FDA decision, or regulatory deadline within the following 30 days? If so, the activity may reflect informed positioning around a known event.
- ☐ Pull the current high-yield bond spread (OAS) from FRED and compare it to the level six months ago. If spreads have widened while equity indices are flat or rising, credit markets are pricing in risk that equities have not yet absorbed. Note which sectors show the widest individual-name CDS spread increases.
- ☐ Check whether any company on your watchlist has experienced a credit rating downgrade or outlook revision in the past 90 days. If the equity price did not react proportionally, the disconnect may represent either a delayed

equity response or a market judgment that the rating action was already priced in. Determine which.

Apply This

Signals to watch for: a sudden spike in out-of-the-money put volume without a corresponding news catalyst, CDS spreads widening for one company while sector peers remain stable, concentrated short-dated call buying that precedes social media promotion of the same stock, and investment-grade bond spreads for a company widening past the threshold where its index classification may change — forced selling by index-tracking funds often follows.

CHAPTER 13

Executive and Insider Intelligence

A company names a new chief executive with a background in oncology drug development. The stock rises on expectations of a strategic turn toward cancer therapeutics. Six months later, the company acquires a small oncology biotech at a premium valuation. The sequence is not accidental. It reflects a familiar pattern in which an executive's functional background and operating habits begin to shape corporate decisions. Most analysis stops at the announcement and misses the structured intelligence embedded in executive histories, compensation design, and insider networks.

This chapter looks past headline appointments to examine how leadership traits translate into concrete decisions. Executives are treated here as agents with recurring tendencies. Their prior performance, incentive structures, and network ties create observable patterns. Those patterns help explain where companies are likely to allocate capital, which strategic initiatives they will emphasize, and when insiders may be acting on information not yet visible in public disclosures.

The work involves reconstructing executive records from archived filings, mapping board interlocks that carry influence and information, and reading insider trading clusters as signs of shared judgment rather than personal bias. It also looks at how compensation structures shape managerial behavior and how network analysis can uncover hidden relationships that affect partnerships and strategy. The aim is to turn executive news from corporate theater into a usable intelligence input for investment analysis.

Executive Background Research and Board Interlocks

A pharmaceutical company appoints a new CEO with deep experience in oncology drug development. The stock climbs on expectations that the company will lean harder into cancer therapeutics. Six months later, it acquires a small oncology biotech at a premium. The pattern shows how executive background can shape corporate action in predictable ways. Research repeatedly finds that executives with particular functional experience make systematically different choices from peers with other backgrounds.

Upper echelons theory provides the basic framework. It holds that corporate strategy reflects the backgrounds, experience, and values of senior executives. A CEO with experience in investment banking and mergers tends to exercise more discretion in financial reporting than peers without that background. Such executives are also more likely to impair goodwill in their first year in office, reflecting a different approach to valuation and risk. The pattern appears across industries and market cycles.

Board interlocks add another layer. An interlock exists when one person sits on the boards of two or more companies, creating a network through which information and influence can travel. Among S&P 1500 firms, nearly 85 percent shared at least one director in the early 2010s. One in eight U.S. interlocks links direct competitors, raising antitrust issues under the Clayton Act of 1914. These ties can also help practices like option-backdating spread across firms.

Analysts map these interlocks to uncover relationships that do not show up in ordinary ownership data. Historical work on late nineteenth-century Boston found that seventeen directors controlled banks holding 40 percent of the city's banking capital. Those same individuals sat on the boards of six insurance companies and five railroads, coordinating activity across an ownership network. Modern board networks show a similar concentration, with dense ties among major corporations forming what researchers have described as one large corporate community.

An interlock does not by itself imply collusion. Most are legal unless they connect direct competitors, and many arise simply because companies recruit experienced directors. Governance researchers, however, often flag busy directors who sit on several public-company boards at once. Their time and attention are divided. Studies have found that firms whose boards are dominated by these busy directors tend to trade at lower valuations and grant higher executive pay.

There is another side to the picture. Studies also show that when directors leave rival boards because of death or mergers, the affected firms suffer an immediate 3 percent drop in return on assets. That equals roughly one-quarter of typical earnings. The effect is strongest when the departing director was not overloaded and could devote meaningful time to each board.

Executive background verification requires more than reading a polished biography. Investigations have uncovered inflated academic credentials, undisclosed civil judgments, tax liens filed in other states, and allegations of financial-crimes investigations in foreign jurisdictions. One North American financial-services firm discovered through public-records searches across several countries that a senior candidate faced possible embezzlement charges in Latin America. The company rejected the candidate before the issue could become its own.

Taken together, executive background analysis and board-interlock mapping offer a strong predictive tool. They help explain why some companies pursue certain acquisition strategies, adopt particular reporting practices, or drift into governance failures. Directors with banking backgrounds tend to form different networks from directors shaped by technology or operations. The effects run through capital allocation, innovation priorities, and corporate oversight. These networks have persisted despite decades of regulatory scrutiny. A 1951 Federal Trade Commission report noted that anti-competitive ties remained stubbornly intact long after the first legislative effort to curb them.

Prior Company Track Records and Performance History

A chief executive joins a new company after leading another business through steady revenue growth while leaving behind a heavily leveraged balance sheet. The pattern is useful because executives tend to carry their operating habits with them. Research shows that leaders who relied on acquisitions to drive growth at one firm often pursue similar deals in the next, even when the industry changes. Their approach to capital, risk, and strategy becomes visible through historical reconstruction.

The process starts with rebuilding the executive's tenure at prior companies from archived SEC filings. That produces a timeline showing when initiatives began and when results followed. An executive may have joined a company in 2018, launched a cost-cutting program in 2019, and reported margin expansion in 2020.

A sequence like that reveals the lag between strategic action and financial effect. It also shows whether the improvement lasted or faded.

Comparison against industry benchmarks provides the needed context. An executive who delivered 15 percent annual revenue growth while competitors averaged 10 percent likely created real operational outperformance rather than simply benefiting from favorable sector conditions. The reverse is also common. If growth matched the industry while leverage rose sharply, the record looks far less impressive once risk is taken into account. The point is to separate company-specific execution from the tide carrying the whole sector.

Financial statements across an executive's tenure show recurring preferences in capital allocation. Some leaders consistently direct cash flow into research and development, building future growth platforms. Others favor buybacks and dividends. A multi-year decline in R&D as a share of revenue may indicate a turn toward financial engineering rather than operating improvement. These preferences often transfer to the next role with surprising consistency.

Departure context also carries intelligence. Executives who leave during periods of strong performance usually present a different risk profile from those who depart during deterioration. A sudden resignation without a clear succession plan can precede negative disclosures that surface months later. Cross-checking departure announcements against later 8-K filings and earnings reports can show whether the executive exited before the market learned about the problem.

Past results do not automatically travel across market conditions. An executive who thrived in a fast-growing industry may struggle in a mature and competitive one that requires a different skill set. The analysis therefore has to test fit, not just record. A turnaround specialist may be strong on cost control and weak on innovation. A growth executive may excel at expansion and flounder when discipline becomes more important than ambition.

Track-record work should also extend beyond the person at the top. Senior lieutenants who follow an executive from one company to another often bring established working habits and a shared view of how to run a business. Their history together can create a management culture that affects everything from capital budgeting to talent development. That helps explain why some leadership transitions work even in difficult settings, while others fail despite polished resumes.

The final judgment comes from weighing recurring patterns against present circumstances. Executives develop signature responses to problems. One may prefer joint ventures over acquisitions when entering new markets. Another may repeatedly choose vertical integration instead of outsourcing. Those repeated strategic choices often reveal more than any single financial metric. They show the executive's underlying view of how competitive advantage is built, and that view is likely to surface again.

Cross-Referencing Insider Selling Clusters

One executive selling shares may reflect tax planning, diversification, or personal liquidity needs. Three executives selling in the same week suggests something different. The distinction separates routine activity from coordinated action. Research covering more than 100,000 sales clusters found that multiple insiders trading together often reflects consensus rather than personal bias.

The analysis starts by identifying clusters, usually defined as three or more insiders trading the same stock within a short window. Sales clusters often unfold across several trading days, with more than 60 percent lasting longer than one session. Purchase clusters look different. Most are compressed into a single day. The contrast reflects the different motives behind coordinated buying and coordinated selling.

Element Fleet Management offers a clear example. Eight insiders, including the acting CEO and the incoming chairman, bought shares in a single month. Over the next year, the stock rose 75 percent while the broader index gained only 1 percent. Cluster buying of that kind indicates that multiple insiders expect appreciation. It carries more weight than an isolated purchase by one executive.

Network analysis shows how this information moves through a company. Insiders form tightly connected groups in which trade-related information can move vertically across ranks and horizontally among peers. Those hidden channels help explain why executives take part in 29 percent of purchase clusters but only 8 percent of sales clusters. Directors show the reverse pattern, accounting for 70 percent of sales clusters.

The surrounding information environment also affects cluster formation. Firms with heavy analyst coverage and concentrated institutional ownership show more frequent cluster purchases. That suggests coordinated trading is more likely in companies already subject to close outside monitoring. Where there are active intermediaries watching insider behavior, insiders may trade in patterns that look more coordinated and less random.

Sales clusters in the month before a stock crash are especially revealing. These coordinated exits often point to information about weakening fundamentals that has not yet reached public disclosure. The short gap between the cluster and the later price decline suggests insiders acting on a shared negative view rather than on portfolio housekeeping.

To separate meaningful clusters from routine activity, analysts have to look at size and role. Small, scattered sales often reflect compensation events or tax obligations rather than information. Transactions by lower-level employees usually carry less weight than trades by executives with broad operational visibility. Who is selling can be as important as how much they sell.

Cluster methodology can also support regulatory review. Network-based approaches detect illegal insider trading by identifying information-sharing patterns that depart from normal communication channels inside a company. These methods can uncover hidden ties that ordinary transaction monitoring misses, revealing coordination among individuals who appear unrelated on the surface.

Purchase clusters tend to produce stronger predictive returns than isolated buys because they reflect several insiders arriving at the same conclusion. The information in those trades often moves into stock prices slowly, even after disclosures become public. That lag creates room for systematic analysis of cluster timing, composition, and sequence.

Option Grant Schedules and Form 4 Filings

A chief financial officer receives a stock option grant on Monday. The filing disclosing it must appear by Wednesday. That two-business-day deadline creates a near-real-time view into executive compensation events. Form 4 tracks changes in beneficial ownership by corporate insiders, including directors, officers, and 10 percent shareholders.

The reporting sequence begins with Form 3, which is due within ten calendar days after a person becomes an insider. Later transactions trigger Form 4 within two business days. That includes option grants, stock purchases, and sales. Form 5 appears 45 days after fiscal year-end to capture exempt transactions that were not reported earlier.

Option grants disclosed on Form 4 reveal the exercise price, vesting schedule, and expiration date. Those terms show how management is being paid and how much future dilution may result. A grant priced well below the current market can suggest that the board expects substantial appreciation. Grants priced at the market often indicate a more restrained view.

Derivative-security reporting also requires disclosure of the underlying security title, share count, exercise price, and exercisable date. The detail allows analysts to estimate future dilution and option value. The ownership figure shown after each transaction also makes it possible to track cumulative insider stakes over time.

Rule 10b5-1 trading plans sometimes appear in Form 4 footnotes. These prearranged plans allow insiders to trade during blackout periods while reducing the risk of insider-trading allegations. Trades executed under such plans usually carry less signaling value than discretionary trades. That distinction affects how selling patterns should be read.

Companies must also disclose in their annual proxy statements whether insiders filed Forms 3, 4, and 5 on time. Late filings may reflect administrative sloppiness, but they can also suggest deliberate obscurity. Repeated delays justify closer attention to governance practices and internal controls.

New directors file Form 3 when they join and Form 4 for any equity grants awarded at that time. Those first filings establish a baseline ownership position for future tracking. The size of an initial grant, relative to total director compensation, can show how strongly the board ties director incentives to shareholder outcomes.

Reporting does not end immediately when an insider leaves. Form 4 obligations continue for six months after someone ceases to be an insider. That rule captures transactions tied to periods when the person may still have possessed material nonpublic information. It closes off one simple route for delayed selling to escape scrutiny.

Form 4 becomes more useful when read as part of a broader pattern. Large option exercises followed by immediate sales usually indicate executives converting paper gains into cash. Option grants that appear just before favorable corporate announcements may suggest confidence in developments not yet widely appreciated.

The SEC's electronic filing system makes Form 4 data public almost as soon as it is submitted. That makes systematic monitoring possible across many companies at once. Automated alerts keyed to unusual filing behavior can flag potential risks or opportunities before the broader market pays attention.

Option grants often follow regular annual or quarterly rhythms tied to compensation-committee meetings. Deviations from those rhythms deserve scrutiny. Unexpected grants in the middle of the cycle can precede major corporate events or accompany efforts to retain key executives.

Form 4 analysis works best when joined with earnings releases, strategic developments, and other insider data. A single filing rarely says much on its own. Patterns across several insiders and several periods are far more revealing. The best signals come from context, not from transaction monitoring in isolation.

Executive Compensation Analysis and Incentives

A proxy statement shows a chief executive receiving total compensation twenty times the industry median. At first glance, the figure may look like evidence of exceptional performance. A closer reading shows that the pay package rewards revenue growth whether or not the growth is profitable, creating an incentive for acquisitions that destroy value. The gap between headline pay and actual design is why compensation analysis belongs in intelligence work.

The Compensation Discussion and Analysis section of the proxy explains the stated logic behind the board's pay decisions. The language often reveals whether directors are focused on short-term stock performance or long-term operating results. Compensation committees routinely cite peer benchmarking, but the chosen peer group may include larger or stronger companies in ways that help justify richer pay.

Realizable pay offers a better measure of what executives actually receive from equity awards over time. This mark-to-market approach compares cumulative compensation with total shareholder return across the same multi-year period. Research shows that companies where realizable pay runs high relative to shareholder returns often underperform industry peers later on.

Pay-for-performance models try to quantify the link between compensation and business results. Common measures include return on invested capital, free cash flow, and earnings growth. Companies that tie pay more tightly to operating performance usually deliver steadier shareholder returns than companies that rely heavily on stock-price targets alone.

Compensation structure also deserves close reading. The balance among salary, annual bonus, and long-term incentives tells you what kind of behavior the board is encouraging. Heavy use of stock options tends to reward risk-taking. Restricted stock with long vesting periods tends to encourage stability and retention. The way payouts respond to below-median performance also shows how the board handles failure.

Target-setting is another revealing area. Some companies use Monte Carlo simulations to test compensation plans under different economic scenarios. That can help boards set goals that are demanding without being unrealistic in volatile conditions. It also reduces the chance of either soft targets that pay out too easily or targets so severe that they lose their motivational force.

Peer-group data from public proxies gives compensation analysis useful context. The comparison works best when firms are similar in size, industry, and financial profile. A more refined approach adjusts for strategic differences such as turnarounds, restructurings, or high-growth phases that may justify some divergence in pay.

A full rewards analysis looks beyond salary and bonus. It includes long-term incentives, benefits, and perquisites. Some companies also include nonfinancial measures, such as customer satisfaction or project completion, especially in service businesses. Those choices show what the board is really trying to reward beyond quarterly earnings.

Several red flags recur. One is a high ratio of executive pay to basic fundamentals such as sales or net income. Research covering a decade of data found that firms with elevated pay-to-fundamentals ratios consistently underperformed lower-ratio peers in both total shareholder return and return on invested capital. Another is the use of discretionary bonuses with no clear tie to performance.

Stock-ownership guidelines are also worth checking. These policies require executives to hold meaningful equity stakes, usually expressed as multiples of base salary. The goal is to ensure that management shares in gains and losses alongside shareholders. The analysis should test whether executives satisfy the guideline through actual ownership rather than through unexercised options that do not expose them to the same economics.

Clawback provisions provide another signal. These policies allow companies to recover incentive compensation tied to financial results that are later restated. Strong clawbacks suggest a board willing to enforce accountability. Weak provisions, or none at all, point to looser oversight of compensation risk.

The strongest compensation analysis looks across several years rather than one pay period. Changes in incentive metrics, performance hurdles, and grant practices reveal shifts in board priorities. Packages that increasingly favor long-term operating measures often align more closely with durable business performance than packages built around short-term price targets.

Network Analysis of Corporate Relationships

Executive background research, insider selling clusters, and compensation analysis each examine individual actors. Network analysis steps back to map the system those individuals operate within — the web of board relationships, shared investors, and prior employment connections that shapes how decisions get made and information gets distributed long before it reaches a public filing.

The intelligence value is specific and practical. Corporate networks predict strategic behavior, reveal undisclosed conflicts of interest, and surface connections that proxy statements technically disclose but rarely make visible in aggregate. Assembling that aggregate picture from public sources is the work of this section.

Board Interlocks: What They Are and Why They Matter

A board interlock occurs when one individual sits on the boards of two or more companies simultaneously. Among S&P 1500 firms, the overwhelming majority share at least one director with another company in the index. One in eight of those interlocks connects direct competitors — a pattern with antitrust implications under the Clayton Act, which prohibits directors from serving simultaneously on competing boards where the effect may be to substantially lessen competition.

For financial intelligence purposes, interlocks matter less as legal red flags and more as information channels. A director who serves on both a pharmaceutical company's board and a major hospital system's board sits at the intersection of buyer and seller. A director shared between a technology firm and one of its cloud infrastructure vendors occupies a position where pricing negotiations involve someone with fiduciary duties to both sides. These structural tensions don't automatically indicate misconduct — but they create the conditions for conflicts of interest that governance disclosures may underrepresent.

Research on the value of these connections is instructive. Studies examining what happens when an interlock is broken — through a director's death, a merger that eliminates one company, or a regulatory forced exit — show that the affected firm experiences a measurable decline in return on assets in the period immediately following. This documents that the connections carry real operational value: information flow, strategic coordination, and access that disappears when the link is severed.

The inverse also holds. When a company recruits a director who already sits on the board of a strategic partner, a key customer, or a potential acquisition target, the appointment signals something beyond governance optics. Track these appointments in real time through the DEF 14A proxy statement and Form 8-K filings — companies must file an 8-K within four business days of a director appointment, and the filing must describe the director's other board affiliations.

Mapping a Company's Network: A Step-by-Step Workflow

The following workflow builds a complete relationship map for any public company using only free sources. It takes two to four hours the first time through; subsequent updates take less than 30 minutes.

Step 1: Pull the proxy statement (DEF 14A). Every director biography discloses their current board seats, their committee assignments, their prior employment history, and their equity ownership in the company. Build a table with one row per director and columns for: name, committee roles, outside board seats, most recent prior employer, years of tenure on this board, and share ownership. This table is your network seed — every entity in the "outside board seats" column is a node to investigate.

Step 2: Search EDGAR full-text for each director's name. Go to efts.sec.gov and search each director's name in quotes. Filter results to the past three years. This surfaces every filing — across every company — where that person is mentioned as an officer, director, beneficial owner, or named party. You will frequently find affiliations that the proxy biography omits or understates: advisory roles at private companies that later become acquisition targets, prior involvement in enforcement actions, or ownership positions in entities that conduct business with your target company.

Step 3: Check for related-party transactions. In the proxy statement and the 10-K (look in the footnotes section titled "Related Party Transactions" or "Transactions with Related Persons"), identify any disclosed transactions between the company and entities affiliated with its directors or officers. Cross-reference those entity names against the director table you built in Step 1. The same director who appears on two boards and whose affiliated entity appears in the related-party footnotes is a conflict of interest cluster requiring further scrutiny — regardless of whether it's disclosed as arm's-length.

Step 4: Pull 13F filings for top institutional holders. Identify the company's top five to ten institutional holders from the most recent 13F data (available through EDGAR or sites like WhaleWisdom and dataroma.com, both free). For each major holder, check whether they also hold significant positions in the company's primary competitors, key suppliers, or disclosed acquisition targets. Shared institutional ownership across a supply chain or competitive landscape creates pressure dynamics and information flows that individual company analysis misses.

Step 5: Extend to prior employers. For each director and named executive officer, search EDGAR for the prior employer named in their biography. Pull that company's proxy for the period when your subject worked there. Were there any enforcement actions, restatements, or going concern flags during their tenure? Did they depart before or after a significant negative event? The prior employer track record section of Chapter 13 covers the analytical methodology — the network analysis step is simply identifying which prior employers are worth examining.

A Worked Example: Mapping a Mid-Cap Software Company

Consider a mid-cap enterprise software company — call it TargetCo. The DEF 14A shows seven directors. Working through the proxy reveals:

- **Director A** (Audit Committee Chair) simultaneously sits on the board of a cybersecurity firm that TargetCo's 10-K lists as a technology partner in the risk factors section. The proxy discloses both affiliations, but nothing flags that the Audit Committee Chair oversees financial controls for a company with a disclosed vendor relationship to their other board seat. Search EDGAR full-text for Director A's name — it returns a Form 4 filing from the cybersecurity firm showing they hold 85,000 shares there. The financial interest is disclosed; the conflict cluster is only visible once you assemble it.
- **Directors B and C** were both appointed 14 months ago, following a 13D filing from an activist investor demanding board refreshment. Pull that 13D — the purpose section describes the activist's specific demands: two independent director seats, a strategic alternatives review, and a cost reduction plan. Check the proxy votes from the subsequent annual meeting. Did Directors B and C vote with management or against it on the executive compensation say-on-pay resolution? If activist-placed directors are voting in lockstep with management on compensation, the governance change may be cosmetic.
- **Director D**'s biography lists their prior role as CFO at a company you don't recognize. Search EDGAR for that company's name — it filed for bankruptcy

two years after Director D departed, and the bankruptcy filing contains creditor allegations about financial reporting irregularities during Director D's tenure. None of this is in TargetCo's proxy. It's in PACER (the federal bankruptcy docket) and in the prior company's 8-K filings from that period.

- **Top institutional holder overlap**: TargetCo's largest shareholder also holds a 9% position in TargetCo's primary competitor. This shared investor has engaged both companies' management teams over the past 18 months based on 13D amendment language from both filings. When the same investor with activist history owns near-threshold positions in two direct competitors, their incentive structure around a potential industry consolidation becomes analytically relevant.

None of these findings comes from proprietary data. Every element is in a free public filing. The network only becomes visible when you stop reading each document in isolation and start reading them as a connected system.

Network Density as a Signal

The degree of interconnection within an industry's director network — how often the same names appear across multiple boards, how many shared investors link competitors, how frequently executives migrate between the same small cluster of companies — is itself informative.

Dense networks in an industry suggest either a legitimate talent concentration (common in specialized sectors like semiconductor manufacturing or pharmaceutical development) or structural relationships that formal filings underrepresent. When the same five investors own major positions in all six publicly traded competitors in a sector, and three of those investors have had private discussions with management teams (sometimes visible in 13D amendment language or activist letters), the network density shapes competitive dynamics in ways that individual company analysis won't capture.

Sudden thinning of a previously dense network is equally significant. When a cluster of directors resign from a company within a short window — especially across different committee roles — the departures create a structural break that warrants an immediate filing review. Mass director exits are disclosed in 8-K filings and often precede governance failures, regulatory actions, or strategic pivots that haven't yet reached the public record.

What Network Analysis Can and Cannot Do

Relationship mapping identifies structural conditions — conflicts, concentrations, information channels, and governance patterns. It does not prove that those conditions produced improper behavior. A director who sits on two competing boards may have received explicit legal clearance. An executive who departed a prior employer before a restatement may have had no involvement in the accounting decisions that caused it. Shared institutional ownership across competitors is the norm, not the exception, in most sectors.

The discipline is in asking better questions, not in drawing premature conclusions. The network map tells you where to look next. The evidence standard for any actual claim still requires primary source documentation — filings, court records, disclosed transactions — not the inference that connected people must be coordinating.

Used correctly, corporate network analysis is one of the most efficient intelligence-gathering techniques available to an independent researcher. A few hours of proxy and EDGAR work surfaces relationship context that months of earnings call analysis may never reveal, because financial performance lags the decisions that network relationships shape.

Key Takeaways

- ☐ Executives replicate their operating playbooks across companies. A CEO who drove growth through acquisitions and leverage at their prior firm will likely pursue similar strategies at the current one. Reconstructing the executive's track record from archived SEC filings reveals capital allocation preferences, strategic tendencies, and risk tolerance patterns that transfer with surprising consistency.
- ☐ Insider selling clusters — three or more executives trading in the same short window — carry far more signal than isolated transactions. Purchase clusters compressed into a single day indicate shared conviction about undervaluation. Sales clusters preceding stock declines by one to three months indicate shared awareness of deteriorating fundamentals not yet public.
- ☐ Board interlocks, shared institutional investors, and prior employer connections form a network that predicts strategic behavior, surfaces undisclosed conflicts, and explains information flows that proxy statements technically disclose but rarely make visible in aggregate. Mapping this network from public sources takes two to four hours per company using the workflow in this chapter.

Fieldwork

- ☐ Run an EDGAR full-text search for the CEO of a company on your watchlist. List every filing — across every company — where their name appears. Check for enforcement actions, prior company restatements, or going-concern flags during their tenure at previous firms. Note any affiliations the current proxy statement omits.
- ☐ Pull Form 4 filings for all insiders at one company for the past six months. Plot the transactions on a timeline. Look for clusters: three or more insiders buying or selling within the same 30-day period. If a cluster exists, check whether a material announcement followed within 90 days.

☐ Build a network table for one company using the five-step workflow in this chapter: proxy statement director bios, EDGAR full-text search for each name, related-party transaction footnotes, top institutional holder overlap via 13F data, and prior employer track records. The table itself — even before analysis — will surface connections you did not expect.

Apply This

Signals to watch for: a new director appointment that creates an interlock with a potential acquisition target or key customer, clustered insider buying by executives with broad operational visibility, the CEO's prior employer showing a pattern of aggressive accounting during the CEO's tenure there, Form 4 option exercises followed by immediate stock sales (converting paper gains to cash), and compensation structures heavily weighted toward short-term metrics with no clawback provisions.

CHAPTER 14

Court Records and Corporate Registries

The previous chapter examined how executive backgrounds and compensation structures shape corporate behavior. That kind of analysis depends on knowing exactly who the relevant actors and entities are. Corporate names change after mergers. Executives move among subsidiaries. Legal disputes are often routed through shell companies built for opacity. Without a reliable way to trace those links, corporate intelligence stays fragmented and often points in the wrong direction.

This chapter takes up the underlying problem of entity resolution. The question is no longer what companies do, but who they are and how they connect across jurisdictions. The work runs through specialized public-record systems that document corporate existence and legal conflict. Those systems hold structured information on formation, ownership, and litigation. Used properly, they turn vague references into verifiable corporate intelligence.

Federal courts and state corporate registries are central sources for that work. Their records provide the factual base against which corporate disclosures and executive narratives can be tested. Legal-administration systems become collection platforms. They reveal recurring behavior that no single filing shows on its own. To use them well, an analyst has to understand both how the systems are built and how their contents should be read.

Public Court Records Research Using PACER

A company faces a securities class action. The complaint sits inside a federal court database that contains more than a billion documents. That system, Public Access to Court Electronic Records, or PACER, is the main electronic portal for federal appellate, district, and bankruptcy court records. It connects to the individual Case Management/Electronic Case Files databases maintained by each court, where the underlying documents are stored. Once an analyst knows how to navigate it, PACER turns litigation research from guesswork into repeatable collection.

Many people assume PACER gives free, instant access to every federal case in one place. It does not. The system charges ten cents per page, capped at three dollars per document. Quarterly fees under thirty dollars are waived. Free access is limited to courthouse terminals, certain academic exemptions, or the RECAP Archive, where users share documents they have already downloaded.

Another common mistake is to assume PACER can be searched nationwide by party name alone. In practice, effective work begins with the PACER Case Locator, a national index updated daily at midnight. The Case Locator tells you which courts hold litigation involving a person or company. Only then does it make sense to move into the individual court records.

Search technique drives both cost and efficiency. The Case Locator accepts searches by case number, party name, Social Security number, Employer Identification Number, nature of suit, and filing-date range. In bankruptcy research, tax identifiers are often essential. A search for "johnson, t" may return two pages and cost twenty cents. Pulling a ten-page docket in case 01-10054 costs one dollar, though date filters can reduce the total. Saved searches and custom landing pages make it possible to monitor multiple parties and jurisdictions over time.

Older cases create a separate problem. Many pre-1999 files still exist only on paper in Federal Records Centers. Retrieving them requires direct contact with court clerks and a sixty-four-dollar retrieval fee per case. That gap needs to be taken into account when the research involves companies with long legal histories or repeated regulatory problems stretching back decades. Comprehensive litigation work often combines electronic retrieval with manual requests for archived records.

The first practical step is to sort litigation by relevance. Securities class actions expose allegations of financial misstatement. Patent suits reveal competitive pressure and innovation risk. Product liability cases may point to future obligations not yet reflected in reserves. Employment-discrimination claims can signal cultural failures that affect retention and operating stability. Each category offers a different kind of intelligence about risk and management quality.

PACER becomes much more powerful when paired with SEC filings. A 10-K may describe a matter as routine litigation without saying much more. PACER may show that the "routine" matter consists of repeated wrongful-termination suits pointing to a deeper HR problem. Bankruptcy dockets can list creditor claims that conflict with the company's account-payable disclosures. Enforcement actions may contain settlement terms that management summaries soften or compress. Court records function as primary sources and often carry more factual detail than the company's own disclosure.

The deeper value lies in patterns across cases. Several suppliers suing the same company for nonpayment may point to cash-flow strain before it appears in quarterly results. A cluster of patent suits against a technology company may suggest either aggressive enforcement or vulnerability to innovation challenges. Regulatory actions involving the same executive at more than one company can reveal a behavioral pattern that follows the person, not just the firm. Those patterns only appear through systematic collection across jurisdictions and over time.

Good PACER work depends on a collection plan. The analyst has to define which forms of litigation are material to the investment thesis. A pharmaceutical thesis may require close monitoring of patent disputes and FDA-related enforcement. A retail thesis may call for consumer class actions and employment claims. Time should be allocated according to likely impact. Some dockets will only confirm what is already known. Others will provide the first useful warning.

Raw court documents still need interpretation. A complaint states the plaintiff's allegations, not established fact. A settlement reflects compromise, not necessarily liability proved on the merits. Docket activity also carries meaning. Bursts of motion practice before a key date, repeated extensions, or sudden shifts in counsel can reveal litigation strategy and resource pressure. The analytical task is to separate procedural theater from substantive evidence, often by comparing the docket with financial statements, regulatory filings, and contemporaneous reporting.

Professional PACER research also requires disciplined documentation. Every document should be logged with retrieval date, jurisdiction, case number, and cost. That creates an audit trail and makes follow-up work faster. Over time, systematic organization turns isolated disputes into broader insight about corporate conduct, industry pressure, and regulatory posture. The federal court system becomes more than an archive of lawsuits. It becomes a real-time feed of corporate risk and opportunity.

Litigation History and Legal Risk Assessment

A company settles a discrimination case for three million dollars. In the financial statements, it appears as a single line item. The underlying court record tells a different story: twelve similar complaints filed against the same manager across three companies over fifteen years. What looked routine starts to resemble a repeated management failure. Litigation-history analysis works at that level. It looks past the individual case to identify recurring behavior, operating weaknesses, and financial vulnerability.

Court records alone do not predict every legal outcome. Duration, procedure, and external shocks all change the economics of litigation. The Myra Clark Gaines inheritance litigation ran for fifty-seven years through repeated appeals and delays. The case is a reminder that legal disputes can sit over an asset for decades. Recessions can alter plaintiff solvency, settlement pressure, and defense posture. Serious risk assessment therefore uses probability-weighted damages and discounted case valuations, combining historical pattern recognition with forward-looking scenarios.

Bankruptcy filings are especially rich sources of financial intelligence. They list assets, creditors, and debt amounts with legal precision. Asset transfers to relatives or shell entities before filing may point to fraudulent conveyance risk. For a trader evaluating a distressed company, the bankruptcy petition itself often provides a cleaner picture of the actual liability structure than the company's own pre-filing liquidity narrative, which tends to emphasize manageable debt and orderly resolution.

Corporate registries add links that litigation records alone cannot show. Secretary of State filings may reveal officer changes before a wave of lawsuits. OpenCorporates may show mergers that shifted liabilities from one entity to another. These connections turn isolated disputes into a recognizable corporate pattern. Repeated supplier-payment suits across multiple subsidiaries may indicate centralized treasury strain rather than local operating problems.

The six-stage OSINT lifecycle gives structure to the work. It starts by defining the litigation exposure that needs to be assessed. From there the analyst identifies sources, collects records through databases and APIs, and preserves an audit trail with timestamps and evidence snapshots. That discipline reduces the risk of cherry-picking only the cases that support the thesis.

Timeline construction is one of the most useful techniques. Arranging corporate events, filings, insider transactions, and litigation milestones in chronological order often reveals relationships that isolated document review misses. When a CFO sells a large block of shares two weeks before a restatement announcement, the sequence matters more than either event on its own. When three suppliers file suits for nonpayment within the same quarter that management describes cash flow as "healthy," the timeline exposes the contradiction. Public records become more powerful when they are arranged in time rather than read one by one.

Commercial risk aggregators can help at the screening stage. Tools such as Moody's Maxsight flag sanctions exposure and adverse media and can quickly surface network connections from very large company databases. These systems are useful for triage. They are not a substitute for judgment. They tell the analyst where to dig, not what conclusion to draw.

Different kinds of litigation point to different kinds of risk. Securities class actions often cluster around earnings surprises and deal announcements. Product-liability suits tend to follow safety incidents after a predictable delay. Employment-discrimination claims often correlate with turnover and weaker cultural indicators. Each category needs its own frame of analysis and its own weight in the overall risk picture.

Artificial intelligence can sort dockets and categorize documents quickly. It is less reliable when the job requires subtle connection-making across cases that appear unrelated on the surface. A human analyst is still the one who sees that several small suppliers suing the same company may indicate deteriorating trade relationships before that change appears in working-capital metrics.

Professional litigation-risk models use exposure analysis, budget projections, and assigned probabilities. They distinguish nuisance cases from lawsuits that threaten the business itself. The question is not simply whether a company is being sued. It is whether the expected value of the claim, the timing of the process, and the surrounding pattern require a change in how the business is understood.

Duration risk is often underestimated. Cases that drag on for more than five years can materially erode returns even when the legal outcome is favorable. The Petersen and Eton Park litigation against Argentina and YPF is one example. The claims involved alleged fraudulent transfers and pre-bankruptcy-style maneuvering. The longer the timeline stretched, the more the economics changed. A three-times return over three years looks very different when spread over a decade.

Legal-risk analysis also connects directly to reserve adequacy. Companies must estimate expected losses from pending litigation in their financial statements. Comparing those reserves with settlement histories and peer practice can show how conservative, or aggressive, management is being. Tracking how reserves change after case resolution also reveals how well management forecasts legal exposure and how effectively it manages litigation.

Corporate Registry Cross-Referencing Techniques

A company called Global Logistics Partners Ltd. appears in Companies House records in the United Kingdom. A seemingly similar entity turns up in Delaware as Global Logistics Partners, Inc., but with different directors. Problems like this are routine in registry work. Cross-referencing connects entities across jurisdictions and databases to reveal ownership, subsidiary networks, and concealed relationships. For a professional analyst, this is not optional cleanup. It is part of the core due-diligence process.

Reliable matching starts with standardized identifiers. Legal Entity Identifiers provide unique twenty-character codes for entities operating globally. Dun & Bradstreet's nine-digit DUNS numbers track supplier relationships across borders. Tax identifiers, including U.S. Employer Identification Numbers and European VAT IDs, anchor the search in something more stable than a company name. Name matching by itself is error-prone. Transliteration, abbreviations, and local naming conventions can produce false matches in a large share of global searches.

Commercial services bring those identifiers together. S&P Global's Business Entity Cross Reference Service links proprietary identification systems to public registries. It connects parent companies and subsidiaries across offshore jurisdictions such as the Cayman Islands and the British Virgin Islands. It also maintains hierarchy information for structures built around majority-control thresholds. Services like this provide the scale required for work that goes beyond manual spreadsheet comparison.

The workflow begins with raw data from the primary registries. Analysts extract names, registration numbers, addresses, and officer data from the relevant jurisdictions. That information then has to be normalized. "Inc." and "Limited" may describe the same business in different places. "Jones and Smith Inc." in one system may appear as "Smith Jones Inc." in another. Without cleaning and standardization, automated matching quickly becomes unreliable.

Identifier mapping turns disconnected records into a network. Querying commercial databases with several identification numbers at once can reveal parent-subsidiary links that do not appear in any single registry. Those links often expose structures designed for tax efficiency or liability isolation. A German manufacturing company may hold intellectual property through a Luxembourg entity, which in turn controls distribution subsidiaries across Asia. Cross-referencing traces the chain rather than leaving it as a set of disconnected local filings.

Automation helps with the scale of the task. Systems built for supply-chain mapping often adapt well to corporate-intelligence work. They allow searches by company name, family group, or business description and present side-by-side comparisons of attributes. Relational databases can store the linkage results and make later projects faster and more consistent. That infrastructure reduces the need to rebuild the same corporate family from scratch every time.

Automation is not enough. Free aggregators such as OpenCorporates are useful for first-pass linkage, but the results still need verification. In high-stakes financial work, analysts should validate the connections through a more formal workflow. That reduces the risk of drawing conclusions from false automated matches and helps preserve a defensible record of how the linkage was established.

Several practical problems recur. Spreadsheets break down under the scale of multi-jurisdictional research. Name matching fails when transliteration changes between writing systems. Static datasets miss later registry updates after mergers, redomiciliations, or reorganizations. Strong workflows address these weaknesses by prioritizing numeric identifiers, maintaining structured databases, and using monitoring tools that capture registry changes over time.

The Library of Congress authority-tracing model offers a useful analogy. In that system, relationship codes generate cross-references showing parent-child links and earlier or later names. Applied to corporate research, the same logic helps trace an entity through mergers, acquisitions, and rebrandings. A company that changed its name three times over twenty years becomes traceable as one continuous subject rather than three unrelated records.

Cross-referencing also supports enhanced due diligence under international compliance standards. Financial Action Task Force rules require beneficial-ownership tracing beyond the twenty-five-percent threshold. Sanctions screening depends on accurate matching across watchlists and registries in multiple jurisdictions. Offshore structures built for opacity become easier to understand when the same identifiers are tracked persistently across databases.

The final output is a network that no single source can show. A pharmaceutical company's Irish R&D subsidiary may connect to Singapore manufacturing operations through a chain of intermediate holding companies. Once those links are established, transfer-pricing strategy, intellectual-property flows, and geographic concentration risk come into view. Cross-referencing turns scattered registry entries into coherent corporate intelligence.

Key Takeaways

- ☐ PACER is a structured research tool, not a free search engine. It charges per page, requires the Case Locator for nationwide searches, and excludes most pre-1999 records. Understanding its mechanics — CIK-equivalent identifiers, date-range filtering, nature-of-suit codes — determines both cost efficiency and collection quality.
- ☐ Litigation patterns across cases carry more intelligence value than any individual lawsuit. Multiple suppliers suing for non-payment signals cash flow strain. Repeated regulatory actions following the same executive across companies reveals behavioral risk. A 10-K that describes "routine litigation" while PACER shows a dozen wrongful-termination suits suggests the company is downplaying systemic problems.
- ☐ Corporate registry cross-referencing solves the entity resolution problem: confirming who a company actually is, how its subsidiaries connect, and whether the names in one jurisdiction match the entities in another. Standardized identifiers — LEI, DUNS, CIK — overcome the false matches that name-based searching produces in 30–50% of cross-border queries.

Fieldwork

- ☐ Open pacer.gov and create a free account if you don't already have one. Search the Case Locator for a company on your watchlist by party name. Note which courts hold cases involving that company, what types of litigation appear (securities, patent, employment, bankruptcy), and whether any patterns emerge across multiple filings.
- ☐ Cross-reference a company's 10-K litigation disclosure against its PACER docket. The 10-K typically describes pending matters in general terms. The court record contains the actual complaint, the dollar amounts claimed, and the procedural history. Note where the legal reality is more serious — or more numerous — than the filing suggests.
- ☐ Pick one director from a company you follow and search their name in OpenCorporates (opencorporates.com). Note any corporate affiliations in

jurisdictions that the U.S. proxy statement does not mention. These connections are often legitimate, but when they intersect with related-party transactions or offshore structures, they deserve closer examination.

Apply This

Treat court records as a verification layer, not a standalone research source. The greatest value comes from comparing what the company discloses about litigation against what the court record actually shows. The gap between the two is where hidden risk lives.

Part 4

International Sources, Fraud Detection, and Alternative Data

The U.S. filing system is the starting point for financial intelligence on American public companies. It is not the endpoint. Corporate structures routinely cross borders, and the consolidated picture in a 10-K leaves the underlying ownership, contractual arrangements, and operating reality scattered across foreign registries, offshore holding structures, and public records that demand different investigative workflows. At the same time, the space between reporting periods—and the physical reality behind reported figures—has become increasingly visible through alternative data sources that sit outside the traditional disclosure regime.

This section extends the toolkit in three directions at once: internationally, into fraud detection, and into the expanding world of non-traditional signals. The chapters cover cross-border structure analysis, the accounting and behavioral red flags that precede major corporate failures, satellite and geolocation data, web traffic and job-posting analysis, and geopolitical risk signals. What ties them together is the same habit that runs through the rest of the book: testing corporate claims against independent evidence.

CHAPTER 15

International Filing Sources and Regulatory Monitoring

A trader who relies only on EDGAR is working inside a hard geographic limit. The SEC's authority stops at the U.S. border. Entire markets remain out of view: London, Toronto, Sydney, Tokyo, each with its own disclosure rules and filing systems.

Different jurisdictions require different information, at different thresholds, on different schedules. Those differences create blind spots around ownership changes, operating risk, and scheduled catalysts.

The answer is to move past a single-source mindset. Professional financial intelligence treats the global regulatory landscape as a set of specialized systems, each built around its own logic and disclosures. A UK private company becomes far more transparent through its Persons with Significant Control register than a comparable private U.S. company ever would. A Canadian mining issuer's material change report on SEDAR+ may contain technical detail that would never appear in an SEC filing. These are not minor variations in format. They determine what becomes public, when it becomes public, and what can be known in time to make a difference.

This chapter maps that terrain. It looks at the disclosure mechanics of the major international exchanges and at the network of U.S. regulators that operate alongside the SEC. The task is not to memorize every form code. It is to understand the structure underneath. Each system reveals a different slice of corporate reality, from broker-dealer compliance failures to scheduled drug-approval decisions. Once those sources are understood together, isolated national disclosures begin to form a usable global intelligence picture.

UK Companies House and European Disclosures

A London private-equity firm is evaluating a UK manufacturing company. On the surface, the target looks healthy. The latest accounts show a profitable business. Then the analyst checks Companies House. The annual accounts were filed three months late. The confirmation statement shows that a new person with significant control acquired a 25 percent stake six weeks earlier. No SEC filing would surface that information for a private U.S. company. In the UK, it is ordinary registry data. It points at both compliance risk and a recent change in control that could alter the terms of a deal.

Companies House operates as a single public registry for all incorporated entities, not just listed issuers. That alone creates a different research environment from the SEC's public-market focus. The core filing is the confirmation statement, submitted annually. It acts as a corporate snapshot, listing directors, registered office, shareholders, and persons with significant control.

The PSC register is the main advantage. It identifies individuals or entities that hold more than 25 percent of shares or voting rights, or that otherwise exercise significant influence. For private companies, this provides ownership transparency that U.S. systems do not match. A Schedule 13D in the United States only applies to public companies, and only once ownership crosses 5 percent. The UK system captures control earlier in the chain for private entities and makes it visible in the ordinary course.

Financial accounts at Companies House vary sharply by company size. Large public companies file full audited accounts with detailed directors' reports. Small companies and micro-entities can file abridged accounts that may omit the profit and loss statement and certain notes. That means the analyst cannot assume all accounts are comparable. The filing itself shows the company's size classification, which helps explain the level of detail provided. A sparse micro-entity filing is not necessarily evasive. It may simply reflect the reporting regime the company is allowed to use.

Across Europe, disclosure runs through more than national registries. The EU's Corporate Sustainability Reporting Directive requires large companies, including some non-EU companies with substantial EU revenue, to make extensive environmental, social, and governance disclosures. Those filings use the European Sustainability Reporting Standards and apply a double-materiality test. Companies must report how sustainability issues affect their financial performance and how their operations affect society and the environment. For financial intelligence, that opens a new body of data on climate exposure, supply-chain controls, and human-rights policies that traditional financial statements rarely capture.

Business registers across Europe are linked through the Business Registers Interconnection System, or BRIS. The system allows cross-border access to basic company data, but each member state still keeps its own registry and access rules. Some systems, such as the Dutch KvK Handelsregister, make extensive data available and use a central KvK number to connect company details with tax identifiers. Others are narrower or require a showing of legitimate interest. Ultimate Beneficial Ownership registers, required under EU anti-money-laundering rules, add another layer. Their accessibility varies by country, so the result is uneven transparency rather than a single European standard.

Jurisdiction applies at a very practical level. An analyst researching a German GmbH will encounter a different disclosure environment from one studying a French SARL. The German Unternehmensregister may provide shareholder lists and management information in one form. French records through Infogreffe may expose a different level of detail on associates and capital. Legal form and jurisdiction both shape what is public.

Brexit added another wrinkle. UK companies listed on EU markets are now treated as third-country issuers. For consolidated financial statements under the EU Transparency Directive, they must use EU-endorsed IFRS. UK GAAP remains acceptable only for the individual financial statements of a UK parent. That distinction is important when comparing a UK issuer with EU-listed peers. The accounting standard in use tells you which regulatory audience the company is prioritizing.

In practice, European research starts by identifying the right jurisdiction and registry. For a UK company, the anchor is Companies House. For a German entity, it is the Unternehmensregister. Each system has its own search logic, document structure, and identifiers. Cross-border groups require more work. A Dutch holding company may own subsidiaries in Belgium and France. The Dutch filing may mention those entities, but the underlying accounts sit in the local registries. It is more fragmented than EDGAR, but it often reveals structures that benefit from exactly that fragmentation.

TSX, LSE, ASX, and Tokyo Exchange Filings

A Canadian junior miner announces a major copper discovery in British Columbia. The stock trades in Toronto. An analyst searching EDGAR will find nothing. The relevant disclosure sits on SEDAR+, Canada's System for Electronic Document Analysis and Retrieval. That platform is the filing system for TSX-listed issuers and covers much more than prospectuses. It includes material change reports, business acquisition reports, and, through the related SEDI system, insider trading reports.

For mining and energy companies, the NI 43-101 technical report is one of the most useful documents. It is a standardized format for scientific and technical disclosure on mineral projects and must be signed off by a qualified person. A press release may highlight high-grade assay results. The later NI 43-101 filing may add the context that matters: sampling method, infrastructure constraints, metallurgy, or permitting complications. The difference between the promotional narrative and the formal technical report can be substantial.

London runs on a different rhythm. The London Stock Exchange uses the Regulatory News Service, or RNS, as the main channel for market announcements. Under the UK Market Abuse Regulation, inside information must be disclosed as soon as possible, generally within thirty minutes of the board becoming aware of it. That creates a faster and more event-driven disclosure culture than the SEC's periodic reporting system. A short seller studying a UK retailer would watch the RNS feed for profit warnings, director dealings, and unscheduled updates, not wait for a quarterly filing.

Dual-listed companies complicate that process. A company listed in both London and Johannesburg may time its RNS announcement to line up with the trading hours of its home market. That can create brief periods of information asymmetry. The information exists, but not yet in the venue where some investors expect it first.

Australia relies on a continuous-disclosure framework through the ASX announcements platform. Listed entities must immediately disclose any information a reasonable person would expect to have a material effect on price or value. The result is a steady stream of announcements, from Appendix 4E preliminary final reports to Appendix 4C quarterly cash-flow reports. For smaller listed companies, especially early-stage firms, the Appendix 4C is particularly useful because it provides a more frequent view of liquidity than annual reporting alone.

A key Australian workflow is to monitor trading-halt requests. Companies often seek a halt pending an announcement. The halt notice may contain no real detail, but the request itself tells the analyst that something material is likely imminent. That is often enough to trigger immediate work.

Japan presents the highest barrier for non-Japanese speakers. The Tokyo Stock Exchange's Timely Disclosure Network, TDnet, is the primary channel for material disclosures. These filings appear in Japanese under the Financial Instruments and Exchange Act. Toyota's quarterly earnings, including operating income and production issues, may appear first on TDnet in Japanese. English versions often arrive later, and sometimes only in summary form.

Since 2009, listed Japanese companies have also filed consolidated financial statements in XBRL through EDINET. That machine-readable data supports quantitative analysis, but the qualitative management discussion remains embedded in the original Japanese filing. The JPX Corporate Governance Code adds another layer, pushing listed companies toward integrated reporting that includes environmental, social, and governance matters. For analysts working Japan, translation lag is not a side issue. It shapes who sees what first.

Each exchange also embeds its own governance logic. The TSX has sector-specific requirements, especially for mining and life sciences issuers. The LSE distinguishes between Premium and Standard listings, with Premium issuers expected to comply with the UK Corporate Governance Code. The ASX requires a minimum free float and adherence to its governance principles. The TSE requires listed companies to maintain an internal audit committee. Those structural differences shape how governance problems appear. In Japan, a governance weakness may show up through audit oversight. In Australia, it may appear in board independence. The first step in any international workflow is therefore not to search for filings in the abstract. It is to identify the exchange, learn its rules, and go to the native platform where the authoritative disclosure appears first.

Regulatory Agency Monitoring Beyond the SEC

A retail brokerage platform suffers a trading outage during a period of severe market volatility. The SEC may become involved later, but the first meaningful regulatory signal often comes from FINRA. As the self-regulatory organization for broker-dealers, FINRA oversees conduct, systems, and compliance at firms serving retail investors. Its disciplinary actions provide early evidence of operational weakness. The monthly disciplinary report, which details fines, suspensions, and settlements, can reveal repeated failures in options supervision, cybersecurity, disclosure, or system resilience long before those issues are framed as broad strategic risk.

The Commodity Futures Trading Commission oversees a different part of the market. Its jurisdiction covers futures, options on futures, and swaps. Its enforcement actions focus on manipulation, fraud, and registration failures in commodity and derivatives markets. The CFTC's case against Deridex over unregistered perpetual contracts is a useful example of how the agency approaches novel digital-asset derivatives. The agency also publishes the weekly Commitments of Traders reports, which show how commercial hedgers, large speculators, and small traders are positioned in futures markets. A sustained buildup in speculative crude-oil longs can point to crowded positioning that may eventually reverse sharply.

Banking supervision runs through yet another layer of agencies. The Office of the Comptroller of the Currency oversees national banks. The Federal Deposit Insurance Corporation insures deposits and monitors bank safety. The Federal Reserve supervises bank holding companies. These prudential regulators issue consent orders and enforcement actions when they identify unsafe practices. An order requiring better anti-money-laundering controls or stronger capital reserves often points to pressure that will surface later in other ways.

FinCEN sits inside the Treasury Department and administers the Bank Secrecy Act. The suspicious-activity reports that banks file under its rules are confidential and unavailable to outside analysts. But FinCEN's public advisories are a different matter. They describe emerging abuse patterns and signal which sectors face tightening regulatory scrutiny. A FinCEN advisory on the misuse of convertible virtual currencies, for example, points to likely enforcement against crypto intermediaries and the public companies connected to them. For a trader, these advisories function as forward indicators of regulatory risk in specific industries.

These agencies do not operate in neat silos. The system is designed with overlap. A broker-dealer may answer to FINRA and the SEC at the same time. If it has a banking affiliate, anti-money-laundering obligations may also draw in FinCEN and a banking regulator. The Financial Stability Oversight Council exists partly to coordinate that overlap. Its annual reports and meeting records often identify vulnerabilities in areas such as hedge-fund leverage or nonbank mortgage servicing before those issues become dominant public narratives.

For a financial-intelligence analyst, the practical implication is simple. Monitoring cannot stop at EDGAR. A serious workflow tracks CFTC releases for manipulation cases, OCC actions for banking-sector strain, and FinCEN advisories for emerging financial-crime risks. Public meeting calendars and comment periods at these agencies also provide advance notice of regulatory change. Taken together, those outputs form a running read on official concern, sector pressure, and fault lines in the financial system, often well before those concerns appear in earnings calls or SEC filings.

FDA Calendars and Healthcare Regulatory Intelligence

A biotech company says the FDA will decide on its lead drug candidate on April 13. The stock trades at twenty-eight dollars. Options volume jumps as traders buy short-dated thirty-five-dollar calls. The trade is built around a PDUFA date, the statutory deadline for FDA review of a new drug application. For professionals, those dates are scheduled binary events. They produce predictable volatility and attract specialized monitoring. The relevant calendars are not simple lists of dates. They are structured databases of pending regulatory decisions, advisory-committee meetings, and related clinical milestones.

The Prescription Drug User Fee Act created these target review dates. Standard review generally runs ten months. Priority review shortens that to six. Those timelines create a narrow and tradable window. A company such as Denali Therapeutics may have a biologics license application for a Hunter syndrome treatment with a PDUFA date of April 5. If that date has already been pushed back from January, the extension becomes information in its own right. It may indicate that the FDA requested more data or that the review is more complex than first expected.

Several platforms package this information in usable form. Benzinga Pro's FDA calendar ties ticker symbols to drug names, event types, and therapeutic areas. FDA Tracker goes further by combining PDUFA dates with clinical-trial timelines and estimates of cash runway. That pairing is significant. A company with six months of cash and a review process likely to run nine months faces a very different risk profile from one with a stronger balance sheet. MarketBeat's calendar adds another layer by tracking events such as supplemental new drug applications, which seek approval for a new use or new formulation of an already approved drug.

Traders tend to use these calendars inside a catalyst framework. They screen for events with strong historical approval odds, such as priority-review or orphan-drug cases, and then compare the calendar with the options tape. A surge in buy-to-open calls above the current stock price, especially with high implied volatility, suggests bullish positioning into the event. The common structure is a vertical spread: long a near-term call and short a higher strike call, often fifteen points away, both expiring just after the PDUFA date.

Advisory-committee meetings often give the market an earlier signal. These panels of outside experts review safety and efficacy data and make nonbinding recommendations to the FDA. A positive vote can lift the stock sharply. A negative one can crush it. The FDA's public calendar of meetings with outside parties also shows which companies are already in discussion with regulators and on what topics. Those meetings can point to regulatory movement before a formal decision date is announced.

PDUFA dates are useful, but they are not mechanical. The FDA does not always announce on the exact deadline, and extensions are common. Another mistake is to treat every healthcare catalyst as equally tradable. PDUFA dates are cleaner because the timing and the binary nature of the event are known. Vague promises of top-line results are much harder to trade because both timing and substance may shift.

Options flow also requires care. Buy-to-open call activity may be bullish speculation. Sell-to-open activity may be hedging or premium collection. The tape only becomes informative once the trade direction and structure are understood.

The FDA's guidance agendas provide another forward-looking source. The Center for Biologics Evaluation and Research, for example, publishes planned draft-guidance topics, including issues such as potency assessment for immunotherapy products. Those agendas show where the agency intends to write new rules. They can affect not just one drug but an entire therapeutic class. For sector analysis, they often count as much as any single approval date.

Healthcare regulatory intelligence works because it turns an opaque administrative process into a sequence of scheduled events. It links the slow mechanics of drug review to the immediate mechanics of options pricing and stock volatility. Once organized that way, it becomes possible to treat regulatory uncertainty not as noise, but as a recurring and analyzable source of market information.

Key Takeaways

- ☐ Each international filing system has its own logic, thresholds, and disclosure rules. UK Companies House exposes ownership of private companies through the PSC register at 25% — information that is invisible for comparable U.S. private entities. Canadian NI 43-101 technical reports on mineral projects contain scientific detail that press releases routinely omit. London's RNS feed operates on a same-day disclosure model that moves faster than the SEC's periodic reporting cycle.
- ☐ European disclosure is expanding through the Corporate Sustainability Reporting Directive, which requires double-materiality assessment — how sustainability issues affect the company and how the company affects the environment. These filings create a new body of intelligence on climate exposure, supply-chain governance, and operational risk that traditional financials do not capture.
- ☐ Regulatory intelligence extends beyond securities regulators. The FDA, FCC, EPA, and FERC each maintain filing systems with scheduled decision dates that function as binary catalysts for companies in their respective sectors. PDUFA dates for drug approvals are among the most tradable regulatory catalysts in the market.

Fieldwork

- ☐ Search Companies House (find-and-update.company-information.service.gov.uk) for a UK-based company or a UK subsidiary of a company you follow. Pull the most recent confirmation statement and check the PSC register. Compare the disclosed ownership structure against what the parent company's U.S. filings describe.
- ☐ If you follow any healthcare companies, go to fda.gov and locate the advisory committee calendar. Identify the next PDUFA date relevant to a company on your watchlist. Note the date, the drug, the therapeutic area, and the expected decision type (approval, complete response letter, or extension).

Then check whether the options market is pricing in a binary event around that date.

- ☐ Search SEDAR+ (sedarplus.ca) for a Canadian-listed company in the mining or energy sector. Pull the most recent NI 43-101 technical report and compare its resource estimates and risk qualifications against the company's most recent press release about the same project. The gap between promotional narrative and qualified disclosure is often substantial.

Apply This

When your research touches a company with operations outside the United States, identify the relevant local filing system before relying solely on SEC disclosures. U.S. filings for foreign private issuers often contain less detail than local filings. The local record — Companies House, SEDAR+, ASX announcements, EDINET — frequently reveals ownership changes, operational detail, or regulatory actions that the U.S. filing omits or summarizes.

CHAPTER 16

Geopolitical Risk Signals and the World Monitor Methodology

A fund manager with a concentrated position in a Taiwanese semiconductor company begins Monday the usual way: earnings estimates, recent 8-Ks, short-interest data. They do not check whether the Taiwan Strait saw unusual military activity over the weekend. They do not look at the USGS feed to see whether a magnitude 7.0 earthquake struck near Hualien early Sunday morning. They do not review UNHCR displacement data showing a steady rise along the Myanmar-China border over the past six weeks.

None of those developments appears in the company's latest 10-Q, because all of them came after it was filed. By the time they are reflected in a regulatory filing, the market will already have moved.

Most investors treat geopolitical risk as too speculative to monitor seriously. They assume it belongs to think tanks, intelligence services, or specialized consultancies with tools beyond the reach of independent researchers. That assumption is wrong.

The core data used by professional geopolitical-risk analysts is largely public, official, and free. The Uppsala Conflict Data Program tracks armed conflict worldwide. UNHCR publishes displacement data by country and origin. The U.S. Geological Survey posts real-time seismic data globally. The Global Disaster Alert and Coordination System classifies major natural disasters by severity.

None of this requires privileged access. The difference between a professional geopolitical monitor and a trader who ignores these sources is not access. It is process, which is the same distinction this manual has drawn from the start.

This chapter maps those sources, shows how to connect world events to specific portfolio exposures, and builds a monitoring routine that makes geopolitical intelligence a repeatable practice rather than a reactive one.

Geopolitical Risk as a FININT Problem

The difficulty in geopolitical analysis is not that the events are unknowable. It is that the sources are fragmented, the noise level is high, and the link between world events and portfolio exposure has to be built deliberately. Most research systems simply do not include that mapping step.

A fund manager holding a mining company with operations in eastern Democratic Republic of Congo does not need a geopolitical consultancy to tell them violence in North Kivu is increasing. They need a process that pulls that signal from public databases, ties it to the company, and prompts the right questions. What is the company's continuity plan? Did it discuss this risk in the latest 20-F? How does the current conflict-event count compare with the last two years?

Those are the same questions the fund manager would ask after reading a risk factor in a 10-K. The source changes. The method does not.

The same intelligence cycle applies here as elsewhere in this book. Define the requirement before collecting. Which geographies matter to which holdings? Collect from the highest-authority sources first: official seismic agencies, UN databases, established conflict datasets.

Then process before concluding. A single conflict-event entry is not enough to revise a thesis. It has to be checked against displacement data, market proxies, peer disclosures, and whatever the company has already said about the jurisdiction in question.

That discipline produces a tangible edge. The reward is not omniscience. It is earlier awareness of changing risk conditions than investors who are waiting for the next filing or earnings call to tell them what already happened.

Connecting World Events to Portfolio Exposures

Before a monitoring routine can work, the analyst has to answer a simpler question: which geopolitical risks are actually significant for the holdings under review? That begins with exposure mapping, and the first source is the company's own filings.

The 10-K's segment disclosures show where revenue is generated. A company deriving forty percent of revenue from one region has a very different geopolitical profile from one whose revenue base is widely dispersed. The risk-factor section often names specific countries or regions when political, regulatory, or supply-chain risks are material.

Those named geographies form the first draft of the watchlist. The latest earnings call often adds detail the annual filing does not require, especially when management discusses regional demand or localized operating pressure.

Supply-chain geography requires a separate pass. Revenue location and operational location are often not the same thing. A technology company may sell mainly into North America and Europe while manufacturing almost entirely in Southeast Asia. A pharmaceutical company may have global sales but source active ingredients from a single country.

The business description and properties sections of the filing often identify major facilities and locations. Import records can sometimes add another layer by showing where goods are actually entering the United States, which may reveal operational dependencies that the filing mentions only indirectly.

Once the map is built, each material jurisdiction goes into the monitoring system as a location to watch. An analyst following a company with major Thai operations watches seismic activity in the region, political developments in Bangkok, and UNHCR displacement patterns nearby. Not because all of them will be definitive, but because systematic watching is cheaper than scrambling after one of them suddenly does.

Physical Event Signals: Earthquakes and Natural Disasters

Physical events are the easiest part of geopolitical monitoring to systematize. The data is authoritative, highly structured, and usually available in near real time. Two sources are central.

The U.S. Geological Survey Earthquake Hazards Program publishes seismic data continuously through a public API. Events of magnitude 2.5 and above appear within minutes and include magnitude, depth, coordinates, tsunami flags, and the reporting network. If an earthquake hits near a company's manufacturing hub, an undersea cable route, or a major port, operations may be affected before the company says a word.

Magnitude matters, but so does depth. Events below 5.0 rarely produce major structural damage. Events between 5.0 and 6.0 can disrupt infrastructure in vulnerable areas. Events above 7.0 in dense industrial regions deserve immediate attention. Shallow quakes, generally under 70 kilometers, tend to cause more surface damage than deeper ones of the same magnitude.

The Global Disaster Alert and Coordination System broadens the field beyond earthquakes. GDACS tracks floods, cyclones, volcanic eruptions, and earthquakes, assigning green, orange, or red alerts based on expected severity. Those classifications are generated algorithmically from population exposure, infrastructure density, and historical impact patterns.

A red GDACS alert for a cyclone approaching a coastal industrial corridor is not background noise. It is actionable intelligence. Many monitoring systems do not surface that information until it has already become a major headline, at which point the disruption is already underway.

The practical workflow is straightforward. Cross-reference GDACS and USGS events against the exposure map built from company filings. In many cases, the impact is indirect. A port closure may reveal more than direct facility damage, and a logistics disruption can affect firms far from the event itself.

The first step after a material physical event is to go back to the most recent company filing. What assets, suppliers, facilities, or logistics nodes sit in the affected area? Have peers already commented through 8-Ks, investor-relations updates, or local disclosures?

Armed Conflict and Political Instability

The Uppsala Conflict Data Program is the strongest public conflict database available. It tracks state-based conflict, non-state conflict, and one-sided violence, coding each event by date, location, fatalities, parties, and conflict episode. The data is accessible by API and download, with the Candidate Dataset providing more current-year coverage.

The categories are important. Organized violence between a government and a rebel group has different commercial implications from factional fighting among non-state actors. Both differ from one-sided violence against civilians. A portfolio exposed to a country needs more than a generic sense that conditions are unstable. It needs to know what kind of instability is unfolding.

ACLED adds a complementary layer with greater frequency and broader event types. It tracks battles, protests, riots, explosions, strategic developments, and civilian targeting, updating weekly. Its coverage is especially strong in Africa, the Middle East, and South Asia.

That granularity is important when exposure is local rather than national. A company distributing consumer goods across sub-Saharan Africa may face rising disruption in a particular district long before country-level indicators show much change. ACLED can make that visible in a way that GDP growth or sovereign ratings never will.

That is a common mistake in this area. Investors often use macroeconomic growth or sovereign credit ratings as shorthand for political risk. Both are backward-looking and too smooth. They can miss precisely the kind of localized instability that disrupts a supply chain or distribution network while leaving national aggregates largely intact.

Event-level conflict data catches what aggregate proxies blur. That is its value.

Displacement and Refugee Data as a Leading Indicator

UNHCR publishes displacement data by country of origin and asylum through a public API. That data often has predictive value because displacement tends to accelerate before instability is fully visible in financial coverage. People leave early. Markets often notice later.

When displacement from a country rises sharply while a company's latest filing still describes that same jurisdiction as a stable growth market, the analyst has a discrepancy to resolve. The filing may simply be stale, but it may also be misleading by omission.

Displacement data is also useful for labor-market analysis. A company may not have facilities inside the immediate conflict zone and still face disruption if its workforce comes from the population now moving out of the area. A manufacturing cluster can lose labor supply well before the company says anything about hiring difficulty or absenteeism.

The combination of conflict-event counts and displacement trends is especially useful. When both are rising together in the same geography, the signal is stronger. More violence and more outward movement from the same origin suggest a deteriorating environment rather than a one-off statistical jump in one series or the other.

That is often enough to justify a closer look even before any company-specific disclosure arrives.

Macro Market Signals as Geopolitical Proxies

Financial markets absorb geopolitical risk into price before the underlying story is always clear. Some market variables can therefore serve as useful real-time proxies, not because they identify the cause, but because they reveal that risk is being priced somewhere.

The VIX is one example. It measures implied volatility in S&P 500 options. Levels above 25 typically correspond to elevated market stress, and levels above 35 often mark acute episodes. The VIX is not a geopolitical index, but sustained elevation without a clear domestic trigger often points to broader external anxiety.

The U.S. Dollar Index offers another signal. The dollar tends to strengthen during episodes of global risk aversion because it remains the dominant reserve and safe-haven currency. If DXY rises without a corresponding Federal Reserve catalyst, capital may be moving defensively in response to geopolitical or financial stress abroad.

That matters for portfolio work because it should prompt a second question. Are currencies tied to the portfolio's exposure map weakening in ways that could hit reported earnings in dollar terms? The geopolitical signal becomes relevant through translation and local operating pressure.

Oil prices also carry geopolitical risk premia directly. The gold-to-oil ratio adds nuance. When gold rises faster than oil during a period of tension, the market may be pricing broader disruption or recession risk more heavily than a simple supply shock. When oil rises faster than gold, the market may be emphasizing supply vulnerability.

That distinction matters for sector positioning in energy, materials, transport, and defense-adjacent industrials. Treasury curves add one more signal. If the curve flattens because the long end falls, rather than because the Fed is easing, large institutional capital may be pricing weaker growth tied to geopolitical friction.

These are not substitutes for primary data from USGS, GDACS, UCDP, or UNHCR. They are calibration tools. A GDACS orange alert combined with rising VIX, firmer Brent, and a stronger dollar is a different signal from the same alert arriving in otherwise calm markets.

Geolocated News and Open-Source Intelligence

Regional and local news often surfaces a developing event before international financial media does. A cyclone threatening a major port will usually appear first in local reporting. A shipping disruption in the Strait of Hormuz may show up first in regional trade publications.

That speed advantage makes a difference if the analyst has already built a geographic RSS list tied to the exposure map. Waiting for Bloomberg or Reuters to decide a story is significant enough to cover usually means waiting until part of the market has already adjusted.

The GDELT Project adds another layer. It transforms global news coverage into structured event data, coding articles by event type, actor, geography, and tone across more than one hundred languages. For analysts with the technical capacity to query it, GDELT provides a live geopolitical event map filtered by country, topic, and sentiment.

A spike in event counts for one country, combined with deteriorating average tone, can indicate that the information environment is worsening faster than official data has yet captured. That does not by itself justify a thesis revision. It does justify a closer look.

Verification still follows the same source hierarchy used throughout this manual. Local reporting is fast but often less certain. A report of an explosion near a manufacturing center should be checked against official emergency sources, company statements if available, and at least one independent corroborating report before it is allowed to affect the thesis.

The workflow is simple. Surface the signal quickly through local media and structured aggregation. Verify it through authoritative sources. Then update the exposure map and monitoring notes accordingly.

Building the Geopolitical Monitoring Routine

The danger in adding geopolitical monitoring is not missing the signal. It is drowning in noise. Watching every disaster feed, conflict dataset, and macro proxy for every country at once produces more information than most research systems can absorb.

The answer is scope. Monitoring has to be tied to material exposure.

The first step is a geographic priority list. For each holding, identify the one to three jurisdictions that matter most for revenue, operations, or supply chain. A twenty-name portfolio may yield only eight to twelve priority jurisdictions. That is manageable.

The second step is assigning cadence. Seismic and disaster feeds are real time and deserve daily review for threshold events in priority jurisdictions. Conflict databases usually update weekly or monthly, so weekly review is sufficient for most portfolio work. UNHCR displacement data moves more slowly and works better as a background indicator checked monthly or quarterly.

Macro market signals belong in the daily market routine rather than in a separate geopolitical session. They are continuous by nature and work best as part of the overall risk picture.

The third step is documentation. When an event crosses the threshold, it should be logged in the same research system used for filings and thesis work. Record the event type, the geography, the holdings exposed, whether the company has said anything, and whether the thesis has changed.

A quarterly geopolitical exposure review should be standard for any portfolio with meaningful international exposure. At that review, the analyst reassesses the jurisdiction list, compares recent event data with the prior quarter, and checks whether any portfolio companies have changed their geographic risk language in recent filings.

That last part is significant. A company that quietly reduces or increases its discussion of a country over several quarters is signaling its own evolving assessment. The filing language itself can become part of the geopolitical evidence trail.

The most common mistake is to wait until the crisis is obvious. An analyst who looks at conflict or disaster data only after the headlines appear is not doing monitoring. That analyst is simply reacting later than everyone else who already saw the same event.

When Geopolitical Risk Enters the Thesis

When a geopolitical development crosses a materiality threshold defined in advance, the analyst should return to the company's latest filing and ask four questions.

First, did the company specifically disclose this risk in the most recent 10-K or 20-F? If not, that is a disclosure lag worth noting. Second, does guidance assume stability in the affected jurisdiction? If so, the operating assumptions embedded in the model may already be stale.

Third, does the company have a practical alternative supply-chain path, labor pool, or customer base that could offset the disruption if conditions worsen? Fourth, have peers with similar geographic exposure already commented through 8-Ks, press releases, or investor updates?

That peer step is often the fastest. When several public companies operate in the same affected geography, one of them will usually disclose first. That disclosure becomes accidental industry intelligence. It says something about the operating environment for every company exposed to the same region, not just the firm that happened to speak first.

Geopolitical signals rarely create a clean binary trade. Their value is usually elsewhere. They improve the quality of scenario analysis behind the position.

A thesis that accounts for the possibility of supply-chain disruption in a specific geography, assigns probability to it, and updates that probability using public data is a better thesis than one that treats the world outside the company as fixed between quarterly reports. The geopolitical layer does not replace the core analysis. It keeps it connected to current reality.

Key Takeaways

- ☐ Geopolitical risk is not an analytical domain reserved for specialists. The primary data sources — USGS earthquake feeds, GDACS disaster alerts, UCDP conflict event databases, UNHCR displacement statistics — are all public, free, and accessible. The edge lies in building a process that connects those data streams to specific portfolio exposures before events reach financial media.
- ☐ Exposure mapping from corporate filings is the prerequisite for meaningful geopolitical monitoring. Until the analyst knows which jurisdictions are material for each holding, the global data flow is undifferentiated noise. The geographic priority list comes from the 10-K's segment disclosures, supply-chain descriptions, and risk-factor language — not from general intuition about which countries seem risky.
- ☐ Market signals — VIX, DXY, oil, gold, and treasury yield curves — are not geopolitical primary sources. They are aggregated signals reflecting the market's collective pricing of a risk environment that primary data sources often show earlier and more specifically. When macro signals elevate without a clear domestic catalyst, the geopolitical primary sources should be the first place to look for an explanation.
- ☐ Geopolitical monitoring is a process, not a reaction. The analyst who reviews conflict event counts quarterly and connects rising UCDP or ACLED event totals to specific holdings before a crisis appears in headlines has a multi-week head start on thesis adjustment. An analyst who begins the same review after a headline crisis has already occurred is receiving public information later than the market, not earlier.

Fieldwork

- ☐ Build a geographic exposure map for one company you currently hold or follow. Use the most recent 10-K to identify every country or region named in segment disclosures, supply-chain descriptions, or risk-factor language. For each named geography, find the corresponding UCDP Conflict Catalog entry and determine whether armed conflict has been coded in that country in any of the past five years. Note whether the company's risk-factor language reflects what UCDP's event data suggests about the operating environment. If the filing language is stable but UCDP event counts have been rising, you have identified an intelligence gap.

- ☐ Go to the USGS Earthquake Hazards Program feed at earthquake.usgs.gov and set a custom alert for earthquakes above magnitude 5.0 in the geographic region of the company you selected. Set a parallel alert from GDACS for orange or red classified events in the same region. Run both alerts for thirty days and note how often events in your monitored geography occur that do not appear in any financial media coverage of the company. That gap measures how much of the physical event landscape is invisible to a researcher who only monitors financial news.
- ☐ Pull the UNHCR displacement statistics for one country where a portfolio company has material operations. Track the total displaced population originating from that country for the past six quarters. Compare the direction of that trend against the language used to describe the same country in the company's two most recent annual filings. If the UNHCR trend is deteriorating while the filing language is stable or improving, you have found an intelligence gap worth monitoring.

Apply This

For every holding with material international exposure, ask: what would have to happen in the physical or political environment of the key jurisdictions before the investment thesis would need to be revised? The answer to that question defines the monitoring threshold. Once the threshold is defined, connect it to a specific, observable data trigger — a USGS magnitude level, a GDACS alert classification, a UCDP monthly event count, or a UNHCR quarterly displacement trend. Geopolitical risk that has not been connected to a measurable data trigger is not intelligence. It is anxiety.

CHAPTER 17

Fraud Detection and Investigative Workflows

The previous chapters set out a system for collecting and processing public financial data. That system turns raw information into structured intelligence. Even the best collection process, however, can be compromised by deception. Financial statements can be manipulated. Corporate structures can be built for opacity. Official disclosures can omit relationships that change the meaning of what has been reported.

This chapter turns from collection to verification. The question is no longer only what the documents say, but whether their claims hold up against independent evidence. That means checking reported numbers against physical assets, identifying recurring patterns of concealment in corporate networks, and using structured checklists to spot discrepancies that point to deeper problems.

The sections that follow lay out specific methods for this work. They show how leaked datasets provide context rather than proof, how reported revenue can be tested against operational evidence, and how red-flag analysis turns suspicion into a set of testable hypotheses. The aim is not to prove fraud conclusively. It is to identify claims that deserve closer scrutiny and to separate reliable intelligence from potentially misleading representation.

Identifying Offshore Structures and Shell Companies

A trader evaluating a mid-cap company notices that its 10-K footnotes disclose a licensing agreement with an entity registered in the British Virgin Islands. The entity has no website, no visible employees, and a name that does not appear in any industry directory. A search on OpenCorporates shows the same registered agent listed on forty other companies at the same address. The licensing fees paid to this entity represent eight percent of the company's operating expenses. Whether or not the arrangement is illegal, it raises a question the financial statements alone cannot answer: where is the money going, and who controls the entity receiving it? Offshore structures rarely operate as isolated entities. They work as networks, and the ones built for opacity share recognizable patterns that a careful analyst can spot using public sources.

A shell company is not illegal by definition. Many are used for legitimate purposes, including intellectual-property holding, cross-border mergers, and family wealth planning. The problem is opacity. A legitimate holding company will disclose its beneficial owners to banks and tax authorities. An illicit shell will try to hide them through layered ownership and carefully chosen jurisdictions. This is jurisdiction shopping: incorporating where disclosure rules are weak and beneficial ownership reporting is thin, not because the business operates there, but because the venue is useful for concealment.

Detection at the institutional level relies on enterprise platforms, but the underlying patterns are visible through free public tools. The shapes to look for are consistent: one address linked to dozens of companies, the same director name appearing across a cluster of entities with no clear operational connection, or subsidiaries registered through nominee officers rather than executives named in the parent company's filings. OpenCorporates allows you to search director names, company addresses, and registration details across more than 200 million entities in over 140 jurisdictions. A search for a director from a company's proxy statement may turn up affiliations in offshore registries that the SEC filing never mentions. The ICIJ Offshore Leaks Database, which is free and searchable at offshoreleaks.icij.org, covers roughly 740,000 offshore entities from the Panama Papers, Pandora Papers, and other major leaks. A match does not prove wrongdoing. It identifies a connection worth tracing further.

Mass registration at a single address is one of the clearest structural red flags. When corporate registry searches reveal that a company's subsidiary or counterparty shares a registered address with dozens or hundreds of other entities, that concentration suggests the address functions as a formation agent's office rather than a place of business. This is something you can check directly. Companies House in the UK shows the registered address for every entity. OpenCorporates and state-level Secretary of State databases in the U.S. provide the same data. If a related-party entity disclosed in a 10-K footnote is registered at an address that also hosts scores of other companies, the transaction deserves closer scrutiny regardless of how it is described in the filing.

Regulatory enforcement patterns offer another lens. When FinCEN or the SEC brings an action against a company for inadequate anti-money-laundering controls or undisclosed related-party dealings, the complaint typically describes the same structural indicators: payments with no clear business purpose, vague descriptions of services rendered, and repeated use of entities whose directors cannot be independently verified. A trader cannot monitor internal payment flows. But a trader can read the related-party transaction footnote in the 10-K, check whether the counterparty entities have a verifiable business presence, and compare the disclosed transaction amounts to what would be reasonable for the stated service. When the description is vague and the amounts are large, the footnote is doing more work than it should have to.

Corporate registry histories also reveal timing anomalies. A subsidiary that was incorporated years ago but shows no filing activity until shortly before a major transaction appears in the parent company's financials may have been created as a shelf entity and activated for a specific purpose. You can check this through Companies House filing histories, state Secretary of State records, or OpenCorporates activity timelines. A long-dormant entity that suddenly appears in a 10-K's related-party footnotes or segment reporting deserves the same skepticism as a revenue spike without a corresponding operational explanation.

Leaked datasets have become part of the workflow. The ICIJ Offshore Leaks Database contains information on roughly 740,000 offshore entities drawn from several major leaks. Analysts cross-check those records against registries and regulatory filings. When a company or its officers appear in both an offshore-leak database and a related-party transaction footnote, the overlap does not prove illegality. It does justify deeper work.

The most useful check for an outside analyst is whether the entity has any visible operational footprint. A subsidiary described as a "technology services provider" should have a website, job postings, or at least a LinkedIn presence with real employees. A "distribution partner" in Southeast Asia should appear in trade databases or shipping records. When none of these traces exist and the entity is receiving material payments from the parent company, the structure looks less like an operational business and more like a conduit. Chapter 18 covers how satellite imagery, shipping data, and job posting analysis can be used to verify operational claims. The same tools apply here: if a company says it has a major partner in a particular country, there should be some physical or digital evidence that the partner operates at the claimed scale.

None of these indicators proves fraud on its own. A company may use offshore subsidiaries for legitimate tax planning, intellectual property holding, or cross-border operations. The question for a trader is whether the structure is transparent enough to evaluate. When a company's corporate network includes entities with no visible operations, directors who cannot be found in any other professional context, addresses shared with hundreds of other registrations, and transaction descriptions too vague to assess, the risk premium should increase. That does not mean sell. It means verify harder, trust the footnotes less, and apply the Appendix B checklist before committing capital.

Revenue Verification and Financial Cross-Referencing

A company reports quarterly revenue growth of 20 percent. Over the same period, accounts receivable rise 40 percent. The gap between reported sales and cash collection is a classic verification problem. Revenue verification begins with the assumption that financial statements are claims, not settled facts. The question is whether those claims hold together across other evidence.

The first step is to test internal consistency. The revenue-recognition footnote explains the accounting policy. A software company using percentage-of-completion accounting should show corresponding progress billings in receivables. A retailer recognizing revenue at the point of sale should show inventory reductions in line with reported sales volumes. When those relationships break down, the revenue number needs closer review.

External verification pushes beyond the company's own statements. A trader cannot access supplier invoices or internal purchase orders, but the public record offers proxies. If a company names its largest customers in the 10-K (or if customer concentration is disclosed in the risk factors), you can check whether those customers' own filings reflect corresponding procurement growth. When a semiconductor company reports a revenue surge from a specific geography, import-export databases and peer filings from companies in the same supply chain should show corroborating activity. If the company's story requires its customers to be buying more, the customers' filings should reflect that. When they do not, the revenue claim needs closer inspection.

Industry systems sometimes provide built-in cross-checks. In oil and gas, accounting software often uses standardized well-numbering systems that map purchaser codes to internal asset identifiers. Those links make it harder to recode revenue manually without leaving an obvious inconsistency.

Physical evidence offers another test. A manufacturer claiming higher production should show increased purchases of raw materials, higher energy use, and more shipping activity. Satellite images of parking lots, thermal signatures at plants, and port traffic data can provide rough but independent measures of operating activity. When financial growth appears without any physical sign of it, the company's claims need to be tested more aggressively.

The revenue-recognition method determines what should be checked. Under the completed-contract method, revenue appears only after the contract is fulfilled. That can work for short projects with clear end points, but it becomes more difficult when warranties are extended or returns remain open for long periods. Under the installment method, revenue is recognized as payments are received, which is more appropriate when collection is uncertain. Each method creates a different verification problem, and the analyst has to work from the accounting policy outward.

The trader's version of reconciliation works through the cash flow statement. Revenue recognized on the income statement should eventually convert to cash. The operating cash flow section shows how much actually arrived. If revenue has grown 20 percent but operating cash flow is flat or declining, the company is booking sales it has not yet collected. Days sales outstanding—accounts receivable divided by daily revenue—quantifies the gap. A DSO that increases quarter over quarter while revenue grows is one of the most reliable public signals that revenue quality is deteriorating. It does not require internal access. It requires two consecutive 10-Qs and a calculator.

A common error is to treat revenue recognition as a purely technical accounting issue. It is a verification issue. Another is to assume that completed-contract accounting is the default for all long-term projects, when in fact it is only appropriate where milestone-based recognition cannot be supported clearly enough.

The best verification combines several methods. Internal checks test whether the accounting policy fits the numbers. External data tests the company's claims against third-party records. Physical evidence checks whether the operations appear to support the story. Payment reconciliation works at the transaction level. Used together, those methods help separate real growth from timing effects, aggressive accounting, or fabrication.

Panama Papers and Leaked Datasets as Contextual Tools

A mining company in Sierra Leone exported millions of dollars in diamonds while owing large sums in local taxes. Public records showed debts of $150 million. The Panama Papers revealed that the operation ran through a shell company called Octea, controlled by billionaire Beny Steinmetz. That link between offshore structure and on-the-ground business turned an ordinary corporate review into a fraud investigation. Leaked datasets often provide exactly that missing connective tissue. They link public disclosures to ownership networks that ordinary filings leave obscured.

The Panama Papers contained 11.5 million documents covering more than 214,000 offshore entities. The materials included emails, spreadsheets, passports, and registration records spanning almost four decades. Journalists at the International Consortium of Investigative Journalists spent a year analyzing the material before publication. The result is now a searchable database used by researchers as a reference tool, not as primary proof.

That distinction is important. The leaks can point to hidden ownership or suspicious relationships, but they do not establish wrongdoing on their own.

The practical method is cross-referencing leaked data with corporate filings and registries. A Spanish infrastructure company may look ordinary on the face of its financial statements. Then the directors' names are matched to Panama Papers records, and those records show offshore entities receiving unexplained payments from company subsidiaries. What looked like normal governance begins to resemble a kickback structure. The leaked data provides the map. The confirmation still has to come from public records.

Banks appear throughout these datasets as facilitators. More than 500 banks were linked to the creation of over 15,000 offshore entities through Mossack Fonseca alone. That law firm specialized in high-volume shell formation, especially in jurisdictions such as the British Virgin Islands. Regulators later used those records to investigate anti-money-laundering failures at institutions including Nordea Bank. The eventual $35 million settlement showed how leaked material can feed formal enforcement.

Researchers now ask whether a company used banks or service providers with documented histories of offshore facilitation. The Mossack Fonseca files showed repeated due-diligence failures, including thousands of entities with owners who were effectively unknown. That kind of opacity separates routine corporate administration from more suspect concealment.

For a trader, the relevance of sanctions-related data is narrower but concrete. If a company you are evaluating operates through intermediaries in jurisdictions known for opacity, and those intermediaries appear in leaked datasets linked to sanctioned entities, the company faces elevated regulatory risk regardless of its own intentions. Enforcement actions against counterparties or banking partners can freeze transactions, trigger compliance investigations, and create material liabilities that the company's own filings may not yet reflect.

Companies with significant government contracts or regulatory dependencies face an additional layer of risk when their officers or directors appear in leaked offshore databases. Offshore structures can create conflicts of interest that ordinary corporate disclosure never reveals. The Iceland prime minister who resigned after the Panama Papers exposed a personal offshore holding that conflicted with his negotiating position is an extreme case, but the principle applies to any company whose leadership has undisclosed financial interests that could affect how they exercise authority. For companies covered in Chapters 21 through 23—those with lobbying, federal contracting, or regulatory exposure—this kind of cross-check is especially important.

Leaked data still needs to be handled carefully. Most offshore entities are used for lawful purposes, including estate planning and international structuring. The Panama Papers documented large amounts of legal tax avoidance, not just criminal evasion. Their value for financial intelligence lies in surfacing hidden connections, not in delivering final conclusions.

The practical workflow starts with a search of the ICIJ Offshore Leaks Database by entity name, director, or address. A positive match triggers deeper work in corporate registries, transaction records, and regulatory filings. Network-analysis tools can then map the relationships across multiple leaks and public sources. That often exposes circular ownership, nominee directors, or fronts for concealed beneficiaries.

Governments have recovered hundreds of millions of dollars in taxes and penalties using information from the Panama Papers. For independent researchers, the value is narrower but still substantial. Leaks can provide the first thread. The rest of the work is to follow that thread through public records until the underlying structure becomes visible.

Cross-Referencing Financials with Physical Evidence

A company reports $50 million of inventory across its distribution network. Satellite imagery shows the main warehouse parking lot empty for weeks. That kind of mismatch is the core problem in physical verification. Financial statements are treated here as claims that need to be tested against the material world.

A trader cannot conduct a physical audit. But the principle behind physical verification—that claims about assets should produce visible evidence—applies to public-source research in a direct way. The question is what physical or operational traces a reported financial result should leave, and whether those traces are visible from the outside.

Satellite imagery is the most direct proxy available to outside analysts. Chapter 18 covers the methodology in detail, but the application here is specific: when a company claims production growth, warehouse expansion, or increased distribution activity, commercial imagery services and free tools like Google Earth's historical view can show whether the physical footprint supports the claim. The Wirecard case demonstrated this principle at its starkest—offices that were supposed to handle billions in transaction volume showed no sign of meaningful activity.

Headcount claims can be tested through job postings and LinkedIn data. A company reporting rapid hiring should show corresponding openings on its careers page, and its LinkedIn employee count should track the growth described in filings. When a company claims to have doubled its engineering team but LinkedIn shows flat headcount and the careers page lists no technical roles, the operational story does not match the disclosure. That mismatch belongs in the same category as a revenue figure that does not convert to cash.

Shipping and logistics data adds another layer. A manufacturer claiming increased production should show corresponding increases in container movements, port activity, or freight bookings. AIS vessel-tracking data, available through platforms like MarineTraffic, can confirm whether a company's shipping patterns match its reported output. Import-export databases can verify whether goods are actually crossing borders in the volumes the company describes. When the logistics trail is quiet while the income statement is loud, the discrepancy is worth investigating.

Energy consumption data provides a final check for certain industries. Utility filings, regulatory reports, and in some cases publicly available metering data can show whether a facility is consuming power at levels consistent with claimed production. A smelter reporting record output while its regional power consumption is flat raises the same kind of question as a retailer reporting record sales while its parking lots are empty.

The broader principle is simple: financial claims that should produce physical evidence can be tested against that evidence using public sources. The test is never definitive from the outside. But a consistent pattern of claimed activity without corresponding physical traces is itself a finding.

One signal that often gets overlooked is the audit opinion itself. When auditors flag material weaknesses in internal controls, that language has specific regulatory meaning: the company's own systems are not reliable enough to prevent or detect material misstatements. A going concern qualification goes further, raising doubt about the company's ability to continue operating. These disclosures appear in the 10-K and can be searched in EDGAR. They are among the strongest publicly available indicators that reported numbers may not reflect reality.

The strongest outside verification combines at least three independent streams. Financial statement ratios test internal consistency. Alternative data—satellite imagery, shipping records, job postings, web traffic—tests operational claims. And the audit opinion, including any qualifications, material weakness disclosures, or auditor changes, tests whether the company's own oversight system is functioning. No single stream is conclusive. Convergence across streams is what produces confidence, and divergence is what produces actionable doubt.

For financial analysts, the practical application is to identify physical correlates of reported metrics. Retail inventory should align with visible store traffic and parking activity. Manufacturing output should line up with container movements and shipping data. Energy production should track pipeline flows and regulatory reports. These proxies are imperfect, but they give the analyst a way to test financial claims without relying entirely on management.

When these streams conflict, the hierarchy is straightforward. Audited financial statements carry the most weight because they are certified by management under Sarbanes-Oxley and reviewed by an independent auditor with legal liability. Physical and operational proxies come next when the methodology is transparent. Social media and unverified press commentary sit at the bottom. A claim supported only by management narrative but contradicted by physical evidence and financial ratios should be treated as suspect until the contradiction is resolved.

Cross-referencing financials with physical evidence turns accounting into something testable. The inventory is either in the warehouse or it is not. The factory is either producing at the claimed level or it is not. The stores are either busy or empty. Numbers on paper become claims about the world, and those claims can be checked.

Fraud Red Flags and Due Diligence Checklists

A company's accounts receivable keep rising while cash collections stay flat. That mismatch between reported sales and actual cash is one of the oldest warning signs in financial analysis. Fraud detection for a trader begins by treating these gaps not as isolated anomalies, but as possible signs of a deeper pattern.

The conditions that make corporate fraud more likely are visible from the outside if you know where to look. Three factors recur across historical cases. The first is financial pressure: companies approaching debt covenants, facing declining cash flow, or dependent on continued access to capital markets have structural incentives to present results in the best possible light. The second is concentrated control: when a founder or CEO dominates the board, chairs the audit committee through allies, or has compensation tied overwhelmingly to short-term metrics, the internal checks that normally catch manipulation are weaker. The third is aggressive accounting: a widening gap between GAAP and non-GAAP results, frequent changes in revenue recognition policy, or growing reliance on estimates and judgments that inflate reported earnings. None of these conditions guarantees fraud. Together, they define the environment where it is most likely to develop. All three are visible in SEC filings.

Financial statement patterns provide the most reliable red flags for outside analysts. Revenue growing faster than cash flow from operations for two or more consecutive quarters is the single most common signal. Accounts receivable rising faster than revenue suggests the company is booking sales it has not collected. Inventory growth outpacing cost of goods sold may indicate channel stuffing or obsolescence being deferred. Gross margins expanding while peers in the same sector show compression raises questions about whether accounting choices, rather than operational improvement, are driving the appearance of profitability. These are all visible in consecutive 10-Qs without any special access.

Governance and disclosure patterns add another layer. An auditor change, especially mid-year or following a disclosed disagreement, is one of the strongest standalone red flags. A going concern qualification in the audit opinion is an explicit warning about the company's viability. Repeated late filing of insider transaction reports (Forms 3, 4, or 5) may reflect either administrative neglect or deliberate obfuscation. Clustered insider selling—three or more executives selling within the same thirty-day window—suggests shared awareness of something the market has not yet priced. Compensation structures heavily weighted toward short-term revenue or earnings targets, with no clawback provisions, create the pressure conditions under which manipulation is most likely.

Related-party transactions disclosed in 10-K footnotes deserve close attention, especially when the counterparty is an entity controlled by an officer or director, the transaction description is vague, or the dollar amounts are material relative to reported revenue. Proxy statement compensation disclosures can reveal structures that incentivize aggressive reporting: uncapped severance tied to revenue targets, performance bonuses that vest on a single metric, or equity grants that accelerate on a change-of-control event. These arrangements do not prove anything by themselves. They define the conditions under which a management team has the most to gain from presenting optimistic numbers.

Operational signals visible from the outside add context. A company claiming expansion while its job postings are declining suggests the growth story does not match the hiring reality. Physical evidence—satellite imagery, shipping data, web traffic—that contradicts reported activity raises the same question from a different angle. Court records showing multiple suppliers suing for nonpayment within the same twelve-month period may indicate cash flow stress before it appears in quarterly results. MD&A language that shifts explanations for underperformance each quarter—the excuse migration pattern described in Chapter 8—suggests management either does not understand the problem or is unwilling to name it.

The Appendix B checklist organizes these signals into a repeatable screening process. It covers three categories: financial statement red flags (revenue-cash flow divergence, receivables growth, margin anomalies, non-GAAP gaps), governance red flags (auditor changes, insider selling clusters, compensation misalignment, board conflicts), and operational red flags (physical evidence contradictions, litigation patterns, corporate structure opacity, MD&A language shifts). The purpose is not to reach a verdict. It is to determine whether a company warrants the normal level of trust or an elevated level of skepticism before committing capital.

Market signals can corroborate or challenge what the checklist surfaces. Short interest above twenty percent, particularly when accompanied by a credible short thesis from an established research firm, suggests that professional capital has reached a bearish conclusion the equity market has not yet absorbed. Credit market signals—CDS spreads widening or bond yields rising for the company while sector peers remain stable—indicate that debt investors, who sit above equity in the capital structure, are pricing in risk that equity holders may be ignoring. These signals do not confirm fraud. They confirm that sophisticated market participants see something worth betting against.

Documentation matters for the trader as much as for the investigator, though for different reasons. When you flag a company through the checklist, log the specific red flags, the sources you checked, and the date. If the thesis later proves correct, the log shows which signals were predictive. If it proves wrong, the log shows where the analysis broke down. Over time, this record becomes a calibration tool: which red flags actually correlate with subsequent problems, and which turn out to be noise? The postmortem framework in Appendix E is built for exactly this kind of review.

The strongest due diligence combines quantitative checks with qualitative judgment. The numbers tell you whether revenue converts to cash, whether margins are sustainable, and whether the balance sheet can support the business. The qualitative layer tells you whether the corporate structure is transparent, whether management's incentives align with shareholders, and whether the company's disclosures match its observable operations. Neither layer is sufficient alone.

The goal is triangulation. Red flags are signals, not proof. A structured checklist keeps the review from drifting and helps focus on the warnings that tend to be most predictive. If revenue rises through aggressive accounting, it should still match cash collections, contract backlog, and operational evidence. If it does not, the question is no longer whether to investigate further. It is whether to hold the position at all.

Key Takeaways

- ☐ Shell company detection depends on pattern recognition across registries, not on any single indicator. Mass-registered addresses (hundreds or thousands of entities at one location), nominee directors with no operational role, and dormant companies suddenly processing large transactions are structural red flags. Legitimate holding structures disclose their beneficial owners. Illicit ones are built to hide them.
- ☐ Revenue verification treats reported numbers as hypotheses requiring independent testing. Internal consistency checks (do accounts receivable match the revenue recognition policy?), external verification (do supplier or customer filings corroborate the company's claims?), and physical evidence (does satellite imagery, shipping data, or energy consumption support reported production levels?) form a three-layer validation framework.
- ☐ Leaked datasets — Panama Papers, Pandora Papers, FinCEN Files — provide context, not proof. They surface connections between entities that regulatory filings may conceal, but the presence of a name in an offshore database does not establish wrongdoing. Their value lies in generating better questions, not in delivering final answers.

Fieldwork

- ☐ Run a company on your watchlist through the Appendix B checklist. Score each red flag as present, absent, or inconclusive. If three or more flags are present, the company warrants deeper investigation regardless of how the stock price is performing.
- ☐ For a company reporting revenue growth, perform a basic internal consistency check. Pull the most recent 10-Q and compare revenue growth to accounts receivable growth and operating cash flow growth. If receivables are growing materially faster than revenue, or if cash flow is flat while revenue climbs, document the discrepancy and check whether the revenue recognition footnote explains it.

☐ Search the ICIJ Offshore Leaks Database (offshoreleaks.icij.org) for the names of directors or officers from a company you are researching. If matches appear, cross-reference them against the company's related-party transaction disclosures and corporate registry filings in the relevant jurisdictions. The overlap itself is not evidence of fraud — but it defines where further verification is needed.

Apply This

Fraud detection is not about proving wrongdoing. It is about identifying claims that do not hold together across independent evidence and escalating those discrepancies into focused investigation. The Appendix B checklist gives you the starting framework. The three-layer verification process — internal consistency, external corroboration, physical evidence — gives you the method.

CHAPTER 18

Alternative Data Sources and Supply Chain Intelligence

The previous chapter focused on verifying what companies already disclose. This chapter pushes the framework forward, into alternative data streams that capture operational reality before it reaches the financial statements. These sources can show production changes, strategic moves, and supply-chain stress weeks or months before quarterly reports confirm them.

Satellite imagery turns physical assets into measurable signals. Job postings and web traffic expose expansion plans and customer interest in real time. Supply-chain mapping connects those signals across firms and industries, revealing vulnerabilities and strategic position inside broader economic networks. Each source offers a different view of the gap between what a company says and what can actually be observed.

The sections that follow show how to collect, process, and interpret these sources. They explain how geospatial intelligence can generate predictive signals in commodity markets, how hiring patterns can reveal unannounced strategic pivots, and how value-chain analysis helps explain why similar companies earn very different returns. The focus stays on turning raw observation into useful intelligence about future financial performance.

Satellite and Geospatial Imagery Analysis

A hedge fund analyst studies satellite images of a large coal terminal in South Africa. Over six weeks, the stockpiles shrink steadily. The images surface before the company's quarterly report says anything about inventory. The analyst then checks shipping data and finds vessel traffic rising at the same terminal. Together, the two signals provide an early read on tightening supply.

Satellite imagery analysis for financial intelligence means systematic monitoring of physical assets through earth-observation data. The work goes well beyond visual inspection. It includes radar, infrared, and multispectral imagery, each of which captures a different form of economic activity. Synthetic aperture radar can monitor ports and shipping lanes through cloud cover. Thermal imagery can reveal plant activity through heat output. Nighttime light intensity can serve as a rough proxy for economic activity in places where official statistics are weak or unreliable.

The commercial satellite market has changed this work. What used to sit mostly inside governments is now packaged for private users. Firms such as SkyFi and Ursa Space Systems aggregate imagery from multiple operators and deliver processed outputs through subscription platforms. Their systems apply machine learning to detect shifts in inventory, industrial output, and agricultural production. An analyst no longer needs to be a remote-sensing specialist to use the data.

Parking-lot analysis was one of the first widely used applications. Analysts counted cars at large retailers to estimate foot traffic before earnings. The same basic approach now extends to container ports, oil-storage sites, and factory complexes. What makes it useful is repetition. A single image can be interesting. A time series of images taken from the same angle over weeks or months becomes much more informative.

Digital surface modeling adds another step. It converts two-dimensional imagery into three-dimensional volume estimates. That allows analysts to measure the size of stockpiles of coal, iron ore, or grain and track how those volumes change over time. The Richards Bay Coal Terminal is a standard example. Repeated imagery shows whether the coal piles are growing or shrinking, creating a near-real-time picture of supply that conventional reporting does not provide.

Geospatial platforms now increasingly use edge computing in orbit. Instead of downloading full image sets for later processing on the ground, satellites analyze part of the data onboard and transmit only relevant outputs. That speeds the workflow and reduces transmission costs. A financial firm can receive an alert about a meaningful inventory change far faster than it could under an older, batch-download model.

The field is more accessible than many people assume. Satellite intelligence is no longer restricted to governments or a handful of large hedge funds. Subscription models have widened access to smaller firms. Another misconception is that usefulness depends on ultra-high visual resolution. In practice, consistency often matters more than visual sharpness. Synthetic aperture radar may be more useful than optical imagery in many settings because it works through weather and darkness.

The difficulty lies in interpretation. Satellite images showing busier factory grounds do not mean much on their own. The analyst still needs context: expected production schedules, normal inventory ranges, and end-market demand. The signal becomes stronger when it is checked against filings, shipping data, and industry reporting. That is what separates a real operational change from ordinary fluctuation.

Agriculture shows how developed the method has become. Multispectral imagery can track crop health through vegetation indices and generate yield estimates months before harvest data is published. Commodity traders use those estimates to anticipate shortages or surpluses. The same technology can also support environmental analysis by monitoring land-use change and deforestation around agricultural operations.

Shipping and logistics provide another mature use case. Analysts monitor vessel counts at major ports and combine them with Automatic Identification System data. AIS transponders broadcast position, speed, and identity. When AIS data is layered over imagery, analysts can confirm vessel locations and sometimes identify spoofing or inconsistent reporting.

Draft data adds another clue. A vessel's draft, the distance from waterline to keel, changes as it is loaded or unloaded. Rising draft implies a heavier cargo. That makes it possible to estimate movement in oil, grain, or bulk commodities before official trade statistics appear.

Container rates often respond first to visible congestion at ports rather than to formal economic releases. The current frontier is data fusion: optical imagery, radar, radio-frequency signals, and ground-sensor data pulled together into one monitoring system. Each source has blind spots. Combined, they produce a more stable picture.

For many financial firms, geospatial intelligence is no longer exotic. It has become a standard part of alternative-data work. At its simplest, satellite imagery offers an independent check on claims about production, inventory, and operating activity. In the right setting, it does so early enough to make a difference.

Job Posting Analysis and Web Traffic Intelligence

A pharmaceutical company announces a new research facility in Boston. The press release stays vague. Its careers page tells a more specific story: thirty-seven openings for oncology researchers with immunotherapy experience. The hiring data reveals the real scientific focus and the likely scale of the buildout before management discusses either in detail.

Companies cannot easily hide their labor needs. Career sites and hiring platforms expose expansion plans, technology priorities, and operating stress in real time. A technology company posting several jobs for quantum-computing specialists may be signaling a strategic push long before it discloses related capital spending. A retailer hiring logistics coordinators in a new region may be confirming expansion plans that the market is still treating as rumor. These are signals about planned activity, not about the past.

Web traffic works differently. It measures customer interest and engagement rather than corporate intent. A streaming platform launches a new original series. Commentary online becomes noisy and speculative. Meanwhile, the platform's site shows a sharp jump in visitors from particular demographic groups during opening weekend. That does not provide final viewership data, but it does offer an early read on audience response before subscriber figures appear.

Job-posting analysis works best as a monitoring exercise, not as a one-off search. An analyst following an industrial-automation firm might set alerts for engineering roles across several hiring platforms. Over three months, openings for robotics-integration specialists rise from two to fourteen while competitors show little change. That divergence suggests an acceleration in automation investment. The insight comes from the trend, not from any one posting.

Web traffic is harder to interpret cleanly. A spike in visits to an e-commerce site may reflect genuine interest, or it may come from bot traffic or a distributed denial-of-service event. To separate the two, the analyst has to look deeper: bounce rate, session duration, referral sources, and conversion behavior.

Bounce rate shows the share of users who leave after one page. Session duration shows how long they stay. Referral source shows how they arrived. Organic search traffic often suggests authentic interest. Direct traffic can imply brand familiarity or repeat use. Referral traffic may indicate attention from other sites, including industry-specific ones. Each source type says something slightly different about momentum and intent.

The strongest signals come from convergence. A bank posts a new role for a director of blockchain integration. Patent filings begin mentioning distributed-ledger technology. Executives start talking more openly about digital-asset infrastructure at industry conferences. Any one of these signals could be incidental. Taken together, they are much harder to dismiss.

Job-posting analysis has its own traps. Not every posted role will be filled. Many firms keep evergreen postings live to build candidate pipelines. Those listings may say little about immediate hiring demand. To separate active recruiting from generic pipeline maintenance, analysts track refresh cycles and posting duration.

A role reposted every ninety days in nearly identical language may be routine. A newly created posting with narrow technical requirements and a short application window is more likely to reflect urgent need.

Web-traffic analysis has a parallel problem. Viral attention can generate a brief surge without any lasting business effect. Analysts need to distinguish vanity metrics from signals tied to revenue. Raw page views tell very little. The more useful combination is traffic growth, depth of engagement, and movement through the conversion funnel.

A fifty percent rise in traffic with steady conversion rates may suggest scalable demand. The same traffic increase paired with collapsing conversion may indicate low-quality traffic or weak customer fit.

Specialist data providers have made collection easier. Thinknum and PredictLeads aggregate job postings across thousands of corporate sites and normalize the formats. They also preserve posting histories that manual checking would miss. Natural-language processing can then sort the roles by function, seniority, and skill, turning unstructured text into something analysts can compare over time.

Web-traffic intelligence has similar intermediaries. Services such as SimilarWeb and SEMrush estimate traffic, audience mix, and competitive position across a large set of sites. Their outputs are modeled rather than drawn from the company's own server logs, so reliability varies. Estimates tend to be better for large consumer-facing sites than for narrow B2B platforms with irregular traffic.

Again, the real value usually comes from combining sources. A software company begins seeing more traffic from university domains. At the same time, it starts hiring sales staff focused on academic accounts. Patent applications reference adaptive-learning tools. Earnings calls begin to hint at education-market expansion. No single data point settles the question. Together they sketch a clear strategic shift.

Timing also matters. Companies often post jobs two to six months before the relevant hiring actually occurs. Web traffic may rise thirty to ninety days before a product launch as marketing ramps. Those lead times allow analysts to anticipate changes before they appear in reported results.

Eventually the formal filings catch up. A quarterly report may mention "strategic investment in emerging technologies" in abstract terms. The hiring data has already shown which technologies. The web traffic has already shown which customers are paying attention. Alternative digital data connects management language to observable action.

Supply Chain and Value Chain Mapping Techniques

A lithium producer in Argentina reports record output. At the same time, a major battery manufacturer in South Korea announces that it is shifting procurement away from South American sources. The miner's stock holds steady on the production headline. The procurement shift tells a different story. Future revenue may now be at risk even if current production is strong. Supply-chain mapping is what allows those two announcements to be read together.

Supply-chain mapping traces the physical movement of materials from extraction to final delivery. Value-chain mapping looks at where economic value is captured along that path. The distinction is important. A company can run an efficient physical supply chain and still capture very little profit. A semiconductor foundry may execute flawlessly in manufacturing while most of the economics accrue to the companies that own the design and intellectual property.

The SCOR model provides one way to structure supply-chain analysis. It breaks operations into five processes: plan, source, make, deliver, and return. Financial analysts adapt those categories to assess vulnerability. A firm dependent on a single supplier for a critical component faces different risks from one with a diversified supply base. Planning choices show up in inventory metrics. Delivery patterns can expose customer concentration when too much volume is tied to a small number of buyers.

Value-chain mapping starts from the finished product and works backward through each stage where value is added. A smartphone's chain runs from retail distribution and marketing back through assembly, component production, semiconductor fabrication, raw-material processing, and mineral extraction. Every step adds cost, but not every step captures the same share of profit. Apple captures a disproportionate share of smartphone-industry profits despite manufacturing very little itself. That fact becomes visible through value-chain analysis, not through logistics alone.

Public records can reveal a surprising amount of the chain. Annual reports identify major suppliers or customers. Import-export databases and customs records show shipment value and direction. Shipping manifests and maritime tracking reveal movement between facilities and ports. Corporate registries help tie entities together when the supplier is hidden behind an intermediate company.

Financial statements add indirect evidence. Accounts-payable aging can suggest payment terms and supplier leverage. Inventory turnover can point to efficiency or bottlenecks. Capital expenditure concentrated in one geography may indicate supply diversification or a coming shift in manufacturing footprint. Footnotes on purchase commitments can reveal dependency on specific suppliers.

A common mistake is to assume the analyst has to map every supplier all the way to raw materials. Usually that is unnecessary. The practical goal is to identify the points where disruption would have a material financial effect. A poultry processor may need visibility into feed suppliers, but not necessarily into the seed producers supplying those feed companies. The key is to stop where the real risk begins to thin out.

Another mistake is to treat supply chains as static. They are constantly changing through renegotiation, geopolitical pressure, shifting input costs, and competitive moves. Continuous monitoring platforms such as Sourcemap try to keep those maps current by tracking supplier relationships, watchlists, and emerging risk signals. A static map can go stale quickly.

Tiered supplier analysis helps organize the structure. Tier 1 suppliers contract directly with the target company. Tier 2 suppliers feed into Tier 1. Tier 3 suppliers sit further upstream and often provide raw materials. Some of the most serious risks sit in those indirect tiers, where visibility is weakest. The 2011 floods in Thailand disrupted automotive production globally because automakers were exposed to specialized Tier 2 and Tier 3 suppliers in the affected region without fully appreciating the concentration.

Supply-chain mapping also supports fraud work. Related-party transactions can hide inside a complex supplier network. A company may buy from a distributor owned by an executive's relative at inflated prices. Once the ownership of major suppliers is mapped, those hidden relationships become easier to spot. Address overlap, family ties, and prior business affiliations can all become visible.

Competitive intelligence comes from the same exercise. Two firms in the same sector may report similar revenue while occupying very different positions in the value chain. One may control a bottleneck technology or a scarce transformation stage. The other may operate in a low-margin, commoditized part of the market. That helps explain why their valuations diverge even when the accounting metrics look similar.

The practical process usually starts with a supplier-assessment questionnaire for Tier 1 vendors, then expands outward to subcontractors and compliance documentation. Site visits provide ground truth when they are possible. Procurement data shows how spending actually flows, which may differ from formal contract structure. Flow charts and geographic maps then make the network readable.

Risk mapping adds another layer. Standard supply diagrams are overlaid with single points of failure, geographic concentration, and regulatory exposure. Third-party services monitor indirect risk through news and regulatory feeds. IoT tracking tools can add real-time visibility into shipments by capturing location, temperature, and handling data through transit.

Some industries now use blockchain-based provenance tools. These systems create tamper-resistant records of custody for sensitive goods such as pharmaceuticals or conflict minerals. In Ghana's gold sector, supply-chain mapping has shown how informal mining feeds into formal export channels without adequate documentation. Once the chain is reconstructed, both revenue leakage and laundering risk become easier to see.

The same logic applies elsewhere. Mapping shows where value escapes taxation, where reporting breaks down, and where legal and illegal flows intersect. Research on liquefied natural gas networks found that collaborative supply-chain strategies tended to outperform isolated operational improvements. Strong financial outcomes were not the result of one tactic applied in isolation, but of coordinated execution across the network.

That is why mapping has to be continuous. Supplier relationships change by batch, by season, and by contract cycle. Automated systems can flag deviations, such as a new supplier appearing without proper vetting or a known supplier disappearing unexpectedly. Those alerts allow risk to be managed before the financial impact becomes visible.

The final payoff is explanatory. Value-chain analysis helps explain why companies in the same industry produce such different financial results. The reason is often not simple operating efficiency. It is strategic position. Companies that control scarce technologies, critical bottlenecks, or proprietary transformation stages capture an outsized share of the economics, even when their physical role in the supply chain looks modest.

Key Takeaways

- ☐ Satellite imagery, job postings, and web traffic each capture a different dimension of operational reality — physical assets, human capital plans, and customer engagement — that financial statements report only after the fact. Their intelligence value is highest when they confirm or contradict what primary filings claim.
- ☐ Consistency matters more than resolution. A time series of satellite images from the same angle over weeks or months is more useful than a single high-resolution snapshot. Draft data on vessels, parking lot counts at retail locations, and thermal signatures at industrial sites all depend on repeated measurement to produce meaningful trends.
- ☐ Job postings cannot be hidden. A company's careers page and public hiring platforms document expansion plans, technology investments, and strategic pivots in real time. Thirty-seven oncology researcher openings tell you more about a pharmaceutical company's priorities than a vague press release about "expanding our pipeline."

Fieldwork

- ☐ Choose one company on your watchlist and check its careers page or LinkedIn job listings. Count the number of open positions by function and location. Compare what you find against the company's most recent strategic guidance. If management emphasized international expansion but all hiring is domestic, that discrepancy is worth investigating.
- ☐ Use Google Earth's historical imagery feature to look at a facility owned by a company you follow — a factory, a distribution center, a retail location. Compare images from two dates six to twelve months apart. Look for visible changes: construction activity, parking lot density, equipment on-site. This exercise builds the habit of thinking spatially about corporate claims.
- ☐ Identify one key supplier or customer for a company in your coverage. Check whether that counterparty's own filings, job postings, or public statements corroborate the relationship described in your target's 10-K. Supply chain

intelligence works best when both ends of the relationship are independently verified.

Apply This

Alternative data is most powerful as a verification layer, not as a standalone signal. A satellite image showing reduced factory activity matters when the company is claiming production increases. A surge in job postings matters when management says they are "rationalizing headcount." The signal becomes intelligence when it intersects with a specific claim from a primary source.

CHAPTER 19

Competitive Intelligence and Industry Research

A company announces twenty percent revenue growth. In isolation, the figure looks strong. But competitor reports show average growth of thirty-five percent across the sector. What looked like strength is, in relative terms, market share erosion. Competitive intelligence moves past analysis of a single company and into the question that matters more: where that company stands within the wider industry.

Patent filings, corporate presentations, conference commentary, and peer benchmarking all help answer that question. Used systematically, they turn scattered corporate communications into structured intelligence about competitive strengths and weaknesses. Patent citations show which technologies attract follow-on investment. Investor day transcripts expose management credibility, especially in unscripted question-and-answer sessions.

Industry conferences work as collective sense-making events. Participants test assumptions, compare implementation experience, and converge on shared views of what is technically possible and how fast adoption is likely to occur. Those discussions reveal timelines, bottlenecks, and maturity gaps that financial statements cannot capture. No single data point is enough. The value comes from the pattern that emerges when multiple sources bear on the same strategic question.

Patent Database Research and Innovation Tracking

A pharmaceutical company has three late-stage drug candidates in development. Its quarterly 10-Qs show rising R&D expense, but they say little about which projects are most promising. Patent filings fill in that gap. They disclose molecular structures, therapeutic uses, and clinical trial designs months before peer-reviewed publication and years before regulatory submission. What looks like opaque research spending begins to resolve into a portfolio of intellectual property that can be tracked, valued, and compared across competitors.

The United States Patent and Trademark Office maintains public databases with millions of patent documents. These filings are often the earliest public record of corporate innovation. Each application includes technical specifications, legal claims, and citations to prior art. Analysts use them to map a company's technology base and to form a view on future competitive advantage. Unlike financial metrics, which describe what has already happened, patent data often points to revenue shifts before they show up.

Forward citations are among the most reliable patent valuation signals. When later patents cite an earlier invention, they suggest that the earlier patent has foundational importance. Highly cited patents tend to correlate with market value and licensing revenue. In pharmaceutical portfolio analysis, patents with above-average citation counts often generate outsized returns. Citation intensity, however, follows an inverted U-shaped pattern. Moderate levels suggest broad relevance. Excessive backward citations may point to narrow scope or a crowded prior-art field.

Portfolio-level queries can reveal strategic change before management acknowledges it in annual reports. An analyst following a semiconductor company might run SQL queries on Google Patents Public Data and aggregate filings by year, technology class, and inventor count. A sharp increase in filings related to quantum computing architectures, combined with new inventor hires from academia, points to a strategic pivot. That signal can appear months before management discusses the initiative on an earnings call or in an investor presentation.

Investors focused on sustainability use specialized taxonomies in patent analysis. The Sustainable Development Innovation framework maps roughly twenty million patents to the United Nations Sustainable Development Goals. That system normalizes innovation output against R&D spending and highlights companies with unusually high patent activity in areas such as carbon capture or renewable energy storage. The resulting scores can support ESG-oriented portfolios while also identifying emerging technological leadership.

Litigation data adds a layer of risk assessment that standard legal disclosure often misses. The USPTO's inter partes review database includes post-grant validity challenges filed between 2010 and 2016. European Patent Office opposition data covers 2007 through 2013. These records show which patents are under serious challenge and how often they survive. A company with several high-value patents in inter partes review faces real uncertainty around future royalty streams. That risk often remains invisible in ordinary risk-factor disclosure until litigation is already underway.

Patent databases can also surface emerging competitors. When Xiaomi moved into electric vehicles in 2021, its patent activity signaled the shift months before the company formally announced it. The filings covered battery management systems, autonomous driving algorithms, and vehicle connectivity, and they appeared in jurisdictions where Xiaomi had previously shown little patent activity. The geographic expansion, along with citations to established automakers' patents, made its competitive intent visible before financial statements did.

Patent abandon rates say something about portfolio discipline. Companies routinely let patents lapse by skipping maintenance payments. High abandon rates in core technology areas may suggest strategic retreat or financial strain. Very low abandon rates across all categories can point in the opposite direction: weak portfolio optimization. The average time from filing to final disposition—grant, rejection, or abandonment—can also be insightful. Long pendency periods may reflect patent office backlogs, but they can also indicate applications encountering repeated rejection and prolonged dispute.

The most advanced work links patent data to financial performance through matching algorithms. These systems connect patent assignees to parent companies while accounting for subsidiaries, acquisitions, and name changes. That makes it possible to run regression analyses of patent metrics against stock returns, profitability, and valuation multiples. The research consistently shows that patent-intensive firms in technology-driven sectors have financial characteristics distinct from less innovative peers, and that citation-weighted patent counts help predict excess returns even after standard risk factors are controlled for.

Trade Show Filings and Conference Presentations

A technology company unveils a new product at a major industry conference, and its stock rises five percent during the presentation. That move often reflects information asymmetry more than the intrinsic significance of the announcement itself. Serious analysis separates routine marketing from disclosures that are material enough to require regulatory reporting. The SEC requires companies to report events that could affect an investor's decision. A product launch or partnership announcement made at a trade show can meet that standard, triggering a Form 8-K within four business days.

Event studies help isolate the effect of those announcements. The method compares actual stock-price movement around a presentation with the movement that prevailing market conditions would have predicted. The difference is the abnormal return attributable to the event. This allows analysts to distinguish between announcements that genuinely change expectations and those that merely confirm what the market already knew. A product launch that restates existing guidance usually produces little abnormal return.

Conference agendas and speaker lists are useful source material in their own right. Organizers publish them weeks before major events. Matching speaker names to corporate filings shows which companies may be preparing meaningful announcements. At the Consumer Electronics Show, for example, keynote slots often precede major product launches or strategic partnerships. When those appearances are cross-referenced against later SEC filings, they create a timeline of material disclosure.

Earnings call transcripts often point back to conference guidance. Management teams regularly discuss investor-conference presentations during quarterly calls. Search tools on transcript platforms can identify references to events such as the J.P. Morgan Healthcare Conference or the Goldman Sachs Technology Conference. Those references often include near-verbatim restatements of guidance first given to institutional investors. Comparing that guidance with later quarterly results helps show whether conference promises turned into operating performance.

Attendance alone is not material. The SEC standard turns on whether the information would matter to a reasonable investor. A company's presence on a trade show floor, without a significant announcement, rarely qualifies. A breakthrough demonstration or a major partnership signing is different. If the event reveals information not previously available through ordinary channels, it may trigger disclosure obligations. The distinction is not the venue but the novelty and materiality of what is said there.

Analyst forecast revisions after conferences provide a useful confirmation signal. Research platforms track changes in consensus estimates across thousands of securities. Watching revisions in the five to ten trading days after a major presentation shows whether analysts incorporated new information. Upward revisions after a product launch suggest analysts viewed the news as materially positive. Downward revisions after guidance presentations suggest skepticism about management's outlook. These shifts often precede broader market recognition by weeks.

Linking conference announcements to revenue requires careful tracking. Management's Discussion and Analysis sometimes refers back to partnerships or channel expansions first announced at a trade show. Following those references over time can connect the announcement to later operating results. A distribution partnership announced at an industry event may not show up in reported revenue until three quarters later. That lag helps explain why some conference disclosures move the market only gradually rather than immediately.

Financial ratios can show whether announced initiatives actually changed the business. Profitability, efficiency, and leverage metrics, compared quarter over quarter, offer objective evidence that goes beyond management's conference narrative. A company that introduces a new manufacturing process at an industry forum may later report improved gross margins. Another that announces expanded credit facilities may show a changed debt-to-equity profile. The numbers test the story.

Safe harbor protection also applies. SEC filings usually include language designed to shield forward-looking statements from liability when accompanied by meaningful cautionary language. Remarks made at conferences outside formal filings receive less protection if they include material non-public information. That difference helps explain why some companies speak more conservatively at investor conferences than in a 10-K. The legal setting shapes the language.

Conference intelligence is most useful when it is part of a larger analytical mosaic. A CES product launch matters more when patent filings show corresponding intellectual property protection. A partnership announcement carries more weight when corporate registry data shows prior ties between the parties. The event itself may be only one tile in the picture. The edge comes from fitting it together with the rest.

Investor Day Transcripts and Strategic Communications

At an investor day, a chief financial officer lays out a plan to return forty-five percent of free cash flow to shareholders while reducing customer churn. That kind of guidance is often more specific than anything found in quarterly filings. Investor day transcripts preserve these communications in a structured form, separating prepared remarks from live Q&A. The prepared section delivers management's chosen narrative about growth, capital allocation, and operations. The Q&A shows how well that narrative survives contact with professional analysts.

Schroders Capital's investor day transcript disclosed realized internal rates of return of twenty-four and twenty-three percent on individual company investments. Those returns outperformed primary fund investments and, in management's telling, reflected "extra value add" from early-mover advantages. The transcript also gave concrete examples, including a hotel investment that achieved one hundred percent growth in revenue per available room through a Marriott partnership. That level of operational detail rarely appears in standard SEC filings. It offers direct evidence of execution.

Citi's services investor day transcript included client case studies showing a one hundred percent win rate on mandates for working-capital optimization across forty-five countries. It also described revenue multipliers from geographic expansion, with some client relationships producing twice the revenue after expansion. The presentation linked those outcomes to resilience during regional bank failures and geopolitical conflict. Strategic goals that might otherwise sound abstract were tied to observable client results.

Analysts use recurring methods to extract intelligence from this material. Some focus on how companies sit at the intersection of several trends, such as income diversification and uncorrelated assets. Others track operational execution by following references to automation, simplified reporting structures, or single-point-of-contact service models. Those approaches turn narrative presentation material into operating metrics that can be compared across competitors.

Investor days are not just marketing exercises. They often contain the first public disclosure of return targets, capital allocation priorities, and operating metrics that later drive analyst revisions. Nor do they ignore macroeconomic pressure. Citi's presentation, for example, showed how a firm could sustain revenue despite regional banking stress and geopolitical disruption, giving investors a more concrete basis for judging business-model resilience.

The Q&A portion is often the most interesting. When analysts repeatedly ask about customer churn, capital expenditure timing, or competitive threats over several events, the pattern itself signals unresolved risk. Management's manner of response can reveal as much as the content. Deflection suggests discomfort. A detailed, data-backed answer suggests confidence. A shift away from pricing pressure and toward innovation may indicate uncertainty about the company's competitive position.

The real value comes from tracking how guidance evolves across multiple events. AT&T's investor day laid out growth targets for service revenue, adjusted EBITDA, free cash flow, and earnings per share. Comparing those targets with later quarterly results provides a straightforward measure of execution. The gap between what management promised and what it delivered becomes a live measure of credibility, and that credibility shapes how the market will treat future guidance.

Activist investors understand this well. Elliott Management's twenty-three-page critique of AT&T dissected the company's Time Warner acquisition, capital allocation, and debt burden by using management's own strategic communications against it. The document highlighted the distance between stated priorities and actual resource deployment. Strategic messaging, once published, can become evidence in a governance fight.

Predictive modeling research goes further. It shows that categorical features extracted from investor day transcripts can forecast next-day stock movements with statistical significance. These models treat prepared remarks and Q&A separately, on the theory that scripted language and spontaneous responses convey different kinds of information.

More advanced work combines text analysis with audio features such as tone and emotional inflection from recorded presentations. That multi-modal approach explains abnormal returns and trading volume better than text alone. Numbers matter, but so does the way management delivers them.

Investor day transcripts are, in the end, commitment devices. They turn aspiration into an observable benchmark and make management accountable for what it has chosen to say.

Industry Conference Intelligence Mining

At a mining conference in Denver, a keynote speaker describes large language models and greater processing power as game changers. The talk contains no material non-public information about any one company. What it does reveal is the strategic direction of the sector. Industry conferences take dispersed corporate signals and compress them into a concentrated view of technological adoption, operating priorities, and competitive position across many firms at once.

The Digitalization & AI in Mining North America Conference in Vancouver draws more than two hundred delegates. Sessions focus on autonomous operations, data analytics, and robotics across the mining value chain. The audience itself is informative. When technical workshops are attended by vice presidents of digitalization, chief technology officers, and data scientists rather than marketing staff, it suggests that companies are committing real resources to those initiatives.

Presentations often include case studies that slip past the usual public-relations filter. A mining technology company may demonstrate predictive maintenance software using actual data from a copper-mine partnership. That can reveal implementation timelines, performance outcomes, and adoption rates that never appear in an annual report. The result is concrete evidence of commercial traction, not just press-release language.

Conference agendas also reveal what an industry is prioritizing. A World Mining Congress webinar that includes several sessions on AI for mineral exploration, reinforcement learning in decision-making, and large language models for supply-chain analysis is signaling a collective shift in attention. That pattern can become visible months before individual companies disclose specific AI investments in quarterly filings.

Speaker affiliations help map relationships. When a Stanford professor appears on a panel with executives from BHP and Microsoft, the lineup itself suggests channels of collaboration beyond any formal partnership announcement. These pairings can point to knowledge transfer and future commercial ties. The BHP-Microsoft work on AI at the Escondida copper mine began as conference conversation before it hardened into formal projects.

The Q&A is often more revealing than the prepared presentation. One executive may answer a question about implementation costs with vague references to "ongoing investments." Another may cite specific cost-benefit ratios from pilot programs. The contrast says something about confidence and project maturity.

These presentations are not just polished marketing. In practice, they force executives to explain technical implementation to an audience that knows the subject. In mining, the language has shifted from talk of "data silos" to "predictive operations" and "AI-ready mining." That change in vocabulary reflects real changes in capability.

Much of this intelligence can be gathered without attending in person. Conference websites often publish slides, recordings, and speaker biographies. Those materials may contain technical specifications, implementation roadmaps, and performance benchmarks that never make it into investor presentations. Collected systematically, they become a comparable dataset across competitors.

The content also reveals adoption timelines and implementation constraints. When several speakers insist that "quality data" is a prerequisite for AI success, they are identifying a sector-wide bottleneck. That helps explain why some mining companies are slower to invest than public rhetoric would suggest. The gap between the language of AI transformation and the admission that data infrastructure is still inadequate produces a more realistic view of the timetable.

Competitive intelligence sharpens when presentation content is compared across firms at the same event. One company may show a fully deployed autonomous haulage system. Another may present only a conceptual framework for future automation. That maturity gap is a competitive signal that financial statements are poorly equipped to show. Often it persists for years before it appears in margin performance.

Tracking speaker movement between companies adds another layer. An executive who presents on digital transformation at one conference and joins a competitor months later carries technical knowledge and strategic priorities into the new role. That kind of personnel signal can provide early warning of competitive change before any formal announcement.

The most valuable conference intelligence may still arise in informal conversations that remote researchers cannot access. Even so, presentation content often hints at those exchanges. When speakers refer to "productive conversations with colleagues" about a shared operational problem, they are pointing to a broader industry effort to solve it.

Industry conferences are, in effect, collective sense-making exercises. Their value does not lie in any one slide or one remark. It lies in the pattern that forms when multiple speakers, from different organizations, keep circling the same technical and strategic problems.

Peer Comparison and Market Positioning Analysis

A technology company reports twenty percent revenue growth. On its own, the number looks impressive. Against a peer group averaging thirty-five percent growth, it looks like market share loss. Peer comparison turns isolated financial metrics into competitive intelligence.

One useful tool is the Jaccard similarity coefficient, which measures overlap between companies based on financial-statement characteristics. Research shows that analysts are more likely to select peers with high financial-statement benchmark scores than peers chosen only by industry classification. A one-standard-deviation increase in this score raises the likelihood of analyst selection by thirteen percent. The method is a way to identify true competitors rather than relying on rough industry labels.

Custom peer groups require matching along several dimensions. Market capitalization captures differences in cash-flow stability and financial flexibility. Growth stage separates mature pharmaceutical companies from clinical-stage biotechs. Value drivers such as return on invested capital or price-to-earnings ratios help create functional comparables. Multi-dimensional matching usually produces more useful peer sets than broad industry buckets.

Before comparison, the data often needs to be normalized. A restructuring charge may temporarily depress one company's earnings. Normalization adjusts for that kind of one-time item across the peer set. Median values can then be calculated for valuation multiples, profitability margins, leverage, and growth. Outliers become targets for further work.

Tesla's forward price-to-earnings ratio reached fifty times earnings in 2023. Ford and General Motors traded at roughly eight to twelve times earnings. That spread reflected investor expectations about relative growth and technological leadership. It also highlighted Tesla's growth premium despite negative EBITDA margins at the time. Gaps of that scale can signal either extraordinary opportunity or speculative excess.

The stacking method formalizes these comparisons. Analysts begin with a peer-group mean or median price-to-earnings ratio, then adjust that baseline for differences in revenue growth, EBITDA margins, and discretionary earnings percentages. The result is a structured estimate of the premium or discount the subject company deserves relative to its competitors.

Financial-statement benchmarking can be decomposed across the income statement, balance sheet, and cash flow statement. Some companies post stronger margins but carry weaker balance sheets. Others produce robust cash flow despite unremarkable reported earnings. Looking across all three statements helps identify where a company is genuinely stronger and where it is more exposed.

Industry membership, by itself, is rarely enough to define a good peer group. Companies in the same industry can sit at entirely different stages of development and operate with different financial structures. A startup drug developer pursuing its first approval is not a clean comparable for a mature pharmaceutical company with a portfolio of approved products. Business model, growth rate, and scale usually carry more weight than the industry code.

Peer analysis also cannot remain static. Competitive landscapes change with regulation, technology, and adjacent entrants. A company may hold its position against traditional competitors while losing ground to firms from neighboring sectors. Only continuous re-benchmarking captures that kind of disruption risk.

Peer comparison in SEC filings extends beyond the numbers. Companies differ in readability, risk-factor language, and ESG reporting. Some disclose customer acquisition costs, unit economics, or other operating metrics in detail. Others provide very little. Those differences in transparency create an information advantage for investors who compare reporting practices systematically.

Analysts tend to favor companies with similar financial-statement structures when choosing peers. That preference reflects a practical truth: comparable accounting treatment makes comparison cleaner. Companies using aggressive revenue recognition or unusual capitalization policies are harder to benchmark because the statements themselves are less structurally comparable.

Market-positioning analysis turns implicit advantages into something measurable. A company with brand strength or technological leadership may be able to charge premium prices. That advantage shows up in gross-margin gaps relative to peers. Tracking those gaps over time helps show whether the company's edge is widening or eroding.

In the end, peer comparison asks a simple question: do a company's valuation multiples make sense in light of its competitive position? Sometimes a discount is deserved because growth is weaker or profitability is lower. Sometimes the market is missing a relative strength. The work is in telling those two cases apart through disciplined comparison.

KEY TAKEAWAYS

- ☐ A company's performance means nothing in isolation. Twenty percent revenue growth looks strong until the sector average is thirty-five percent. Peer comparison, sector mapping, and competitive positioning analysis provide the context that turns company-level data into market intelligence.
- ☐ Patent databases are the earliest public record of corporate innovation. Forward citations — later patents citing an earlier one — are among the most reliable signals of foundational importance. Filing patterns across technology classes, inventor counts, and geographic expansion reveal strategic pivots months before management discusses them on earnings calls.
- ☐ Investor day transcripts contain the most specific forward-looking guidance a company issues outside of SEC filings. The prepared remarks deliver management's scripted narrative. The Q&A reveals how that narrative holds up under professional scrutiny. Comparing guidance from investor days against subsequent quarterly results provides a direct, measurable test of management credibility.

FIELDWORK

- ☐ Search Google Patents (patents.google.com) for a company on your watchlist. Filter by the past three years. Note which technology classes dominate the filings and whether the mix has shifted. Check if any patents have been cited by competitors' subsequent filings — that forward-citation pattern signals foundational technology.
- ☐ Find the most recent investor day transcript for a company you follow (search the company's IR page or a transcript provider). Read the Q&A section first. Identify which topics drew repeated analyst questions and whether management's answers were specific or evasive. Then check whether the guidance given at the investor day was confirmed or contradicted by the next two quarterly results.
- ☐ Build a simple peer comparison table for one company: three to five direct competitors, with columns for revenue growth, operating margin, valuation

multiple (EV/EBITDA or P/E), and leverage (debt/EBITDA). Note where your target company is an outlier in either direction. Outlier positions — particularly premium valuations without corresponding margin or growth advantages — require explanation.

Apply This

Competitive intelligence answers the question that single-company analysis cannot: is this company gaining or losing ground? Every metric in your dossier should have a peer comparison attached. Revenue growth relative to sector, margins relative to competitors, R&D intensity relative to innovation output. Without that context, company-level analysis is incomplete.

CHAPTER 20

Social Media and Retail Sentiment Analysis

Social media presents a paradox for financial analysis. It generates enormous volumes of stock discussion, yet most of that discussion contains little or no real information about company fundamentals. The noise is constant, and it easily overwhelms whatever signal may be present.

The problem is not just measuring sentiment. It is separating genuine retail conviction from narratives designed to move prices. Coordinated networks can manufacture the appearance of consensus by posting in sync across accounts and platforms, using recommendation systems to amplify misleading claims.

The distinction usually appears less in the content itself than in the pattern around it. Genuine grassroots enthusiasm tends to vary in timing, language, and participant background. Manipulation networks tend to converge across all three.

Price action alone rarely resolves the issue. A real burst of retail momentum and a manipulated spike can both produce sharp short-term gains. The difference usually emerges in volume patterns, options activity, and cross-sectional comparisons with related securities.

Manipulated rallies often appear without any corresponding fundamental development. At other times, they show concentrated buying in narrow instruments rather than broad participation. Those patterns become clear only when several data streams are analyzed together rather than read one at a time.

Reddit, StockTwits, and X/Twitter Signal Extraction

A pharmaceutical stock begins trending across three platforms at once. Reddit posts insist that breakthrough trial results are imminent, StockTwits sentiment gauges show ninety-five percent bullishness, and X accounts with financial verification badges begin amplifying the story. The stock jumps fifteen percent in pre-market trading.

Yet none of these platforms contains the trial data itself. That information remains confidential until the company releases it. The basic challenge of social media signal extraction is deciding whether the market is reacting to information or to a coordinated narrative.

Each platform shapes the signal differently. Reddit's threaded format allows users to build detailed theses, but voting dynamics often reward emotional force more than analytical quality. During the GameStop episode, technical analysis drew little engagement while memes about "diamond hands" collected thousands of awards.

StockTwits works through ticker-specific real-time feeds. Its bullish-bearish meter offers a simple sentiment reading, but that reading often follows price rather than anticipates it. Extreme bullish readings can look informative while doing little more than mirror a move already underway.

X, and the financial subculture often called fintwit, mixes professional analysts with retail participants. Verification has become a weaker marker of credibility because paid badges no longer distinguish expertise in any meaningful way. Retweet patterns can show how quickly a thesis spreads, but high-follower accounts often publish their views one to three days after institutional options activity is already visible.

By then, sophisticated money may already be in position. What reaches retail users as apparent discovery may be nothing more than late-stage amplification. The sequence is often more revealing than the post itself.

Useful signal extraction depends on method, not casual observation. Volume and velocity provide a first screen. A five- to tenfold increase in ticker mentions over twenty-four hours deserves attention, but it can reflect either genuine catalyst discovery or coordinated promotion.

The distinction begins to sharpen when the activity is checked against regulatory calendars and news databases. If no scheduled event or credible disclosure corresponds to the surge, the attention is more likely manufactured than organic. Social media excitement without any external anchor usually deserves skepticism.

Language helps refine the picture. Posts built around phrases like "inevitable," "sure thing," or "moon" usually reflect speculative enthusiasm rather than researched conviction. More credible commentary tends to acknowledge specific risks while still making a directional case.

A post saying, "Love the company but margins compressed three hundred basis points year over year," carries more weight than unqualified optimism. That kind of balanced language appears more often in smaller forums such as r/SecurityAnalysis, where users work through filings and valuation models. It appears less often in mass-audience communities driven by momentum, identity, and performance theater.

Account behavior often reveals the manipulation more clearly than the content. Multiple accounts created in the same week, all posting identical or near-identical thesis language, point to coordinated inauthentic behavior. These campaigns often appear before secondary offerings or insider unlock periods, when fresh retail demand can absorb impending selling pressure.

Another warning sign is a cluster of anonymous accounts with little posting history suddenly flooding one ticker with high-frequency messages. When the same pattern appears across several platforms at once, it creates the appearance of broad enthusiasm. What looks distributed may in fact be tightly organized.

Time-series analysis helps clarify the relationship between sentiment and price. When bullish posting peaks three to five days before earnings, the actual results often disappoint the social-media consensus. Retail participants may be extrapolating stale information rather than incorporating anything new.

Celebrity endorsements offer another timing clue. When a financial personality with a large following suddenly promotes a company they have never discussed before, recent Form 4 filings may show that they bought shares within the previous month. The public post follows the position.

A contrarian filter improves signal quality. Posts containing specific financial metrics often receive far less engagement than narrative-driven content. A detailed analysis citing revenue growth, leverage, and year-over-year comparisons may struggle to attract one hundred upvotes, while a meme about the same stock collects thousands.

That disparity says a great deal about platform incentives. Comments correcting factual errors and providing citations are often heavily downvoted in strongly bullish communities. Skepticism becomes socially costly at exactly the moment it is most useful.

One of the most persistent mistakes is to equate high engagement with a correct thesis. Tesla short theses accumulated more than fifty thousand upvotes during a period when the stock rallied seventy percent. Platform algorithms reward emotional reaction, not predictive accuracy.

Another mistake is to assume that communities will correct misinformation through voting. In practice, voting often reinforces prior belief rather than filtering for truth. Posts claiming that certain technical setups "never fail" can receive awards even when their historical failure rates exceed sixty percent.

Social media works best as one input among several. Real signals emerge when online chatter lines up with other forms of evidence. Unusual options activity preceding social-media discussion may indicate institutional positioning leaking into retail channels.

Regulatory filings showing executive purchases before a celebrity endorsement help confirm sequence and motive. Satellite imagery showing increased activity at a facility, combined with social-media speculation about expansion, creates converging evidence. Social media alone rarely offers actionable intelligence, but it can reveal shifts in crowd psychology before price fully adjusts.

Identifying Coordinated Inauthentic Behavior

A cryptocurrency begins trending across social platforms with identical claims about an imminent exchange listing. Twenty accounts created within the same hour all post the same message: "Major exchange listing confirmed for next week – last chance to buy before announcement." The profile pictures differ, but the phrasing does not.

This is coordinated inauthentic behavior. The term comes from Meta's enforcement framework, where it refers to deceptive coordination designed to distort public perception. In financial markets, the goal is often to manufacture urgency and false consensus.

That differs from ordinary misinformation. A single account spreading false information is simple deception. A network of accounts acting under centralized control creates artificial amplification, and that is usually detected through behavior and network structure rather than content alone.

These operations often mix fake profiles, authentic accounts, and duplicated personas to create the illusion of independent support. Macedonian actors used this approach when they coordinated with a U.S. company to push for-profit fake news through personas that misrepresented their location. The tactic works because people respond not only to claims, but to apparent agreement.

Detection begins with behavior. Newly created accounts with sparse profiles posting identical content in narrow time windows are an obvious warning sign. Older accounts that suddenly shift into out-of-character financial promotion may have been compromised.

Researchers studying the Fediverse have documented campaigns in which sock-puppet accounts mass-follow targets or flood discussions to simulate grassroots support. A sock puppet is a fake identity controlled by a single actor for exactly that purpose. The goal is not simply to spread a message but to alter the perceived balance of opinion.

Content synchronization is often the clearest marker. Identical narratives, links, and hashtags appearing at the same time across multiple accounts strongly suggest centralized direction. Low-quality financial content tends to be amplified in repetitive, patterned ways that are difficult to explain through normal user behavior.

Platforms such as Meta use automated systems to identify these synchronization events and then apply human review to determine whether the accounts are actually linked. Their enforcement actions have removed dozens of coordinated networks operating across multiple countries, including campaigns that used mass reporting as part of broader influence or espionage efforts. The same detection logic applies, on a smaller scale, in financial promotion campaigns.

The Nisos framework goes further by combining signature discovery with telemetry analysis. It overlays technical indicators across accounts and outlets to expose hidden connections. Shared IP addresses or device fingerprints across supposedly independent profiles can serve as early indicators of coordination.

Pattern mapping can reveal control even when wording changes slightly from post to post. Telemetry-based location and identity attribution can also help distinguish domestic commercial operations from foreign influence campaigns. The market may react similarly to both, but the motives and resources behind them differ.

In financial markets, coordinated behavior is usually tied to profit. Fraud networks use clusters of accounts for scams, micro-targeted advertising, and sentiment manipulation. They often exploit personal data harvested from earlier breaches to make the pitch feel tailored and credible.

Post-Cambridge Analytica investigations showed how synchronized messaging could shape behavior at scale. The Cambridge Analytica case itself illustrated how psychological profiling and platform coordination could be combined to influence sentiment. In market settings, the same logic is used to elevate low-quality financial content and manufacture credibility around it.

It is easy to mistake grassroots enthusiasm for coordination, so the distinction requires care. Organic trends can involve many people arriving at similar conclusions independently. What makes a campaign coordinated is centralized control, not mere similarity of opinion.

Another common error is to focus too narrowly on individual accounts rather than on the network they form. A single fake account is ordinary deception. A network designed to manufacture agreement creates something more powerful and more dangerous.

Platform enforcement frameworks usually distinguish between domestic, non-government coordination and foreign or state-backed activity. Meta uses different tiers for those categories, with different escalation paths. Domestic coordination often centers on commercial gain, including market manipulation.

Foreign operations usually pursue broader geopolitical objectives. The technical methods overlap, but the scale, resources, and intent may differ sharply. On the platform itself, though, the visible behavior can look remarkably similar.

Practical identification depends on several signals at once. A cluster of account-creation dates around a specific event can indicate planning. Posting times synchronized to the minute across different time zones often suggest automated scheduling.

Identical grammatical errors or unusual phrasing across nominally unrelated accounts point to copy-and-paste operations. Engagement loops, in which the same accounts repeatedly like, share, and endorse one another, create artificial visibility. The appearance of support is generated by design.

Regulatory filings can add a financial layer to the picture. Accounts promoting a stock often appear just before secondary offerings or insider unlock periods. That timing suggests awareness of coming selling pressure that retail buyers may not anticipate.

The campaign creates demand just as better-informed holders prepare to sell into it. Social media does not create the exit opportunity by itself, but it can supply the necessary liquidity. In many schemes, that is enough.

Network-analysis tools help make these structures visible. Shared followers, repost patterns, and comment interactions often reveal hub-and-spoke arrangements in which central accounts direct a cluster of peripheral profiles. In a true hub-and-spoke structure, the center distributes the narrative and the periphery repeats it.

Organic communities usually look different. Their connections form through genuine interaction rather than centralized instruction. The difference is visible not only in what people say, but in who always seems to speak after whom.

The strongest detection systems combine automated screening with human judgment. Algorithms can flag anomalies in posting behavior at scale. Human analysts can then interpret the strategic objective of the content and the signs of deception that simple rules miss.

Sophisticated operators change vocabulary, cadence, and account design. But the underlying behavioral signatures tend to persist. Coordinated inauthentic behavior distorts markets by manufacturing the perception of consensus and pushing price discovery away from analysis and toward engineered sentiment.

Genuine Retail Momentum vs. Manipulation Detection

A stock rises twenty percent in a single session. Social media lights up with excitement about the company's breakthrough technology, and trading volume jumps to five times normal levels. The question is whether the move reflects genuine retail momentum or manipulation.

The answer rarely appears in the price move alone. Genuine momentum can persist because many investors independently reach similar conclusions about a company's prospects. Manipulated spikes are usually designed to create temporary demand so promoters can sell into it.

Genuine retail momentum often leaves recognizable technical traces. Volume builds steadily alongside the price move, showing broad participation. RSI may climb above seventy, indicating overbought conditions, while indicators such as MACD remain aligned with the trend.

On-balance volume should rise with price if the move reflects real accumulation. When that happens, the rally is being supported by actual participation rather than by a hollow spike. Walmart's 2021 rally showed that pattern after the company announced its largest annual dividend increase in a decade along with a three-for-one stock split.

The stock posted a bullish MACD crossover and an RSI above seventy. Volume confirmed that both retail and institutional investors were responding to a clear fundamental development. The move was extended, but it was not empty.

Manipulated rallies often fail the same volume test. Price jumps while volume stagnates or declines, suggesting that the move lacks broad participation. In some cases, manipulators engineer an initial burst of activity to trigger algorithms and then withdraw liquidity, leaving the appearance of self-sustaining momentum.

The collapse comes later, when retail holders discover there is no real support beneath the price. The key is whether volume continues to validate the rally after the breakout, not just during the first burst. A move that cannot recruit additional participation usually cannot sustain itself.

Cross-sectional momentum analysis provides another filter. Genuine momentum often appears across a group of related stocks within a sector or theme, reflecting a broader market view about the industry. A sharp move in one stock, with no corresponding movement in peers, is more suspect.

The Jegadeesh-Titman framework ranks stocks by prior returns and goes long recent winners while shorting laggards. Adapted for retail analysis, it can be rerun weekly to distinguish durable leaders from names that briefly spike and fade. What persists across a basket is different from what erupts in isolation.

Regime shifts in volatility expose weak momentum. Momentum strategies tend to work in stable, trending markets and break down when volatility rises. Manipulators exploit that by creating temporary trends that cannot survive once conditions normalize.

ADX is useful here. Values above twenty-five suggest a trend with some staying power, while lower readings imply a weaker move more vulnerable to reversal. The 2022 drawdown in technology stocks exposed how many supposed momentum names had little true trend strength once volatility returned.

The quality of discussion on retail platforms also helps separate the two. Genuine momentum usually produces disagreement, technical analysis, and arguments grounded in fundamentals. Manipulated campaigns lean on repetitive price targets, urgency language, and synchronized posting.

Message-board history often makes the difference visible. Platforms that let users inspect posting records and engagement patterns make it easier to distinguish organic enthusiasm from manufactured consensus. A community with memory is harder to game than a feed with none.

Options activity provides another check. Genuine momentum often coincides with rising open interest in call options across several strikes and expirations. Manipulated rallies may instead show concentrated buying in short-dated, far out-of-the-money calls.

Unusual options activity that appears before social-media promotion is especially suspicious. The absence of corresponding put hedging points to speculative positioning rather than informed risk-taking. Here again, the sequence is as significant as the size of the trade.

Fundamental cross-checking remains the most reliable filter. Genuine momentum usually follows something identifiable: an earnings surprise, a product launch, a regulatory approval, or an analyst upgrade. Those events give investors something concrete to evaluate.

Manipulated rallies often rest on vague rumors about unnamed partnerships or unspecified technological breakthroughs. The simplest test is whether the claims can be anchored in SEC filings, company releases, or credible reporting. If the story cannot be anchored, the price move deserves doubt.

The signal strengthens when several technical indicators line up. RSI above seventy by itself may only show that the stock is stretched. But when MACD crosses bullishly, moving averages support the trend, and volume confirms the move, the case for sustained momentum becomes stronger.

Practitioners often work through a checklist: primary trend confirmation, alignment across indicators, rising volume, limited divergence, and confirmation across timeframes. That does not eliminate false signals. It does reduce them.

The way a move decays is often revealing. Genuine momentum tends to accelerate, pause, and then either continue or consolidate. Manipulated moves are more likely to go vertical and then collapse once the promotion stops.

Rate of change helps expose that difference. Persistently extreme readings without any corresponding fundamental development often point to artificial acceleration rather than durable demand. A stock that can only rise faster is often close to failure.

Retail sentiment also has to be read in the context of each platform. Different communities have different cultures, and those cultures shape the quality of the momentum. Some forums reward careful fundamental analysis, while others reward short-term excitement and tribal reinforcement.

The same stock can therefore produce very different signals on Reddit, StockTwits, and specialized investment forums. Platform culture does not determine what is true, but it does influence how enthusiasm is produced, rewarded, and sustained. That is analytically useful in its own right.

Historical precedent helps because manipulation leaves recurring traces. Pump-and-dump schemes tend to follow the same structure: rapid price appreciation, exaggerated social-media claims, weak underlying participation, and a sharp collapse once promoters sell. The tactics change around the edges, but the pattern remains familiar.

The strongest detection combines quantitative screening with qualitative investigation. Automated systems can flag suspicious patterns in price, volume, and social-media activity. Human analysis can then examine promoter history, company fundamentals, and market structure around the move.

Sophisticated manipulators adapt around simple rules, but they still leave recognizable traces in sequence, structure, and behavior. Genuine retail momentum is collective judgment applied to public information. Manipulation is something else: a transfer mechanism designed to move wealth from followers to promoters through an artificial price move.

Key Takeaways

- ☐ Social media sentiment is a barometer of crowd psychology, not a research database. Its value lies in measuring how retail participants feel about a stock, not in discovering fundamental information about the company. Treat it as one data stream among many, never as a standalone signal.
- ☐ Coordinated inauthentic behavior is identifiable through structural patterns: accounts created in the same time window, identical or near-identical language across posts, high-frequency posting about a single ticker by accounts with no prior history, and timing that coincides with secondary offerings or insider lock-up expirations. The content may look organic. The metadata usually does not.
- ☐ Genuine retail momentum differs from manipulation in volume structure, not in price action. Real momentum shows steady volume increases alongside price advances, broad participation across strike prices in the options chain, and correlation with identifiable fundamental catalysts. Manipulated spikes typically show concentrated activity in narrow instruments, volume that fades after the initial move, and no corresponding fundamental development.

Fieldwork

- ☐ The next time a stock on your watchlist surges on social media attention, apply the cross-reference test before reacting. Check: Is there a scheduled catalyst (earnings, FDA date, contract renewal) that explains the attention? Does the options chain show broad participation or concentrated short-dated activity? Is there any corresponding regulatory filing or press release? If the social media surge has no anchor in the public record, treat it as noise until proven otherwise.
- ☐ Pick a stock with active discussion on Reddit or StockTwits. Read twenty posts about it. Classify each as analytical (cites specific metrics, acknowledges risks, references filings) or promotional (uses urgency language, cites no sources, makes unqualified predictions). Calculate the ratio. Communities

where promotional content dominates analytical content by more than 3:1 are unreliable signal environments.

Apply This

When social media activity correlates with other intelligence sources — unusual options flow preceding the discussion, regulatory filings confirming the catalyst, insider purchases aligning with the timeline — the convergence strengthens the signal. When social media is the only source pointing in a given direction, the signal is weak regardless of how loud it is.

Part 5

Policy Intelligence and the Political Economy Layer

The regulatory environment is not a neutral force acting on business from the outside. It is produced by institutions—Congress, federal agencies, executive departments—that are responsive to organized interests, staffed by people who move between public and private roles, and shaped by political pressures that leave extensive public records behind. For any company whose economics depend on government contracts, favorable rulemaking, or the continued absence of adverse legislation, this political-economy layer is as material to the thesis as the income statement, and far more legible in public data than most analysts assume.

This section examines the three government databases that make that layer visible: the Lobbying Disclosure Act system, USAspending.gov's federal contracting record, and the STOCK Act's congressional trading disclosures. Together they show how industry, government, and capital interact to shape regulatory outcomes, support contractor revenue, and, at times, surface in the personal investment activity of the officials charged with oversight.

CHAPTER 21

Lobbying Intelligence

A pharmaceutical company reports strong pipeline progress in its annual filing and describes the regulatory environment as stable and manageable. In the same quarter, it quietly doubles its lobbying spend in Washington. Its retained firms file disclosures naming the House Energy and Commerce Committee, the Senate Finance Committee, and the Centers for Medicare and Medicaid Services as covered agencies.

The issue descriptions in those filings identify the Inflation Reduction Act's drug-pricing provisions and Medicare Part D negotiation authority. Nothing in the 10-K or the earnings call frames this as urgent. The lobbying record does.

Most investors treat lobbying disclosures as political background noise rather than financial intelligence. That is a mistake. When a company begins spending heavily to influence a specific law, rule, or agency, it is making an internal judgment that the outcome could materially affect the business.

That judgment often surfaces in lobbying before it appears in investor-facing language. Spending is harder to explain away than tone. A company can sound calm on an earnings call while simultaneously paying multiple firms to work a problem it clearly does not consider routine.

The Lobbying Disclosure Act system produces more than twenty thousand filings a year. Those filings show who is lobbying, for whom, on which issue codes, with which agencies or congressional bodies, and for how much money. The underlying database is public, machine-readable, and available through a free API maintained by the Senate Office of Public Records.

The method is the same one used throughout this manual. Define the requirement first. Collect from the primary source. Cross-reference the result against the company's filing record. Then ask the essential question: does the company's lobbying behavior match the regulatory story management is telling investors?

The Lobbying Disclosure Act Framework

The Lobbying Disclosure Act of 1995 created the modern federal lobbying-registration system. The Honest Leadership and Open Government Act of 2007 strengthened it by tightening registration thresholds, increasing the reporting cadence from semiannual to quarterly, and adding stricter rules on gifts and political contributions.

The filing obligation begins when a lobbying firm expects to receive at least three thousand dollars from a single client in a quarter for lobbying activity, or when an organization lobbying on its own behalf expects to spend fourteen thousand dollars or more in that quarter. Below those levels, no filing is required.

That threshold is analytically useful. It means the official record captures organized and sustained lobbying better than incidental contact. For investment work, that is usually what counts. A company that crosses the filing threshold has already signaled that the issue has become important enough to justify structured federal engagement.

Two forms carry most of the intelligence. Form LD-1 is the registration statement filed when a new lobbying relationship begins. It identifies the registrant, whether a retained firm or an in-house operation, the client, the issues involved, and the agencies likely to be contacted.

LD-1 is important because it is often the first public sign of a new regulatory concern. A company that has never previously registered a lobbying engagement, or that suddenly hires a new firm focused on one agency or committee, is signaling that some issue has moved from passive monitoring to active response.

Form LD-2 is the quarterly activity report. It is filed by January 20, April 20, July 20, and October 20, and it reports the income earned by the lobbying firm or the expenses incurred by the in-house team, the issue codes involved, a narrative description of the issues lobbied, the names of the lobbyists on the account, and the covered agencies and officials contacted.

Form LD-203 adds a second layer. It is filed semiannually and discloses political contributions made by registered lobbyists and their employers to covered officials. It is less central to most company-level monitoring, but it can be useful when the analyst wants to understand the wider political network around a particular lobbying campaign.

All three forms are maintained in the public database of the Senate Office of Public Records. They are searchable manually at lda.senate.gov and available through a structured API at the same domain, with no authentication required for basic read access.

The Senate LDA API: Structure and Access

The LDA API is the primary collection tool for systematic lobbying work. It exposes the full Senate database through endpoints organized around the key entities: registrants, clients, filings, and lobbyists. Each supports filtering, which makes it possible to narrow the universe before pulling detailed records.

The filings endpoint is usually the best place to start. A query filtered by client organization name returns all relevant LD-1 and LD-2 filings across all registrants. That matters because large companies often retain several firms at once, each handling different parts of the same regulatory agenda.

A major technology company may have five or six firms active in a single quarter. One may be working tax issues, another antitrust, another telecommunications, another trade. The endpoint surfaces the whole pattern in one structured response.

Date filtering is important because the value is often comparative. Pulling the quarter immediately before an earnings call and comparing it with the prior four or six quarters can reveal whether lobbying intensity has changed meaningfully. If the company's language to investors has remained flat while the filings show a sharp increase in effort, the discrepancy deserves attention.

The income and expense fields in each LD-2 provide the spending dimension. Retained firms report income in rounded increments. Amounts below five thousand dollars appear as zero, and larger amounts are rounded to the nearest ten thousand.

That limits precision, but not direction. An in-house operation reporting eight hundred thousand dollars in lobbying expense in a quarter is not meaningfully comparable to one reporting eighty thousand. The trend is what counts, not the missing granularity.

The registrant endpoint adds another layer by showing which firms a company has engaged, when those relationships began, and whether any have lapsed. A company that hires a firm with deep ties to a specific committee or agency is making a targeted decision, and that decision is visible in the public record well before management chooses to frame the issue for investors.

The 79 Issue Codes: A Regulatory Map

Every LD-2 filing assigns one or more of seventy-nine standardized issue codes to the lobbying it reports. These are not improvised labels. They are the official taxonomy maintained by the Secretary of the Senate, and every filer has to use them.

That standardization is what makes the database scalable. An analyst can query all filings using a particular issue code and immediately see which organizations are active in that policy area. The code does not tell the full story, but it does make the universe manageable.

The codes span the full range of federal policy. TAX covers taxation. FIN covers financial institutions, investments, and securities. HCR covers health issues broadly, while PHA focuses on pharmacy. DEF covers defense, TRA trade, ENE energy, ENV environmental matters, TEL telecommunications, IMM immigration, BNK banking, INS insurance, AVI aviation, and AUT the automotive industry.

For investment analysis, the codes serve three purposes. The first is company-specific monitoring. If a pharmaceutical company files under PHA and HCR while naming CMS and FDA as covered agencies, the filing is plainly describing active engagement with its core regulators.

The second is sector pattern analysis. Pulling all filings under a particular code for a given quarter shows who in the sector is active and at what apparent intensity. The third is competitive intelligence. Two companies may file under the same code and still be managing different risks if their issue descriptions or agency targets diverge.

The code alone is not enough. It tells you the domain, not the substance. The real value lies in reading the issue description attached to it.

A filing coded TAX that describes lobbying on a specific Internal Revenue Code provision affecting foreign base company income is analytically rich. A filing coded TAX that merely states support for lower corporate rates is much less so. The code filters for relevance. The description carries the content.

Agency Reach: What the Contact List Reveals

Each LD-2 identifies the houses of Congress and executive agencies contacted during the quarter. This field is one of the least used and most informative parts of the filing. It shows where the company believes the real decision points are.

On the legislative side, filers often identify specific committees rather than Congress in the abstract. Senate Finance, House Ways and Means, Senate HELP, and House Energy and Commerce appear frequently, and each maps to a clear area of jurisdiction. When a company is in contact with Senate Banking and House Financial Services while a banking proposal is moving through Congress, the filing places that company inside the live legislative process.

On the executive side, the agency list may include HHS, CMS, FDA, EPA, FCC, FERC, Treasury, DOJ, FTC, or USTR, among others. Each agency named is a direct signal about where management believes near-term regulatory pressure or opportunity sits.

The pattern becomes more useful over time. A company that names the EPA quarter after quarter has persistent environmental exposure built into the lobbying record. A company that suddenly adds DOJ and FTC, alongside antitrust issue codes, is signaling a regulatory problem that may not yet have appeared anywhere in investor-facing disclosure.

Agency reach also helps define the character of the campaign. Lobbying concentrated on committees suggests an effort to shape legislation before it is enacted. Lobbying concentrated on agencies suggests rulemaking, implementation, interpretation, or enforcement concerns.

A company doing both at once is usually dealing with a higher-stakes issue. The problem has moved through more than one institution, which often means the regulatory pressure is broader and more material than a single-agency dispute or a narrow piece of legislation.

Quarterly Filing Cadence and Trend Analysis

The quarterly cadence of LD-2 filings creates a usable time series. The deadlines—January 20, April 20, July 20, and October 20—anchor the collection schedule. Each filing covers the prior quarter, so there is some lag, but it is usually no worse than the lag in 10-Q reporting and often shorter.

Trend analysis works best over eight to twelve quarters. A single quarter can reflect a one-time campaign, a fee renegotiation with a retained firm, or a temporary spike around a vote or comment period. The longer series strips out some of that noise.

A company spending two hundred thousand dollars a quarter on lobbying two years ago and eight hundred thousand dollars a quarter now has made a real decision. The reason may not be clear from the spending figure alone, but the directional change is hard to dismiss as incidental.

The pattern of issue-code rotation adds another layer. Most companies have a base set of codes that appear almost every quarter, reflecting their permanent regulatory environment. Others appear only briefly, tied to a specific bill, rulemaking, investigation, or threat.

Those temporary codes are often where the best intelligence sits. They mark the live moments in the company's regulatory history. Tracking when they appear and disappear creates a timeline of what management considered worth fighting.

Termination filings matter too. When a lobbying relationship ends, that date is worth comparing with later regulatory developments. The issue may have been resolved favorably, dropped, or simply reassigned to a different firm. The timing often helps sort those possibilities.

Reading Individual Lobbying Filings

The specific issue-description field is where the filing becomes most useful. It is free text, and the quality varies. Some descriptions are almost useless, offering only something like "issues related to healthcare policy." Others identify a bill by number, describe the exact provision at issue, and name the agency responsible for implementation.

The more specific the description, the more analytically valuable it is. Specialized Washington firms often file with more precision than general in-house operations. That is not a hard rule, but it is common enough to take note of.

The individual-lobbyist field adds another dimension. Every person who worked on the account during the quarter is listed, along with prior covered-government employment over the preceding twenty years, if applicable. That revolving-door disclosure often says something important about the kind of access the client is buying.

A technology company that hires a former FTC commissioner is not making a generic lobbying hire. It is signaling something specific about the regulatory relationship it is trying to manage. The same is true when a bank hires former Senate Banking staff or a defense contractor hires a former Pentagon official.

Cross-referencing those names against OpenSecrets can deepen the picture. The LDA filing shows who is on the account. OpenSecrets often shows the career history, political contributions, and broader network around that person. The two together are more informative than either alone.

Industry Coalitions and Competitive Intelligence

Lobbying records also reveal competitive dynamics inside regulated sectors. Trade associations file separately from member companies, which means the public record captures both the individual campaign and the coordinated industry response.

The Chamber of Commerce, the American Petroleum Institute, PhRMA, the American Bankers Association, and similar groups all file LD-2s. When a company is active on a regulatory issue, checking the corresponding trade-association filings helps determine whether the company is working inside a broader coalition or fighting a more isolated battle.

That distinction is important for the thesis. An issue being lobbied by five major companies and their trade association is less likely to produce an outcome that harms just one of them. A company lobbying alone, with no visible industry support, is often dealing with something more company-specific and harder to diffuse across the sector.

Competitive divergence is one of the most revealing patterns in the database. Two companies may file under the same issue code but target different agencies or committees. That usually means they are not facing the same regulatory problem, even if the broad policy domain looks identical from a distance.

Reading the issue descriptions and the covered agencies together often makes that difference clear. One company may be trying to shape general legislation. Another may be responding to a live agency inquiry or an enforcement risk. The market often does not see that distinction until much later.

Connecting Lobbying Data to the Investment Thesis

The core analytical move is simple. Compare the regulatory story management tells investors with the regulatory behavior visible in the lobbying record. If the company says the environment is stable while doubling its spend on the very rule that governs its pricing, the two records are in tension.

In that situation, the lobbying record is usually the more behaviorally honest source. SEC-reviewed language can remain calm for many reasons. Resource allocation is harder to fake. Companies do not spend heavily and specifically unless they think the issue matters.

The inverse is also useful. A company that has lobbied aggressively on one issue for several years and then terminates that activity while issuing more optimistic guidance may be signaling that the fight has been resolved, perhaps in its favor, before the formal disclosure catches up.

At the sector level, the issue-code system becomes a regulatory dashboard. A sudden rise in DEF filings across defense contractors often precedes appropriations or procurement developments. A sharp increase in TRA filings among companies with international supply chains often appears before tariff or trade-policy changes become obvious to the broader market.

These patterns are often visible in the data before they become headlines. That is the point. Lobbying intelligence is useful not because it predicts every outcome, but because it shows where companies are devoting effort before they are ready to describe the problem or opportunity directly.

Building a Lobbying Monitoring Routine

The quarterly LD-2 calendar defines the monitoring schedule. After each filing deadline—January 20, April 20, July 20, and October 20—the analyst should pull the latest filings for every company on the active watchlist using the LDA API, filtered by client name and recent filing date.

For an established watchlist, this does not take long. A focused thirty-minute review after each filing deadline is often enough. The purpose is not exhaustive policy analysis. It is to compare the new quarter with the prior one across three dimensions: total spend, new issue codes, and new covered agencies.

New issue codes deserve immediate attention. If a company that normally files under TAX, FIN, and TRA suddenly adds HCR or ENV, something has entered its regulatory environment that was not there before. The first step is to read the issue description attached to the new code.

If that description names a bill, proposed rule, or guidance document, the next move is to find the primary source—Federal Register notice, congressional bill text, or agency release—and assess what the underlying action could mean for the company financially. The lobbying filing identifies the issue. The government source defines the substance.

Changes in covered agencies are the second major alert category. A company that suddenly adds DOJ, FTC, or a banking regulator is signaling new institutional contact. If the issue description is vague, checking whether the agency has recently opened an inquiry, issued a notice, or acted against peers often clarifies the context quickly.

OpenSecrets is a useful overlay for analysts who want faster orientation without building queries from scratch. It provides multi-year expenditure charts, individual lobbyist profiles, and cross-referenced contribution data. It is not a substitute for the primary LDA record, but it makes the first pass through a new company or issue much faster.

Key Takeaways

- ☐ Lobbying disclosures operate on a quarterly cadence and are largely independent of the editorial choices that shape earnings-call language. When a company's lobbying record and its investor-facing narrative are in tension, the lobbying record is the more behaviorally honest document — because spending money is harder to rationalize than language choices.
- ☐ The seventy-nine LDA issue codes provide a standardized regulatory taxonomy for the entire federal policy domain. Querying the Senate LDA API by issue code across all filers reveals sector-wide regulatory engagement patterns that can surface legislative and regulatory risk before individual company disclosures acknowledge it. New issue codes appearing in a company's filings for the first time are the highest-priority signal in the quarterly review.
- ☐ The covered agencies field in each LD-2 maps where the regulatory engagement is directed. Legislative branch contacts signal prospective legislative risk; executive branch contacts signal rulemaking or enforcement risk. A company adding a major regulatory agency to its covered list for the first time is disclosing, through its behavior, that a new institutional relationship has become necessary.
- ☐ Lobbying intelligence works best as a corroborating or contradicting layer alongside SEC filings and earnings-call analysis. The analytical value comes from the comparison between what management tells investors and what the company's resource allocation in the lobbying record reveals. The gap between those accounts is where investigation should begin.

Fieldwork

- ☐ Go to lda.senate.gov and run a manual search for one company you currently hold or follow. Review its LD-2 filings for the past eight quarters. Build a simple table tracking total lobbying expenditure per quarter, the issue codes present in each filing, and the covered agencies listed. Note any quarter where a new issue code or a new agency appeared for the first time. For that quarter, read the specific issue description and identify the underlying legislative or regulatory action being targeted.

- ☐ Using the Senate LDA API at lda.senate.gov/api/v1/filings, query for all filings using a single issue code directly relevant to an industry you follow. Filter by a twelve-month date range. Sort the results by income amount descending. Identify the five companies spending the most on that issue in the period. Compare those five names against the companies you would have identified as most exposed to this regulatory domain based on their SEC filings alone. Note any names that appear prominently in the lobbying data but have not highlighted the same issue in investor-facing communications.
- ☐ Pull the LD-203 contribution filings for the same company you analyzed in the first exercise. Compare the political contribution recipients against the members of the congressional committees identified as covered agencies in the same period's LD-2 filings. The overlap between lobbying targets and contribution recipients defines the company's specific congressional engagement strategy, which is often more precisely targeted than either record suggests on its own.

Apply This

When starting a lobbying-intelligence review on any company, ask three questions in order. First, is lobbying spend rising, falling, or holding steady over the last eight quarters? Second, do the two most recent filings contain any issue codes that did not appear at all in the prior year? Third, do any covered agencies appear for the first time, and does their jurisdiction suggest a regulatory risk the company has not yet acknowledged in its SEC filings?

If the answer to the second or third question is yes, the next place to go is the specific issue-description field tied to those new codes or agencies. That is where the filing becomes useful. Management narratives describe the regulatory environment the way management wants investors to see it. Lobbying filings describe it the way the company's own spending decisions do.

CHAPTER 22

FEDERAL CONTRACTING INTELLIGENCE

An analyst covering a mid-size defense technology company sees a familiar story: strong revenue growth, expanding margins, and a backlog management describes as robust on every earnings call. The analyst builds a discounted cash flow model and initiates a position. What they do not do is check USAspending.gov to see what that backlog actually consists of.

Eighteen months later, the company misses revenue guidance by twelve percent. The explanation, buried in the 10-Q, is that the primary indefinite-delivery, indefinite-quantity contract supporting roughly forty percent of revenue was recompeted, and the company was not selected as an awardee. The recompete had been scheduled for two years.

The public record had flagged the risk well before the miss. USAspending.gov showed the award to a competing team three months before the earnings disappointment, and SAM.gov had posted the solicitation in draft form nine months before that. The analyst was not missing hidden information. They were missing a process.

Federal contracting is among the most thoroughly documented markets in the world. Every contract award above the simplified acquisition threshold, every modification, every obligated dollar, and every period of performance flows into the Federal Procurement Data System and then into USAspending.gov, where it becomes public at the transaction level. The data can be organized by agency, recipient, NAICS code, contract type, award date, and a range of other fields.

For any company materially dependent on federal spending, that record provides a level of revenue visibility that management's own communications often do not match. The difference between modeling a government contractor from earnings calls and modeling it from the contract record is the difference between listening to the narrative and reading the actual source of the revenue.

Why Federal Contracting Is a FININT Problem

Federal contracting intelligence is a FININT problem because the data is public, useful, and persistently underused. Most analysts covering government contractors rely on backlog disclosures, appropriations news, and broad budget commentary. Those sources matter, but they operate too high above the contract layer that actually drives revenue.

What counts in practice is more specific. Which vehicles does the company hold? What are the ceiling values and what has actually been obligated? When do base periods and option periods expire? How much of the apparent backlog is theoretical, and how much is funded? Is the company's position inside a competitive vehicle improving or weakening?

Government contractors face risks that most civilian companies do not. Revenue can be delayed or disrupted by appropriations fights, continuing resolutions, stop-work orders, terminations for convenience, and bid protests that push start dates back by months. Each of those risks leaves a public trace.

Appropriations status is public. Contract modifications, including stop-work and termination actions, appear in FPDS-NG and flow into USAspending.gov. GAO protest decisions are published by GAO. None of this requires a proprietary subscription. It requires knowing where to look and how to connect the pieces.

USAspending.gov: Structure and Access

USAspending.gov is the public spending database created under the Federal Funding Accountability and Transparency Act of 2006 and expanded under the Digital Accountability and Transparency Act of 2014. It covers four main categories: contracts, grants, indefinite-delivery vehicles, and loans. The data is available through the website and through the API at api.usaspending.gov, which is free and open for most practical use.

Contract data originates in FPDS-NG, the Federal Procurement Data System. Agencies are required to report contract awards within thirty days of execution, and those records include the awarding agency and sub-agency, recipient name, obligated amount, base and all-options value, period of performance, place of performance, NAICS code, product or service code, contract type, set-aside status, competition status, and parent award if the action is a task order.

The awards endpoint lets the analyst filter by recipient, agency, fiscal year, award type, and NAICS code in combination. The recipient profile endpoint aggregates total federal spending to a single company across agencies and award types, which makes it possible to see how exposed the business really is to federal revenue in the aggregate.

Indefinite-delivery vehicles require special care. An indefinite-delivery contract, blanket purchase agreement, basic ordering agreement, or Federal Supply Schedule may carry a ceiling that looks enormous, but that ceiling is only a theoretical maximum across the vehicle. It is not revenue, and it is not a commitment to any single contractor.

The only dollars that matter are the ones actually obligated through task orders. USAspending.gov distinguishes between the parent IDV record and the task orders beneath it. Analysts who stop at the parent record and anchor on the ceiling figure systematically overstate the company's real position, and the mistake is entirely avoidable.

Contract Types and What They Reveal

The contract type field in FPDS-NG is one of the most revealing attributes in the record. It says a great deal about revenue quality, margin structure, and operating risk. A company with the same top line as a peer may be a very different business once the contract mix is understood.

Fixed-price contracts place cost risk on the contractor. The government pays a defined amount for a defined deliverable, and if execution turns out to be more expensive than expected, the contractor absorbs the overrun. Fixed-price work can produce stable revenue, but it turns execution problems into margin pressure before they ever become revenue problems.

Cost-reimbursement contracts work differently. The government reimburses allowable costs and adds a negotiated fee, which may be fixed, incentive-based, or award-based. Cost-plus work is common in research, development, and complicated systems integration, and it tends to produce more predictable revenue at lower, more regulated margins.

Time-and-materials contracts sit somewhere else again. They pay set hourly rates for labor categories plus actual material cost, which makes them common in IT support and professional services. Their vulnerability is utilization: revenue drops when billable staff are between task orders.

Governmentwide acquisition contracts and other large multiagency vehicles introduce another layer of confusion. A company announcing that it has won a place on a major GWAC is only saying it is eligible to compete for task orders, not that it has won any meaningful revenue. The real competitive picture appears only when the task-order flow beneath that vehicle is tracked over time.

Reading Award Data: From Obligation to Revenue

The most important distinction in federal contracting data is the one between ceiling value and obligated amount. Ceiling value is the largest theoretical number attached to the vehicle. Obligated amount is money the government has actually committed.

Company press releases almost always emphasize the larger number. A ten-year IDIQ with a large all-options value sounds impressive, but the base-period obligation may represent only a small fraction of that amount. Option years require affirmative government action and carry no guarantee.

USAspending.gov reports the base and all-options value alongside the obligated amount and the period of performance. Those three figures together tell the revenue story the press release usually obscures. The analyst who reads only the headline number is not reading the contract.

Modifications add the second layer of intelligence. Agencies modify contracts when they add funding, exercise options, change scope, adjust the period of performance, issue stop-work orders, or terminate performance. Each of those actions enters FPDS-NG and appears in the public record.

Tracking modifications over the life of a major award shows whether the government is fully using the vehicle, partially funding it, or letting it drift. A multi-year program with no meaningful modifications for several quarters may not be producing the revenue management's rhetoric implies. A stop-work order or termination can show up in the data before the company is forced to discuss it in a quarterly filing.

Agency Concentration and Revenue Risk

Agency concentration is one of the most important structural risks in any government contractor, and USAspending.gov makes it directly measurable. The recipient profile lets the analyst calculate what percentage of total federal revenue comes from each agency and how that distribution has shifted over time.

Heavy concentration in one agency is a real business risk whether or not management emphasizes it. A company deriving sixty percent of federal revenue from the Department of Defense, with most of that tied to one program office, is exposed to a remarkably narrow set of budget and procurement decisions. That concentration exists in the data whether the company chooses to frame it as such or not.

The by-agency and by-state filters also support competitive work. If a company describes itself as a leading provider in a service area but a competitor is receiving two and a half times the obligated dollars from the same agency in the same NAICS category, the marketing language is overstating the position. The contract record is the better source.

Continuing resolutions add another layer of concentration risk. Under a CR, agencies are often constrained from starting new programs, increasing funding above the prior year, or exercising certain options without further authorization. A contractor dependent on new starts is more exposed to CR delay than one whose book consists mainly of already-funded ongoing work.

That distinction is visible in the record. Period-of-performance data, contract type, and modification history together show whether the company's revenue base is mature and funded or dependent on program starts that may be postponed by budget timing.

Competitive vs. Sole-Source Analysis

The competition field in FPDS-NG shows whether an award was made competitively or on a sole-source basis. That distinction goes directly to revenue durability. Sole-source contracts usually reflect a situation in which the agency believes only one vendor can meet the requirement.

That can create highly defensible near-term revenue. But sole-source status does not last forever. Agencies come under periodic pressure from inspectors general, GAO, and internal procurement review to open work to competition, and when they do, the incumbent may discover that a comfortable revenue stream was never as secure as it appeared.

Competitive history matters for that reason. A company's win rate on competitive bids over multiple years gives a clearer picture of business-development strength than management's own language about "pipeline" or "capture" success. If the firm repeatedly loses recompetes in its core categories, the problem is visible long before management is forced to call it out.

Set-asides create a different kind of protection. Contracts reserved for small businesses, 8(a) firms, HUBZone businesses, or service-disabled veteran-owned small businesses narrow the field of competition and can help a company defend market share in ways that are not obvious from a standard financial model. That eligibility is verifiable through SAM.gov and through the set-aside field in the award record.

The SAM.gov Layer: Registrations, Exclusions, and Opportunities

USAspending.gov shows what has already been awarded. SAM.gov shows what is coming and who is even eligible to receive it. Every contractor seeking federal business needs an active SAM registration, renewed annually.

A lapsed registration is rare, but when it happens it can disrupt both payment and new award eligibility immediately. It may take time for the financial impact to become visible in SEC disclosure, but the operational problem begins at once. Any analyst following a government-dependent company should verify that the registration remains active.

The SAM exclusions database is even more serious. It lists entities that have been suspended, debarred, or otherwise excluded from federal awards and assistance. For a government contractor, debarment is effectively existential. Suspension, though temporary, can be nearly as damaging while it is in force.

Those records are public and searchable. Due diligence on a government-heavy company should include not just the parent entity, but key subsidiaries and key executives as well. The risk is too severe to leave unchecked.

SAM.gov also contains the opportunities database, which replaced FedBizOpps. It publishes solicitations, presolicitation notices, sources sought announcements, and draft requests for proposal across the federal government. For forecasting, this is one of the most valuable forward-looking sources available.

A company whose core IDIQ is approaching recompete will usually become visible in SAM.gov months before the award decision later appears on USAspending.gov. Monitoring solicitations in the contractor's key NAICS codes and agencies turns the process from backward-looking record review into something closer to genuine early warning.

Bid Protests as an Early Warning Signal

Federal bid protests are formal legal challenges to contract awards or proposed awards. The GAO protest database publishes final decisions and makes them searchable by company, agency, and docket number. For revenue timing, protest activity is significant, even when the protest is ultimately denied.

A sustained protest can force a re-evaluation or re-award of the contract. For the incumbent, that threatens revenue; for the challenger, it can create upside. But even a denied protest can still matter because, in most cases, filing at GAO triggers an automatic stay of performance while the protest is pending.

That delay can push revenue out by three to six months. A contractor with a recently won program under protest has a timing risk that management may not spell out with the same precision. The legal record often says more about near-term revenue than the guidance does.

Court of Federal Claims protests are less common, but when they occur they are often more consequential. They are filed in federal court rather than at GAO, and the dockets are available through PACER. They do not create the same automatic stay, but injunctions are possible, and the existence of the case is itself an important signal.

Institutional analysts following defense services often monitor both GAO and CFC activity as routine practice. Cross-referenced against USAspending.gov award data, the protest record shows which awards are secure, which are delayed, and which are vulnerable.

Connecting Contract Data to the Investment Thesis

Contract data matters to the thesis in three ways. It verifies revenue, it gives a forward-looking view of likely award flow, and it identifies structural risks such as agency concentration and impending recompetes.

A company describing its federal business as growing strongly should show increasing obligations in the relevant agencies and service categories. If management's growth narrative and the public obligation record move in different directions, the analyst has a discrepancy to resolve before trusting the model. The discrepancy may have an innocent explanation, but it is the beginning of the work, not the end.

Forward analysis combines known vehicle holdings from USAspending.gov with the solicitation pipeline in SAM.gov. If the analyst knows which contracts the company holds, when they expire, and which recompetes are coming, the revenue forecast becomes much more grounded than one built entirely from management guidance and generalized backlog language.

Risk identification centers on the two most dangerous conditions in the portfolio. One is heavy dependence on a single agency or even a single program office. The other is reliance on a large vehicle that is nearing recompete. Both are visible in public data before they are fully acknowledged in company-level risk disclosure.

Building a Federal Contract Monitoring Routine

The monitoring routine is quarterly at the review level and event-driven at the alert level. The quarterly review should line up with each 10-Q cycle. Pull the

USAspending recipient profile for each contractor on the watchlist and compare the most recent four quarters with the prior year.

Check total obligations, agency mix, and contract-type distribution. Compare the trend in new obligations with management's discussion of backlog and pipeline. Then review SAM.gov for solicitations tied to the company's major vehicles and GAO for protest activity involving the company either as awardee or protester.

The event-driven layer is more immediate. The USAspending API can be queried on a rolling thirty-day basis for each company, producing a log of new awards, task orders, and modifications. A material new award that has not yet appeared in a press release is worth noting, especially if it falls within a program the analyst has already mapped.

SAM.gov can be monitored through subscriptions by agency or NAICS code, which often surfaces recompetes six to twelve months before the eventual award. The protest databases complete the picture by identifying which recent awards are likely to be delayed, contested, or reopened.

Taken together, the system relies on three streams. USAspending.gov provides the obligation and modification record. SAM.gov provides the opportunity pipeline and eligibility layer. GAO and CFC dockets provide the legal vulnerability map.

For government contractors, that combination produces a view of revenue quality and risk that is often more detailed and more timely than the company's own SEC disclosure.

Key Takeaways

- ☐ The federal contracting record is a primary source for revenue analysis of government contractors that operates independently of SEC filings and company communications. USAspending.gov reports every contract obligation, modification, and task order within thirty days of execution, providing a near-real-time revenue picture that management guidance summarizes but rarely matches in granularity.
- ☐ The critical distinction between ceiling values and obligated amounts determines whether a contract award represents actual revenue or theoretical maximum exposure. An IDIQ ceiling is not revenue. Only obligated task orders are revenue. Analysts who model government contractor revenue from contract ceiling figures will systematically overestimate the revenue base until they drill down from the IDV parent to the task order layer in the underlying data.
- ☐ Agency concentration and contract vehicle expiration are the two most material structural risks in a government contractor's portfolio, and both are directly computable from USAspending.gov's recipient profile and award-level data. A company with heavy concentration in a single agency and a large IDIQ approaching recompetition within the next twelve months has material revenue risk that may not be visible in its backlog or guidance disclosures.
- ☐ The SAM.gov solicitation database provides the forward-looking complement to USAspending.gov's historical record. Monitoring SAM.gov for presolicitation notices and draft RFPs in a company's core NAICS codes converts the federal contracting research routine from backward-looking obligation tracking into a genuinely predictive revenue pipeline analysis.

Fieldwork

- ☐ Go to USAspending.gov and use the recipient search to pull the full federal spending profile for one government contractor you currently hold or follow. Identify the top three agencies by obligated dollars in the most recent fiscal year and calculate each agency's share of the company's total federal obligation. Compare that concentration profile against the customer diversification language in the company's most recent 10-K. Note any gaps between the filing's description and what the obligation data reveals.

- ☐ From the same USAspending.gov recipient profile, click through to the award-level data for the company's largest single contract vehicle. Find the base and all-options value alongside the cumulative obligated amount, and calculate what percentage of the theoretical ceiling has been obligated to date. Then check the period-of-performance end date for the base period and each option year. Assess whether the remaining option years represent a revenue opportunity or whether the contract is in its final period and approaching recompetition.
- ☐ Go to the GAO bid protest database at gao.gov and search for the company's name as either the awardee or the protesting party in the past three years. Note how many protests have been filed against its awards, how many were sustained, and how many are currently pending. Cross-reference any sustained protests against the company's revenue disclosures in the corresponding quarter to assess how the company communicated — or did not communicate — the impact to investors.

Apply This

When analyzing any company with material federal revenue, build a contract concentration table from USAspending.gov before reading the company's own backlog and pipeline disclosures. The table should show, for each of the top five agencies, the total obligated dollars in the past four quarters, the contract vehicle or vehicles generating that revenue, and the period-of-performance end date for each base period.

If any single agency represents more than twenty-five percent of estimated total revenue, or if any contract vehicle generating more than fifteen percent of estimated federal revenue has a base period expiring within the next twelve months, those are the first questions to raise on the next earnings call. If management's answers do not match what the public record shows, the discrepancy defines the next round of research.

CHAPTER 23

Congressional Trading and Regulatory Capture

In January 2020, several members of Congress attended a closed-door Senate Intelligence Committee briefing on a novel coronavirus spreading in China. In the weeks that followed—before public guidance described the outbreak as a pandemic threat and before equity markets had sold off in any serious way—some of those members sold meaningful equity positions or bought put options tied to broad U.S. market exposure.

Those trades were disclosed under the STOCK Act. By the time journalists and researchers pieced them together, weeks had passed and the market had already moved. The information had been public the entire time. Almost no one was watching it.

The Stop Trading on Congressional Knowledge Act of 2012 requires members of Congress, their spouses, and dependent children to disclose securities transactions above one thousand dollars within forty-five days. That creates a structured public record of how elected officials with direct oversight of whole industries allocate personal capital.

Read alongside committee assignments, lobbying disclosures, campaign-finance records, and the broader dynamics of regulatory capture, those filings form a coherent intelligence picture of where political power and financial interest meet. This chapter is not about insider-trading law. Whether a particular member violated the STOCK Act is a matter for enforcement.

The problem here is methodological. How do you collect and analyze the public disclosure record in a way that identifies patterns of congressional activity in sectors under direct legislative oversight? How do you understand regulatory capture not as a scandal but as a structural condition? And how do you use both without pretending they are more predictive than they are?

The STOCK Act System: What Is Disclosed

The STOCK Act became law in April 2012 after academic work showed that congressional portfolios had historically outperformed market benchmarks and public scrutiny turned toward the gap between legislative access and disclosure requirements. The law covers members of the House and Senate, certain senior congressional staff, executive-branch employees, and federal judges.

The disclosure requirement applies to transactions in stocks, bonds, commodity futures, and options above one thousand dollars. Covered persons must file a Periodic Transaction Report, or PTR, within forty-five days of the trade date. Each PTR identifies the asset, the transaction type, the approximate trade date, and the dollar amount using one of eight standardized ranges.

Those ranges run from one thousand to fifteen thousand dollars, then fifteen thousand to fifty thousand, fifty thousand to one hundred thousand, one hundred thousand to two hundred fifty thousand, two hundred fifty thousand to five hundred thousand, five hundred thousand to one million, one million to five million, and above five million. Widely diversified mutual funds and government securities are exempt.

That range system limits precision. An analyst cannot tell whether a senator bought forty thousand dollars of a pharmaceutical stock or forty-nine thousand. At larger sizes, the uncertainty becomes more pronounced. The value of the record therefore lies less in exact position sizing than in pattern: timing, sector, committee role, and repetition.

Late filing is common. The penalty is two hundred dollars, which is small enough that chronic late filers can treat it as friction rather than deterrence. Some disclosures arrive more than ninety days after the transaction. The filing is still useful, but it is not a real-time signal. It tells you what happened, not what is happening.

Annual Financial Disclosure forms add the broader balance-sheet context. Filed separately each year, they provide a more complete inventory of assets, liabilities, and income, and they serve as the baseline against which PTR activity can be interpreted.

House and Senate Disclosure Databases

The House disclosure system is maintained through the Office of the Clerk at disclosures.house.gov. PTRs and annual financial disclosures for House members and covered staff are available there. Since a modernization effort in 2020, those records have also been available in structured CSV and XML form, which makes them much easier to analyze systematically.

Senate annual disclosures are filed with the Secretary of the Senate and published through senate.gov. The Senate PTR system remains more cumbersome. It is still largely PDF-based, which has made bulk analysis more labor-intensive than the House equivalent.

Several private platforms now sit on top of the raw government data and make it easier to work with. CapitolTrades provides a consolidated database covering both chambers, searchable by member, ticker, sector, and committee assignment. QuiverQuant offers a similar dataset through its interface and API, with historical coverage back to the STOCK Act's early years.

These tools are useful, especially for monitoring at scale, but they are not the source of record. For any discrepancy, the House and Senate disclosure systems remain authoritative. The aggregator is an access layer. The filing is the document that counts.

The practical collection method depends on the question being asked. If the goal is company-specific monitoring, querying by ticker will surface all congressional transactions in that security. If the goal is sector analysis, industry-level filtering gives a broader view. The most useful approach, though, is often committee-based, because committee role is what gives the trades their analytical weight.

Committee Assignments: The Analytical Key

A member of Congress buying a pharmaceutical stock is one thing. A member of the Senate Finance Committee or the Senate Health, Education, Labor and Pensions Committee buying the same stock while that committee is marking up drug-pricing legislation is another. The committee assignment is what turns the trade from background activity into a possible information signal.

Committees are where Congress does its real work. The Senate Banking Committee shapes financial regulation. House Energy and Commerce has jurisdiction over health care, telecommunications, and energy. Senate Armed Services drives defense authorization. House Ways and Means controls tax legislation.

Members of these committees receive briefings, conduct oversight, and deliberate on legislation and agency conduct before the wider market has any reason to focus on the issue. Their trades in sectors under direct committee jurisdiction therefore carry a different kind of significance from identical trades made by members with no relevant oversight role.

The overlap should be examined in both directions. A member who begins accumulating positions in a sector soon after joining the committee that oversees it presents a more interesting pattern than one who has held the position for years. Timing is important because access changes with the assignment.

Seniority counts as well. Chairs, ranking members, and subcommittee leads have broader agenda control and deeper access than rank-and-file members. A Finance Committee chair buying pharmaceutical shares while CMS is engaged in a pricing rulemaking has a different information profile from a junior senator with no committee leadership role.

Committee assignments and leadership roles are public. They appear on House and Senate committee websites, and membership changes are published in the Congressional Record. Those records should be treated as part of the disclosure file, not as incidental context.

Reading Periodic Transaction Reports

A single PTR, read by itself, usually says very little. The value emerges in patterns across time, across members, and against the background of subsequent legislative and regulatory events. A PTR is only useful once it is placed in context.

That context starts with the member's committee assignment. It also includes whether the filing was timely, whether the same security has been traded repeatedly, and whether multiple members with relevant committee roles have traded the same sector in the same window.

The amount range is important to look at, but only within reason. Trades in the one-thousand-to-fifteen-thousand-dollar band may reflect household diversification, spousal activity, or routine rebalancing. They are usually too small to carry much weight in isolation. Larger trades, particularly those in the fifty-thousand-to-one-million-dollar range and above, suggest more deliberate positioning.

The upper ranges matter even if the exact size remains uncertain. A trade reported at one million to five million dollars is analytically significant even without precision. At that point, the issue is not fine-tuning the position size. It is understanding why a member with that level of access was willing to make such a large allocation.

Spousal and dependent-child disclosures add ambiguity but not irrelevance. Members sometimes describe those transactions as outside their direct control. That claim may be true, but it cannot be independently verified from the filing.

For analytical purposes, household trades in sectors under committee oversight should remain in the dataset. The information environment of a congressional household is not cleanly separable from the member's own access.

Sector Clustering and Pre-Legislative Signals

The most useful pattern in congressional trading data is sector clustering. That means a concentration of purchases or sales across multiple members in the same sector during a defined period, close to a legislative or regulatory event in that sector.

The pattern can run either way. Members of Armed Services buying defense names before authorization markup is one version. Members of Finance selling health care names before movement on drug-pricing provisions is another. In each case, the significance lies in the convergence of timing, sector, and committee access.

The legislative calendar provides the reference frame. Committee hearing schedules are public. Bill cosponsorship records appear on Congress.gov. Floor votes and markup sessions are announced in advance and recorded officially.

Those events are not background noise. They are the catalysts against which trading activity has to be measured.

An analyst who has assembled PTR data, committee assignments, and the legislative calendar in one place can identify these windows before they become press narratives. That does not mean the analyst can predict the outcome of every vote. It means the analyst is no longer confined to hindsight.

Beyond Trading: Understanding Regulatory Capture

Congressional trading is the visible edge of a broader problem that matters more for long-term analysis: regulatory capture. Capture is not mainly a story of one scandal or one illicit trade. It is a structural alignment in which agencies and congressional committees begin to reflect the interests of the industries they oversee more than the public interest they are supposed to protect.

The mechanism is usually not overt corruption. It is repeated contact, revolving employment, campaign money, and a gradual convergence in worldview between regulator and regulated. Over time, the industry's assumptions become the assumptions of the people overseeing it.

The classic structure has three actors: the industry, the agency, and the congressional committee with jurisdiction. The industry lobbies the agency through formal comments and informal contact. It lobbies the committee through the LDA system. It funds campaigns through PAC contributions reported to the FEC. It hires former regulators and staff, and it often serves as the labor pool from which future regulators and staff are drawn.

That circular movement of people and money creates a durable form of alignment. For the analyst, the question is not moral but operational. Given the degree of visible capture in a sector, how should the probability of an adverse regulatory outcome be adjusted?

In a heavily captured industry, proposed harmful regulation is more likely to be delayed, diluted, or quietly abandoned. In a sector where capture is weak—where the agency is adversarial, enforcement is active, and personnel flows are less industry-dependent—the same proposal has a better chance of surviving implementation more or less intact.

The Revolving Door as a Data Source

Senior executive-branch officials must file financial disclosures when they enter and leave government service. Those filings, available through the Office of Government Ethics, identify the private employers they came from. Exit records can then be cross-referenced against later private-sector jobs.

The lobbying system creates a companion record on the other side. Under the LDA, lobbyists must disclose covered government positions held during the prior twenty years. That makes it possible to trace the movement of people from committee staff, agencies, and senior executive roles into industry lobbying positions.

Congressional staff careers can often be reconstructed through a mix of LinkedIn, lobbying filings, committee directories, and OGE material. That movement is not incidental to capture. It is one of the ways capture operates in practice.

The pattern can be quantified. For a given agency, an analyst can ask what share of senior officials over the past decade came directly from the regulated industry and what share left for the same industry. High rates in both directions are not proof of corruption, but they are a workable operational measure of capture risk.

Enforcement behavior provides a harder measure. SEC litigation releases, FTC complaint records, FDA warning letters, and EPA enforcement data are all public. For any regulated sector, the analyst can track enforcement frequency, fine size, and whether repeat misconduct triggers stronger penalties or merely nominal ones.

An agency that repeatedly imposes small penalties for serious violations is not describing itself as captured. But its behavior may be consistent with a captured posture regardless of the rhetoric attached to it.

Connecting Congressional Intelligence to the Investment Thesis

Congressional trading and regulatory capture belong in the thesis at different levels. Trading is a tactical signal. It may offer short- to medium-term directional information about legislative outcomes that can affect specific securities.

Capture is a structural variable. It belongs in the long-term probability distribution of regulatory outcomes for an industry. It affects how the analyst should think about multiple expansion, policy risk, and the chance that a threatened rule will actually survive implementation.

The strongest tactical congressional signal combines three things: committee relevance, security-specific trading rather than broad ETF exposure, and meaningful size within a short window before a known legislative catalyst. When a senior member of Senate Finance discloses a large pharmaceutical purchase shortly before a markup session that later stalls a provision threatening pricing power, the sequence is visible in the PTR record, the committee calendar, and the vote history.

The point is not that every such sequence implies illicit conduct. It is that the analyst who assembled those data streams in advance is working from a different position than the analyst who sees the story only after it becomes a media scandal.

On the structural side, capture analysis shapes the discount applied to regulatory threats. A proposed rule should not be valued solely by asking what it would do if implemented exactly as written. It should also be valued by asking how likely that implementation path really is in the political environment surrounding the industry.

A hostile proposal in a high-capture sector has a lower probability of surviving intact than the same proposal in a low-capture sector. That difference can be estimated from public evidence: lobbying intensity, PAC concentration, revolving-door patterns, and enforcement history. Ignoring those inputs leads to systematically distorted estimates of regulatory risk.

Building a Congressional Monitoring Routine

The monitoring routine has three parts: a pre-vote alert system, a quarterly disclosure review, and an annual capture assessment. Each serves a different purpose, and together they create a workable process rather than an occasional burst of curiosity.

The pre-vote alert system begins with the legislative calendar. Committee hearings, markups, and other events likely to move sector prices should be tracked in advance. In the sixty to ninety days before those events, the analyst checks new PTR filings from members on the relevant committees.

That work is not complicated, but it has to be regular. Committee websites update hearing schedules and markup notices weekly. CapitolTrades or the House disclosure portal can then be checked for new activity by the members with jurisdiction over the affected sector.

The quarterly review follows the slower rhythm of the disclosure system itself. Once enough time has passed for quarter-end trades to be reported—usually sixty to ninety days after the quarter closes—the analyst pulls the current Congress's PTR activity in sectors relevant to the portfolio. The main output is clustering: who traded, in what sector, with what committee role, and in what sequence.

The annual regulatory-capture assessment is broader. For each heavily regulated industry in the portfolio, the analyst should review five data points: the revolving-door rate for the primary agency and the key congressional committees over the prior two years; total lobbying spend from the industry under the LDA record; campaign-contribution concentration from industry PACs to committee members using FEC data; enforcement frequency and penalty severity from the agency's own public enforcement record; and the trailing-year congressional trading pattern in the sector by committee members.

Those five inputs produce a practical capture score, even if it remains qualitative. When all five point in the same direction, the result should change the thesis. If every indicator suggests high capture, then the probability that an adverse rule survives unchanged should be marked down explicitly rather than left as an unexamined assumption.

Key Takeaways

- ☐ The STOCK Act requires disclosure of securities transactions exceeding one thousand dollars within forty-five days of execution, creating a structured public record of congressional capital allocation. The forty-five-day lag and amount-range reporting make the data always retrospective and imprecise in position sizing, but the patterns it reveals — particularly when filtered by committee assignment and mapped against the legislative calendar — are not available from any other public source.
- ☐ Committee assignment is the analytical key. A member trading a sector directly under their committee's oversight is a categorically different analytical subject from a member with no relevant committee responsibility. Mapping PTR data against committee assignments and the legislative calendar — hearing schedules, markup sessions, floor votes — is the process that identifies the most analytically significant patterns and converts disclosure aggregation into actionable intelligence.
- ☐ Regulatory capture is a structural condition visible in public data through revolving-door employment patterns, campaign contribution concentration from industry PACs to oversight committee members, enforcement action frequency and fine levels, and lobbying intensity from LDA disclosures. Calibrating capture for a specific industry and agency produces a structural input that shapes how much weight to assign to proposed adverse regulations in the long-term investment thesis.
- ☐ Congressional trading, lobbying disclosures, and campaign contributions are three parallel public records independently documenting different aspects of the relationship between an industry and its political environment. When all three converge simultaneously — lobbying spend rising, contributions flowing to relevant committee members, and those same members accumulating positions in the affected sector — the mosaic is substantially stronger than any individual data stream and warrants active investigation of the underlying legislative dynamics.

Fieldwork

- ☐ Choose one heavily regulated industry in your current portfolio or watchlist. Go to CapitolTrades.com and pull all congressional transactions in the top five companies by market cap in that sector over the past twelve months. Filter the results to include only members sitting on a committee with direct oversight jurisdiction. Note the number of transactions, the directional balance between purchases and sales, and whether any clusters of activity coincide with known legislative or regulatory events during the same period.
- ☐ Go to the House committee website for the relevant oversight committee. Download the current member roster and note each member's seniority ranking. Cross-reference the five most senior members against their PTR filing history at disclosures.house.gov for the past two years. For each member who traded in the sector, calculate the approximate window between the disclosed transaction date and the next significant legislative calendar event in the sector. Ask whether the timing pattern is consistent with trading ahead of known catalysts or independent of the legislative calendar.
- ☐ Go to fec.gov and run a PAC contribution search for the industry or trade association PACs most active in the sector. Filter contributions to members of the relevant oversight committee in the most recent election cycle. Calculate what percentage of each committee member's total PAC receipts came from the industry they oversee. Compare that concentration figure against each member's trading record in the sector from the PTR data and note whether high contribution concentration correlates with active trading.

Apply This

When evaluating a proposed adverse regulation affecting a portfolio holding, do not estimate the probability of implementation from the text of the proposal alone or from the agency's stated intent. Before assigning odds to the rule as written, run a regulatory-capture assessment. Check the revolving-door rate in the agency's senior leadership using OGE filings, the level of industry lobbying on the relevant LDA issue code, the concentration of industry PAC money going to oversight committee members in FEC data, and the agency's enforcement history to see how aggressively it has actually acted against industry interests.

A proposed rule in a high-capture sector should be treated differently from the same rule in a low-capture sector. The former has a lower probability of surviving implementation unchanged, and that difference can be estimated from public data rather than guessed at impressionistically. Ignore that layer, and the base-case thesis will tend to overstate regulatory risk in some sectors and understate it in others.

PART 6
PROFESSIONAL PRACTICE

Collecting intelligence is not the same thing as practicing a discipline. An analyst can absorb every technique in the preceding sections and still have no real process for organizing research, writing a thesis, monitoring positions, or reviewing what failed. In that case, what they have is an impressive toolkit with nowhere solid to use it. This section is about building that workbench: the habits, documents, and feedback loops that turn individual acts of research into a repeatable professional practice.

The chapters cover thesis construction, monitoring routines, and postmortem review, along with case studies that apply the full framework to situations where the public evidence existed before the market reached its conclusion. The aim is not to describe professional practice from a distance. It is to give the reader the working parts needed to build one.

CHAPTER 24

Research Organization and Documentation Systems

A trader opens a blank spreadsheet to research a semiconductor company. The first decision is what information to collect and where to put it. That moment marks the line between amateur research and professional financial intelligence. Company dossier templates provide the structure that turns scattered public data into usable intelligence.

Professional analysts usually organize research around a three-statement financial model. This Excel-based framework integrates the income statement, balance sheet, and cash flow statement into a single dynamic system. It includes preformatted sections for historical data drawn directly from SEC filings, with formulas that automatically calculate key ratios and metrics. When an analyst enters revenue figures from a 10-K, the model calculates gross margin, operating margin, and net income percentage without manual work.

That standardization improves consistency across projects and reduces calculation errors. It also makes comparison easier when the analyst is covering several companies at once. A good template does not eliminate judgment, but it removes avoidable friction.

The sum-of-the-parts model serves a different purpose. It is designed for conglomerates and diversified businesses whose segments need to be valued separately before they can be added together. An analyst working on a multinational industrial company might create separate tabs for aerospace, energy equipment, and industrial automation, using segment-reporting data from the annual report.

The model then combines those segment valuations into a total. That makes it easier to see which divisions are driving enterprise value and which ones may be candidates for divestiture. In practice, the framework is as useful for identifying weak assets as for highlighting strong ones.

Beyond financial models, a full company profile pulls many different sources into one reference document. These profiles usually include sections for company overview, market statistics, leadership, products, and significant corporate events. They also serve as the central repository for executive biographies from proxy statements, patent filings from USPTO databases, litigation history from court records, and supply-chain relationships drawn from trade publications. What results is a broader picture than the financial statements can provide on their own.

Templates are not meant to be rigid. The best ones balance standardization with adaptability, keeping the core structure intact while allowing the industry-specific sections to expand or contract as needed. The backbone remains the same—financial statements, key ratios, management background—but the details shift with the business model.

A pharmaceutical dossier needs space for clinical-trial pipelines, FDA approval calendars, and patent-expiration schedules. A retail company template needs more attention to store-count trends, same-store sales, and geographic expansion. The template should adapt to the company, not force the company into a generic shell.

Research files extend beyond the dossier itself. Professional analysts usually maintain separate folders for primary-source documents, including SEC filings, earnings-call transcripts, regulatory announcements, and court records. Those source files link directly to specific claims or figures inside the dossier.

If the dossier notes an unusual related-party transaction, the supporting folder should contain the exact page from the 10-K footnote where the transaction is disclosed. That documentation chain creates an audit trail strong enough to withstand scrutiny. It also allows rapid verification when speed is essential.

Quarterly board-deck templates are another organizational tool adapted for research. These slide-based frameworks track key performance indicators across reporting periods and display them through standardized charts and graphs. A trader following a software company might use one to track annual recurring revenue growth, customer acquisition costs, lifetime-value ratios, and churn over several quarters.

The visual format often makes directional change easier to see than a spreadsheet does. A margin inflection or deterioration in churn can stand out immediately when shown in a consistent chart. For that reason, board-deck style reporting often works well alongside the underlying model.

A good organizational system also includes catalyst tracking. This section lists scheduled earnings releases, FDA decision dates, patent expirations, regulatory hearings, and court milestones. Each entry includes the event date, expected significance, and links to background material.

That forward-looking element turns the dossier from a historical record into a monitoring tool. It gives the analyst a way to connect static research to upcoming market-moving events. The file begins to function less like an archive and more like a live operating system.

Depth matters, but accessibility matters just as much. The most comprehensive research file is useless if nothing can be found quickly during market hours. Professional systems rely on consistent naming conventions, clear folder hierarchies, and indexed cross-references.

When news breaks about an executive departure, the analyst should be able to move directly to the leadership section and find the executive's background, compensation, and recent Form 4 filings. That speed is crucial because the market rarely waits for tidy research conditions. Good organization shortens the distance between new information and informed judgment.

The last layer is version control. Research files change as new information arrives through filings, earnings releases, and market developments. Systems that track version history, record the source and date of each update, and maintain change logs reduce confusion about what is current.

That discipline becomes especially important when several analysts work on the same company or when the research spans a long period. Without it, even a well-built file becomes unreliable. With it, the dossier remains a working record rather than a pile of overwritten assumptions.

These frameworks turn raw public data into structured intelligence through systematic collection, categorization, and linkage. The dossier is not a static report. It is a living research platform that supports ongoing analysis, hypothesis testing, and decision-making under time pressure.

Sector Mapping and Peer Comparison Frameworks

A trader reviews a specialty chemicals company that has just reported strong quarterly earnings. The stock trades at a premium to the broader industry. That premium may reflect a real competitive advantage, or it may reflect the fact that the company has been placed in the wrong peer group.

The chemicals industry is not a single economic unit. It contains commodity producers, specialty formulators, and advanced-materials developers, each with different cost structures, growth profiles, and valuation logic. A company placed in the wrong peer set can end up misvalued by more than thirty percent.

Sector mapping establishes the competitive landscape before the analyst begins comparing financial metrics. The modern baseline for that work is the Global Industry Classification Standard. GICS divides the market into eleven sectors, twenty-four industry groups, sixty-nine industries, and one hundred fifty-eight sub-industries.

Those distinctions are not cosmetic. A producer of industrial gases may sit under Materials, Chemicals, and Commodity Chemicals, while a company making semiconductor-grade specialty gases may fall under Information Technology, Semiconductors, and Semiconductor Equipment. Valuation multiples and growth expectations differ sharply between commodity businesses and technology-linked applications.

GICS is updated every year to reflect market change. New categories such as fintech and cryptocurrency infrastructure have been added as business models evolved. That constant revision is itself a reminder that sector mapping is not fixed.

Analysts often go beyond standard classifications. For more granular work, especially in sustainability analysis, they may build custom sector maps using the ISIC+ framework. That system extends traditional industry codes with more specific environmental and social impact categories.

A renewable-energy developer, for example, cannot be understood through a broad sector label alone. Its position depends on technology type, regulatory jurisdiction, subsidy dependence, and grid-integration constraints. A solar-panel manufacturer and a wind-turbine producer may share a GICS category while facing very different supply chains, input costs, and competitive pressures.

Peer comparison starts with correct grouping, but it does not end there. State Street Global Advisors developed a sector business-cycle approach that evaluates forty-nine industry portfolios across six standardized metrics. These include earnings growth, valuation multiples, profitability measures, and leverage.

The process converts raw data into z-scores so that comparisons remain meaningful across different accounting practices and business models. A consumer-staples company with strong cash flow and low growth ends up with a different profile from a technology company with high growth and negative earnings. The value of the approach is that it identifies outperformance on specific dimensions rather than relying on a crude rank order.

Financial-system mapping adds another layer. The Office of Financial Research built a multilayer map showing how institutions connect through funding, asset, and collateral networks. A similar approach can be applied to industrial sectors to identify which companies function as critical nodes inside supply chains or distribution systems.

A semiconductor-equipment manufacturer may look peripheral if judged only by revenue. Structurally, though, it may sit at a bottleneck that affects multiple technology sectors at once. Positions like that create pricing power and competitive moats that do not show up clearly in standard ratios.

The Boston Consulting Group matrix offers a more strategic way to look at sector portfolios. It sorts business units by market growth and relative market share. Stars occupy high-growth markets and hold leading positions, cash cows produce steady profit in mature markets, question marks compete in growth markets without leadership, and dogs sit in weak positions in low-growth segments.

Used on a diversified conglomerate, the matrix helps show which divisions create value and which consume capital without adequate return. It is not a valuation model by itself, but it helps frame capital-allocation questions. That framing often matters before any spreadsheet output does.

Sector cycles also move unevenly. Historical work across multiple economic cycles shows that consumer staples and utilities tend to behave defensively during downturns and then lag during recoveries. Technology and consumer discretionary often lead early-cycle expansions and suffer more during contractions.

Energy and materials usually perform better in late-cycle periods when inflation pressure builds. These patterns persist because sectors respond differently to interest rates, commodity costs, and consumer confidence. Company-specific performance makes more sense when placed inside that cycle.

A common mistake is to treat peer groups as static. Industry boundaries move with technological disruption, regulatory change, and competitive convergence. Telecommunications, for example, evolved from landline providers to broadband infrastructure firms and then to integrated media platforms.

Peer groups have to move with that shift. Traditional telecom operators may now need to be compared with cable companies, satellite firms, and wireless carriers, not just with one another. That is one reason GICS is reviewed annually and companies are reclassified as business models change.

Dynamic peer comparison means tracking classification changes alongside financial performance. When a biotechnology company receives approval for its first commercial product, its peer set should widen beyond development-stage biotech. It now belongs, at least in part, in a comparison set that includes commercial pharmaceutical businesses.

That transition often brings a change in valuation multiple, but the correct benchmark depends on which pharmaceutical companies actually resemble it. Specialty pharma companies with similar product portfolios and sales forces are usually more useful comparables than large diversified drugmakers with very different risk and growth profiles. The peer set has to fit the economics, not just the label.

Effective sector mapping uses both quantitative and qualitative factors. The ACCA-CFA Institute sector-analysis framework examines twenty-one industries through several lenses. In mobile gaming, the key drivers may be user-acquisition costs, retention, and monetization mechanics; in utilities, the focus shifts to rate structures, capital-expenditure needs, and weather.

Each sector also carries its own red flags. Renewable-energy companies may be overly dependent on subsidies, semiconductor-equipment firms may face concentration risk, and pharmaceutical companies may be exposed to patent cliffs. Those differences help explain why companies with similar headline metrics can still deserve very different valuations.

The final output is usually a structured peer-comparison table. It organizes competitors across financial ratios, growth metrics, valuation multiples, and strategic-positioning scores. More advanced versions add supply-chain dependencies, regulatory exposure, and technological capability.

That table should not be treated as a static snapshot. It works best as a living document that updates with every earnings cycle and every major corporate development. When a competitor announces an acquisition or receives a regulatory approval, the table shows how the event changes the sector for everyone else.

Catalyst Tracking Systems and Event-Driven Workflows

A pharmaceutical stock trades sideways for months while the market waits for Phase 3 trial results scheduled for the second Tuesday of the next quarter. That is a classic catalyst: a known future event capable of moving the stock sharply regardless of outcome. The difference between noting the date and building a workflow around it is the difference between reacting to news and preparing for it.

Professional systems sort catalysts by type, probability, and expected market impact. Earnings announcements are scheduled events with near-certain timing but uncertain results. FDA decisions are often binary, with narrower timing windows and more asymmetric outcomes.

Corporate actions such as mergers, spin-offs, and dividend changes follow their own legal and operational timelines. Each category requires a different workflow. A spin-off may trigger a price move on announcement, but the actual separation can take months and create a series of additional filings, votes, and operational milestones.

The Bookmap platform shows how more advanced traders combine catalyst tracking with order-flow analysis. It can monitor small-cap stocks for news events such as FDA approvals while also displaying liquidity and market depth. When a biotech company announces positive trial results, the platform shows whether aggressive buyers are actually consuming sell-side liquidity.

That matters because it helps distinguish genuine momentum from a false breakout. Roughly half of machine trades in such situations may be non-directional high-frequency activity rather than conviction buying. Price movement without order-flow confirmation can be misleading.

Catalyst workflows often follow a three-phase sequence: scan, confirm, and trade. Scanning means monitoring regulatory calendars, earnings schedules, and corporate-event databases. Confirmation means checking the catalyst against supporting evidence such as unusual options activity, insider transactions, or institutional positioning.

Only then does the trade phase begin. At that stage, the analyst or trader executes a preplanned strategy built around the probability distribution of outcomes. The value of the workflow is that it reduces improvisation when the event actually arrives.

Event-driven trading does not rest on headlines alone. In practice, serious systems look for order-flow confirmation before treating a catalyst as real. The TD Securities CTA Position Tracker, for example, shows how commodity trading advisors can amplify a fundamental catalyst through algorithmic momentum strategies.

When Saudi Arabia and Russia announced supply cuts, the news itself was the first catalyst. CTA trend-following systems then reinforced the move and helped create an overshoot. Traders using the tracker were not simply reacting to the headline; they were positioning for the machine-driven flows likely to follow it.

Crypto firms use specialized tools built for the same logic. The Catalyst Python library supports backtesting and live trading across multiple exchanges. Funds use it to ingest minute-level data and move directly from historical analysis into real-time execution.

That allows event-triggered trades to be built around technical setups, news sentiment, or on-chain signals inside a single framework. Data ingestion, analysis, and execution become part of one closed loop. A catalyst can trigger a predefined response instead of requiring a fresh decision each time.

Regulatory compliance adds another layer. Under the Market Abuse Regulation, suspicious transactions tied to possible manipulation around corporate events must be reported immediately. Proprietary trading firms therefore need surveillance systems that can keep pace with algorithmic execution and newer forms of agentic AI.

Those systems capture market data across complex electronic venues and use visualizations or Markov State modeling to detect abnormal behavior before, during, and after a catalyst event. The workflow is not only about finding opportunity. It is also about staying inside the rules while markets move quickly.

Spin-offs are a good example of a multi-stage catalyst. When General Electric announced its plan to separate into three companies, the initial announcement moved the stock immediately. But the real process unfolded over roughly eighteen months through filings, shareholder approvals, and operational separation.

Each stage created its own trading opportunity with a different time horizon and risk profile. A tracking system has to keep all of that in view. Positioning around the first announcement is not the same as positioning around the final separation.

Dark-causality analysis adds a more advanced layer by uncovering hidden interactions between assets during catalyst events. Traditional correlation measures often fail in nonlinear markets under event-driven stress. More sophisticated methods can reveal asymmetrical relationships, such as credit default swap spreads moving ahead of equity prices before visible news appears.

Those hidden links become especially important during systemic stress, when risk is concentrated across dealer balance sheets and asset classes. A catalyst in one market may show up first somewhere else. Analysts who can trace those connections get a better view of where pressure is actually building.

Catalyst tracking works best when it is embedded in the broader research system. A company dossier should include sections for known catalysts, probability assessments, and planned responses. Sector maps help identify similar catalyst types across an industry, and peer comparisons show how related companies have reacted to comparable events in the past.

That integration gives each catalyst context. It is no longer an isolated date on a calendar, but part of a larger operating picture. The research system becomes a place where event timing, probability, and competitive context come together.

The end product is a prioritized event calendar with attached trading plans. Each entry includes catalyst type, date, probability, expected market impact, and planned position adjustments. High-probability binary events may justify larger positions with clear exit rules, while lower-probability situations may call for smaller speculative exposure or options structures.

In that form, random news flow becomes something more manageable. The trader is no longer waiting passively for headlines. The calendar becomes a structured portfolio of event-driven opportunities with defined risk parameters.

Company Dossier Templates and Research Files

A trader opens a blank spreadsheet to research a semiconductor company. The first decision is what information to collect and where to place it. That moment separates amateur work from professional-grade financial intelligence. Company dossier templates provide the framework that turns scattered public data into actionable intelligence.

Professional analysts usually build around a three-statement financial model. This Excel-based framework links the income statement, balance sheet, and cash flow statement inside one dynamic system. It includes preformatted sections for historical data taken from SEC filings, with formulas that calculate key ratios and metrics automatically.

When revenue from a 10-K is entered, the template can immediately calculate gross margin, operating margin, and net income percentage. That kind of standardization improves consistency across research files and reduces avoidable errors. It also lets the analyst focus on interpretation rather than arithmetic.

The sum-of-the-parts model is built for a different kind of company. Conglomerates and diversified businesses often have to be valued one segment at a time before the total can be understood. An analyst covering a multinational industrial company might create separate tabs for aerospace, energy equipment, and industrial automation, each built from segment data in the annual report.

The model then combines those pieces into an aggregate valuation. That makes it easier to see which segments are creating value and which may be candidates for sale or restructuring. In practice, it also forces the analyst to think clearly about what kind of business each division really is.

Beyond models, the broader company profile gathers many different forms of information into one document. These profiles usually include company overview, market statistics, leadership, product information, and major corporate events. They also hold executive biographies from proxy statements, patent records from the USPTO, litigation history from court filings, and supply-chain information from trade sources.

That consolidation produces a multidimensional view of the company. The financial statements remain central, but they no longer sit alone. The dossier becomes a place where financial, legal, strategic, and operational data can be read together.

Research files also need a supporting documentation system. Professional analysts usually keep separate folders for primary-source material such as SEC filings, earnings-call transcripts, regulatory announcements, and court records. Those source documents should link directly back to claims and figures inside the dossier.

If the dossier flags an unusual related-party transaction, the exact page from the 10-K footnote should be available in the supporting folder. That creates an audit trail that can withstand scrutiny and speed up verification. When pressure rises, the analyst does not have to go hunting for the source.

Quarterly board-deck templates provide another useful format. These slide-based frameworks track key performance indicators across reporting periods and present the trends in standardized charts and graphs. A trader covering a software company might use one to follow annual recurring revenue growth, customer acquisition costs, lifetime-value ratios, and churn over time.

The visual format often makes changes easier to detect than a spreadsheet alone. A deterioration in customer economics or a shift in retention can appear quickly when plotted consistently across quarters. That makes the board-deck format especially useful as a companion to the model.

The organizational system should also include catalyst tracking. That section lists earnings dates, FDA decisions, patent expirations, regulatory hearings, and court milestones. Each entry should include timing, expected significance, and links to the supporting background material.

That forward-looking component changes the role of the dossier. It is no longer only a record of what has happened. It becomes a dynamic monitoring tool that helps the analyst prepare for what may happen next.

Good dossier design has to balance depth with accessibility. A research file can be exhaustive and still fail if the analyst cannot find the right information quickly during market hours. Professional systems rely on consistent naming conventions, clear folder structures, and indexed cross-references.

When news breaks about an executive departure, the analyst should be able to move immediately to the leadership section and find the executive's background, compensation data, and recent Form 4 filings. That speed is part of the research edge. Information that cannot be retrieved fast enough is often no better than information not collected at all.

The final layer is version control. Research files change as new filings, earnings releases, and market developments come in. Systems that track version history, record the source and date of every update, and maintain change logs reduce confusion about what is current.

This becomes especially important when several analysts are working on the same company or when the research spans a long period. Without update discipline, even strong research degrades. With it, the dossier remains a reliable working platform.

These frameworks turn raw public information into structured intelligence through systematic collection, categorization, and connection. The resulting dossier is not a static report. It is a living research system built to support continuing analysis, hypothesis testing, and decision-making under time pressure.

Key Takeaways

- ☐ A company dossier is not a report. It is a living research platform with eight functional sections — overview, financials, leadership, filing analysis, competitive landscape, catalyst calendar, thesis and risk register, and source log — each serving a different analytical purpose. The Appendix A template provides the structure. The discipline of maintaining it provides the value.
- ☐ Sector mapping determines whether your peer comparison is valid before any financial analysis begins. GICS classifications are a starting point, not a conclusion. A semiconductor-grade specialty gas manufacturer classified under Materials may actually compete with firms in Information Technology. Placing a company in the wrong peer group creates valuation errors that cascade through the entire analysis.
- ☐ Catalyst tracking turns known future events — earnings dates, FDA decisions, patent expirations, contract renewals — from calendar entries into structured trading opportunities. The difference between noting a date and having a pre-defined response for each possible outcome is the difference between reacting to news and positioning ahead of it.

Fieldwork

- ☐ Open the Appendix A template and complete Sections 1 through 3 (Overview, Financial Summary, Leadership) for one company using only primary sources. Time yourself. The first dossier takes two to four hours. Subsequent updates take less than thirty minutes per quarter. The exercise reveals which sources you are fluent with and which require more practice.
- ☐ For the same company, complete Section 6 (Catalyst Calendar). List every known upcoming event with a date, expected significance, and — for each — what outcome would confirm your thesis, what would weaken it, and what would invalidate it. This pre-commitment prevents the common failure of rationalizing unexpected results after the fact.
- ☐ Identify the three closest peers for your target company. Check whether all three share the same GICS sub-industry classification. If they do not,

determine which classification better reflects the actual competitive landscape and use that grouping for your peer comparison table.

Apply This

The dossier and catalyst calendar are the infrastructure that connects every other technique in this book. Without them, individual research efforts remain disconnected — a filing analysis here, an insider transaction there, a satellite image somewhere else. The template creates the place where all of those inputs converge into a single, updatable picture of the company.

CHAPTER 25

Thesis Development and Risk Management

Collecting information is only the beginning. The harder part is turning raw material into a coherent investment thesis and then managing that position as conditions change. That is where a great deal of research breaks down.

Analysts often accumulate documents, transcripts, models, and notes, yet still struggle to reduce that material to a clear and testable hypothesis. They identify risks in the abstract but have no disciplined way to monitor them or decide when those risks have invalidated the original case. The result is a body of research without a decision structure.

The real work begins when research has to become judgment. A professional process does not rely on conviction alone. It converts evidence into argument, documents the chain of support, identifies what could disprove the case, and sets objective conditions for adjusting or exiting the position.

That structure is important because markets rarely invalidate a thesis all at once. More often, the case erodes through a sequence of small contradictions, missed signals, or unchallenged assumptions. A disciplined framework makes those points visible early enough to make a difference.

Macro Context Integration and Geopolitical Signals

A semiconductor company beats quarterly earnings expectations, and the stock rises five percent. At the same time, its largest manufacturing facility sits in a region facing escalating trade restrictions with its primary export market. The earnings release says nothing about those tensions.

That gap between reported performance and macro context is where a great deal of analysis goes wrong. Geopolitical conditions are often treated as background noise or as something too broad to model. In practice, they can alter supply chains, capital allocation, margin assumptions, and long-term market access.

Serious frameworks now treat geopolitical analysis as part of core financial intelligence. The multipolar geopolitics model starts from the idea that major powers are pursuing increasingly divergent interests, fragmenting trade rules, creating new alliances, and redirecting capital. Companies respond by building what practitioners sometimes call geopolitical muscle: the habit of folding political risk into strategic and financial decisions.

The US Inflation Reduction Act and the tariff regime around it are one example. These policies were not simply domestic economic tools. They emerged from rivalry with China and reshaped incentives across manufacturing, energy, and industrial investment.

That change had to be reflected in forecasts. Economists revising growth expectations had to account for how subsidies and tariffs altered plant location, sourcing, and sector profitability. Investors who reallocated capital into domestic manufacturing were responding not to an isolated policy event, but to a geopolitical realignment.

Integration requires more than noticing that politics and markets are connected. A European automaker may post strong quarterly numbers while also negotiating access to Mercosur, Indonesia, and India. Those trade talks are not a side issue. They are part of Europe's response to weak growth, strategic dependence, and a more fractured global order.

Financial analysis has to ask what those relationships do to the model. Access to two billion potential customers changes demand assumptions. Broader sourcing options alter supply-chain resilience and long-term margin expectations. The trade agreement is not just a headline; it becomes a variable.

It is no longer safe to treat globalization as a stable force that automatically produces deeper interdependence. Executives now talk in terms of friend-shoring, trusted partners, and strategic redundancy. European imports from China have flattened in some sectors even as trade with other Asian and European partners has grown.

That is not simply an efficiency story. It reflects strategic realignment under political constraint. At the same time, data and services flows continue to expand even as technology controls and intellectual-property restrictions tighten between rival powers.

The Global Cooperation Barometer offers one way to quantify the fracture. It tracks trade and capital flows, innovation transfer, climate cooperation, natural-capital coordination, and health security. For investors, the value lies in turning vague geopolitical unease into measurable stress across systems that matter to portfolios.

A more immediate layer comes through recurring geostrategic reports. These monthly analyses translate political instability into business exposure. When tensions rise around Venezuela, NATO cohesion weakens, or middle powers shift their foreign-policy posture, those changes feed into assumptions about trade access, energy cost, or regulatory risk.

Oil offers a clear illustration. Middle East tensions around the Strait of Hormuz pushed crude prices nearly eight percent above seventy-eight dollars per barrel. Because that corridor carries more than a fifth of global petroleum flows, the move had immediate implications for freight, refining, and Asian import dependence.

But the first move in price is not the whole story. Historical analysis shows that unless geopolitical conflict produces a sustained energy shock, equity markets often recover within months. The distinction between temporary disruption and structural damage is what determines whether the event belongs in a short-term reaction or a long-horizon thesis revision.

Defense spending provides another signal that can be modeled. NATO's commitment to raise spending to more than double earlier levels as a share of GDP by 2035 creates clear demand implications for defense contractors in Europe, Japan, and Korea. Even there, the analysis cannot stop at the announcement, because political commitment and fiscal capacity are not the same thing.

Macro integration works only when the geopolitical signal changes the assumptions inside the model. Inflation affects cost of goods sold and wage pressure. Interest-rate expectations reflect central-bank responses to trade fragmentation and commodity stress. Downside cases should include political shocks as modeled drivers, not as vague external surprises.

Thesis Memo Writing Structure and Evidence Standards

A venture capital firm receives a memo recommending an investment in a financial technology company. The document runs fifteen pages and opens with a claim that the platform can scale advisor technology into one hundred billion dollars of assets under management by 2025 while sustaining forty percent annual revenue growth. Claims at that level cannot rest on narrative alone.

A serious investment memo has to force the argument into structure. The standard form usually runs fifteen to twenty-five pages, but the point is not length. It is to make sure the recommendation can survive scrutiny from someone who reads only the first page and then starts asking hard questions.

The opening page carries the burden of the whole case. It should state the company, the sector, the stage, the proposed transaction, the key metrics, and the recommendation, including expected return. If that page makes a bold claim, the rest of the memo has to prove it.

The next section usually covers company background and market opportunity. This is where the analyst defines the business model, explains the product, and sizes the market. The useful discipline here is bottom-up reasoning rather than inflated top-down market estimates.

Financial analysis follows. That section usually presents three to five years of historical financials, then builds a forward model based on specific operating drivers rather than arbitrary growth assumptions. Revenue composition, gross margins, operating expense, cash flow, customer acquisition cost, and lifetime value all belong here because they explain how the economics actually work.

A good memo does not summarize whatever information happens to be available. It lays out a proposed investment, the people involved, the terms, the benchmarks, the risks, and the portfolio logic. It is an argument, not a scrapbook.

Competitive positioning deserves its own section. That means identifying direct and indirect competitors, defining any durable advantage, and assessing market share with enough precision to matter. Terms like moat only belong on the page if they describe something concrete, such as switching costs, regulatory licensing, or proprietary data.

Evidence standards separate serious memos from polished speculation. Every major claim should be backed by data, charts, or clearly attributed sources. Assumptions must be labeled explicitly as base, upside, or downside cases so that the reader can tell the model from the rhetoric.

Historical context also plays a role. Three to five years of operating history give the analyst a way to distinguish trend from noise. Forward projections then have to rest on visible drivers such as pipeline conversion, pricing assumptions, retention, expansion revenue, or market-share gains.

That is what turns a memo into something decision-useful. A sales team asking for a revenue analysis from 2010 through the first quarter of 2022 does not need a rearrangement of known data. It needs interpretation: where growth came from, what changed, what looks anomalous, and what follows from that.

Risk belongs inside the memo, not in an afterthought at the end. The memo should identify financial, market, legal, and operational risks, then specify what would mitigate them and what would not. In credit work, that may include global cash flow, proposed risk rating, and covenant structure; in venture or equity work, it may mean customer concentration, churn, dependency on one product, or regulatory exposure.

A professional memo also needs a Plan B. If one of the key assumptions fails, the reader should know what happens next. That requirement often exposes the weakness of a thesis before capital is committed.

Valuation and deal terms come near the end. This section should explain why the chosen method fits the asset, whether that is discounted cash flow, comparable companies, or precedent transactions. It should also set out the proposed investment size, equity stake, control provisions, and any relevant term-sheet protections.

Exit logic belongs here as well. A credible memo should sketch realistic exit scenarios, likely timelines, and return outcomes under different assumptions. That exercise often reveals whether the proposed entry valuation is grounded or merely convenient.

The last test is whether the body of the memo actually supports the first page. Every large claim in the executive summary should trace to evidence in the sections that follow. When that standard is enforced, the act of writing becomes a form of analytical pressure-testing rather than just presentation.

Risk Registers and Pre-Defined Exit Conditions

A trader buys a semiconductor stock after strong quarterly earnings. The thesis emphasizes revenue growth, operating leverage, and competitive positioning. Three weeks later, a key supplier files for bankruptcy protection and the stock falls fifteen percent before the open.

Without a framework, the trader is forced into improvisation. Is the selloff noise, or does it invalidate the thesis? That question is much easier to answer if the supply-chain dependency was already identified, monitored, and tied to a predefined response.

A risk register turns that reactive moment into a structured process. It is a living inventory of the threats to an investment thesis, organized by probability, impact, and ownership. Each risk receives a description, a monitoring responsibility, and a distinction between inherent risk and residual risk after mitigation.

That structure moves risk out of the realm of vague concern. A supplier-distress entry, for example, might describe instability caused by a demand downturn, identify alternate sourcing as the mitigation plan, and assign early warning indicators such as payment-term extensions or quality-control complaints. The risk is no longer theoretical. It becomes something observable.

Most financial risk registers sort exposure into market, credit, liquidity, operational, and regulatory buckets. A trading desk may discover that it has cluster risk because it owns exposure to the same issuer through equity, bonds, and funds. A probability-impact matrix then makes it easier to decide which risks demand immediate attention and which can be monitored at a lower frequency.

Predefined exit conditions should connect directly to that same structure. These are not generic stop-loss rules. They are thesis-specific tripwires tied to the actual assumptions that justified the trade in the first place.

In pharmaceuticals, an exit condition might be the failure of a lead clinical trial or a regulatory delay beyond a specified date. The stock may move sharply before either condition is confirmed, but the actual trigger is the failure of the business assumption, not the market's emotion. That is the difference between reacting to volatility and responding to deterioration.

Monitoring frequency should also vary with the risk. High-probability, high-impact threats may need daily review. Low-probability strategic risks may only require quarterly reassessment. What counts most is that every risk has a cadence and an owner rather than disappearing into collective awareness.

Residual risk ratings are especially useful because they force the analyst to distinguish between gross exposure and net exposure after controls. A position may carry high market risk in the abstract but only medium residual risk once hedges or supplier alternatives are in place. That distinction should influence position size.

The register also has to evolve. New information from filings, calls, channel checks, or price action may raise or lower the probability of a risk that already sits in the system. If supplier strain intensifies after an earnings call, the register should change, and that change should feed directly into the exit conditions and position sizing.

The final discipline is traceability. Every exit condition should link back to a specific risk entry with a clear monitoring responsibility. That prevents arbitrary trading decisions while making it easier to act decisively when an assumption has actually broken.

Evidence Logs and Source Chain Documentation

A research note says a pharmaceutical company's new drug will receive FDA approval within three months. The note cites an unnamed industry consultant. Another analyst reads it, builds that timeline into a valuation model, and the stock rises on the expectation. When approval does not arrive, no one can trace the original claim.

That failure is not unusual. It is what happens when research is built on assertions that cannot be reconstructed. Professional intelligence work depends on evidence logging precisely because market narratives often spread faster than their sourcing can be checked.

An evidence log creates a forensic record for every important fact used in a thesis. It records not just the information itself, but where it came from, how it was collected, and when it was captured. That sounds procedural, but the point is analytical: conclusions should rest on a chain that can be inspected later.

Take a retail-company supply-chain investigation. Satellite imagery may show reduced truck traffic at a distribution center, while a supplier bankruptcy filing appears in court records. Each item belongs in the evidence log as a separate entry, with the image source, capture time, coordinates, case number, filing date, and collection method recorded in plain terms.

That separation is important because evidence should not be confused with conclusion. The observation is one thing; the inference about operational stress is another. A clean log keeps the two apart until the argument is ready to be made.

The source chain is what connects the evidence into a finding. An analyst may notice unusual EDGAR download patterns around a company's 10-K footnotes, then see elevated put activity in the options market, then read a short-seller report that cites the same footnotes two weeks later. Each item alone may be weak. The sequence tells a stronger story.

Forensic accounting work shows the value of this method. A retail company's accounting backup may reveal vendor lists and ledger entries, while the system's own audit logs show that specific line items were modified after the original posting date. A defensible investigation records the original extraction, the timestamp of the changes, and the personnel codes attached to them.

The best logs are structured rather than narrative. Each entry should identify the exact source, the collection method, and the retrieval timestamp. Those fields are basic, but they become crucial when dealing with time-sensitive information or when a question resurfaces months later.

Verification status deserves its own field. A media report about a contract award may remain in the log, but it should be marked as pending until a company filing or an independent source confirms it. That does not mean unverified information is useless. It means its weight should be visible.

The PRISMA framework from academic review work offers a useful analogy. It requires documenting the search strategy, the inclusion and exclusion decisions, and the path from raw literature to final conclusion. Applied to financial intelligence, that means recording not only the sources kept, but the ones discarded and the reasons they were rejected.

Done properly, evidence logging is not bureaucratic drag. It reduces duplicated effort and makes it much easier to revisit a question later without rebuilding the research from scratch. It also forces contradictions into the open early, when they are still manageable.

This becomes especially important with social media and alternative data. A sentiment analysis built from online posts should record the platforms used, the time window, the sampling method, and the location of the raw archive. Otherwise the conclusion cannot be revisited when the method improves or when someone challenges the representativeness of the sample.

Source hierarchies also need to be explicit. Regulatory filings sit at the top tier for corporate factual claims because they are institutional, attributable, and legally consequential. Financial media sits lower unless independently verified, while social media usually belongs at the bottom tier for factual assertion, even if it may still be useful for tracking narrative momentum.

Making those tiers explicit prevents a low-quality source from quietly carrying too much analytical weight. A Tier 1 SEC filing and a Tier 3 anonymous forum post should not enter the workflow as though they were equivalent. The log should make that impossible to miss.

The system becomes most useful when it links directly to the thesis memo and the risk register. A claim in the memo should point to specific log entries. A risk in the register should point to the sources used to monitor it. That is what creates a closed loop rather than a pile of disconnected documents.

The result looks less like a notebook and more like the appendix to a legal brief. Another analyst should be able to reconstruct the reasoning from the raw material. In markets where narrative often gets ahead of fact, that kind of source discipline is a durable analytical edge.

Disconfirmation Practice and Scenario Planning

A venture capital firm reviews a software startup with strong growth and a compelling story. The lead partner becomes enthusiastic. Instead of moving directly to deal terms, the investment committee spends the next meeting asking why the company might fail.

That is disconfirmation practice. It means deliberately searching for evidence that challenges the initial thesis rather than letting the research drift toward confirmation. Without that discipline, even intelligent teams begin to assemble arguments around the position they already want to hold.

The value of the practice is not psychological hygiene for its own sake. It is that most investment mistakes do not come from a lack of supporting evidence. They come from failing to notice that the evidence was one-sided or that the contrary case was never seriously developed.

A pharmaceutical example makes the point. A thesis memo may emphasize the market potential of a lead drug and favorable trial statistics. Disconfirmation practice requires the analyst to search just as hard for signals that point the other way, such as patent disputes, adverse regulator behavior in adjacent products, or competitor filings that suggest similar drugs are being delayed.

Those findings should be recorded alongside the supporting evidence. The burden is then on the analyst to explain why the thesis survives them. That changes the tone of the work. The case is no longer a sales pitch. It becomes a disciplined argument under pressure.

Scenario planning extends the same principle into the future. A weak version of the exercise reduces everything to best case and worst case. A useful version builds several plausible futures around internally consistent drivers and then asks what each one would do to the economics of the investment.

For a retailer, one scenario may involve weakening consumer demand and excess inventory. Another may combine inflation with wage growth strong enough to preserve purchasing power. The point is not to name every possibility, but to create a set of futures that are coherent enough to test.

Venture firms often apply this through structured stress testing at the committee level. Teams ask what adoption metric would disprove the growth narrative, what competitor move would undermine the moat, or what cost structure would turn scale into a burden instead of an advantage. The investment is challenged before it is owned.

The same practice works in public markets. Analysts often overweight reports that support their existing position while dismissing critical research as flawed or biased. A disconfirmation framework forces them to document why contradictory analysis does not invalidate the thesis rather than simply ignoring it.

Credit analysis shows the predictive value of this method well. Analysts may model several economic scenarios for a borrower, including interest-rate shocks, commodity volatility, and supply-chain disruptions. Each scenario produces different coverage ratios, covenant outcomes, and downgrade risks.

This is not list-making. The work is iterative, and it depends on varied inputs. In its best form, it resembles a pre-mortem: assume the investment has already failed, then work backward to identify the most likely cause.

At the portfolio level, scenario planning becomes a way to test concentrations and hidden vulnerability. Firms run what-if exercises across entire portfolios to see how they would behave in a market drawdown or a sector-specific shock. The technology collapse of 2022 and 2023 exposed how many portfolios had treated correlation as diversification.

To make the work actionable, the scenarios need challenge goalposts. These are specific metrics that would indicate a scenario is beginning to unfold or that a thesis is losing validity. For a growth stock, it might be two straight quarters of falling customer acquisition. For a value thesis, it might be a worsening cash-conversion cycle.

The expectancy-disconfirmation model from behavioral science is useful here. It compares actual outcomes with prior expectations and sorts them into positive disconfirmation, simple confirmation, or negative disconfirmation. In financial terms, that can be applied to earnings, guidance, macro releases, or customer metrics.

The real value of disconfirmation practice appears when the evidence shifts gradually. Most thesis failures do not begin with one dramatic event. They begin with small data points that create discomfort and then get rationalized away.

A disciplined system records those contradictions as they appear. Over time, the accumulation becomes visible as a pattern rather than a feeling. That is what turns discomfort into something decision-useful.

Scenario planning earns its keep when markets move against the position. A trader who has already imagined the stress cases can decide quickly whether current conditions match a known scenario or whether genuinely new information has arrived. That speed can be the difference between a controlled adjustment and a panicked exit.

Key Takeaways

- ☐ A thesis memo is not a summary of research. It is a structured argument with five components: the opportunity, why it exists, the supporting evidence, what could disprove it, and the specific action that follows. Writing the memo forces logical rigor that mental conviction does not. If the thesis cannot survive being written down, it cannot survive contact with the market.
- ☐ Risk registers convert vague concerns into monitored variables. Each risk entry includes a description, a probability estimate (high/medium/low), an impact assessment, and — critically — the specific observable event that would confirm the risk is materializing. Pre-defined exit conditions tied to those triggers prevent the common failure of holding a deteriorating position because the original research "felt thorough."
- ☐ Disconfirmation practice is the most valuable and least practiced analytical discipline. Actively seeking evidence that contradicts your thesis — before entering a position — identifies weaknesses that confirmation bias would otherwise hide. The strongest theses survive structured opposition. The weakest collapse under the first serious challenge.

Fieldwork

- ☐ Write a full thesis memo for one position using the five-question structure. Spend at least as much time on "What could prove it wrong?" as on the supporting evidence. If you cannot articulate three specific risks with observable triggers, the thesis is underspecified.
- ☐ Build a risk register for the same position. List the top five threats, assign each a probability and impact score, and define the specific data point or event that would confirm each risk. Set a calendar reminder to review the register after the next quarterly filing.
- ☐ Before your next new position, conduct a deliberate disconfirmation exercise. Spend thirty minutes searching only for evidence that your thesis is wrong. Check competitors' filings for contradictory data. Search for bear cases on

the company. Read the most critical analyst report you can find. Document what you find. If the opposing evidence is stronger than you expected, adjust your position size accordingly.

Apply This

The thesis memo, risk register, and disconfirmation exercise work as a system. The memo forces clarity. The register converts the memo's identified risks into monitored conditions. The disconfirmation exercise stress-tests both before capital is committed. Skipping any one of the three weakens the other two.

CHAPTER 26

Monitoring Systems and Automation

The previous section established frameworks for building an investment thesis and managing risk. Those frameworks only work if they are tied to ongoing observation. A risk-register entry about supplier concentration requires regular checks on supplier health, and a thesis built on market-share expansion requires continuous tracking of competitor moves.

Without that follow-through, the framework hardens into paperwork. The gap between planned risk management and actual position oversight is where a great deal of independent research breaks down. The file looks complete, but the position is no longer being watched in a disciplined way.

The problem is not deciding what matters. It is creating a repeatable way to watch the right things across different time horizons and source types. Good monitoring turns occasional checking into a routine that surfaces relevant developments before they become market events.

The best systems do not try to eliminate effort altogether. They reduce the time spent searching and increase the time spent interpreting. Coverage has to be broad enough to catch change, but narrow enough to preserve focus.

Manual routines, lightweight alerts, public APIs, and no-code automation all solve different versions of the same problem. The point is not to build the most sophisticated system. It is to create information flows that continue to function when markets are quiet and when they are under stress.

Monitoring Routines and Standard Operating Procedures

A research analyst begins every Monday the same way. First comes the SEC's EDGAR database for weekend filings on watchlist companies, then pre-market futures and Asian closes for overnight developments, and then the calendar of scheduled corporate events for the week. That twenty-minute sequence is a monitoring system, not a habit of casual checking.

Standard operating procedures turn sporadic information gathering into a repeatable form of intelligence collection. They also reduce the cost of switching from one position to another because the workflow stays stable even when the companies change. The routine does not have to be elaborate to be useful.

Effective monitoring usually works across three time horizons. Daily routines focus on immediate events and live data, such as SEC filings before the open, earnings-call transcripts as they are posted, and unusual options activity during the session. Weekly routines widen the frame to include portfolio performance, watchlist changes, technical breakdowns, activist filings, and developments that do not need minute-by-minute attention.

Monthly routines are more strategic. They include updates to short-interest data, review of insider-transaction clusters, and changes in sector maps or peer groups as industry conditions evolve. The broader the time horizon, the less the emphasis shifts to reaction and the more it shifts to pattern recognition.

The principle of separation of duties fits this work well. One person may handle regulatory filings while another follows credit-market signals or supplier data. That kind of division reduces monitoring fatigue and creates natural verification points when the findings are brought back together.

The edge usually comes from consistency rather than from access. Analysts who follow structured routines tend to detect material developments earlier than those relying on ad hoc checks, not because the information is better, but because the coverage is. A known source watched regularly will often outperform a better source watched irregularly.

The tools can be simple. RSS readers for SEC filings, recurring reminders for earnings periods, and spreadsheet templates for insider activity are often enough to create a solid baseline. More advanced setups may add APIs, dashboards, and automated alerts, but complexity is not the same as discipline.

Automation does not make routines obsolete. It changes their shape. Automated systems still need validation against primary sources, and they still produce false positives that require judgment to filter.

The strongest operators keep manual spot checks even in heavily automated environments. That creates a layered process rather than blind dependence on one feed. A simple checklist performed every day is usually more valuable than an elaborate system touched only when something feels urgent.

The real test comes in stress. When volatility rises and information accelerates, a structured routine prevents attention from fragmenting. Analysts with an established sequence continue checking the highest-priority sources in order instead of chasing every headline or alert.

A monitoring system that works only when nothing is happening is not a system. It needs redundancy, priority, and enough restraint to keep the analyst from drowning in updates. Under pressure, routine is what keeps signal from dissolving into noise.

Optional Automation Using Public APIs and RSS Feeds

A research analyst receives an alert at 4:05 p.m. Eastern time. The message says a chief financial officer has filed a Form 4 showing the sale of fifty thousand shares, and it arrives within minutes of the SEC posting the document. No one refreshed EDGAR manually and no one set a special reminder.

That is what optional automation looks like in practice. A simple script or feed monitor watches the SEC's RSS output and triggers a notification when a filing matches predefined criteria. The value is not elegance. It is that repetitive checking has been turned into a reliable information stream.

Public APIs make that possible by turning static sources into machine-readable feeds. The Federal Reserve Economic Data API can update dashboards automatically when CPI or employment figures are released, and tools such as the Financial Modeling Prep API provide access to historical filings, ratios, and market data without constant downloading and spreadsheet cleanup.

Each API comes with limits. Rate caps, latency, data freshness, and access restrictions shape what the system can do in practice. A useful setup begins not with the fanciest feed available, but with a clear sense of what has to be monitored and how quickly it has to be seen.

RSS feeds provide a simpler form of automation. The SEC maintains feeds for filings tied to specific CIK numbers, and those feeds can be routed through ordinary readers or alert services without writing any code. That is often enough to build a passive monitoring layer for a priority company or sector.

The weakness of RSS is volume. A single company can generate a steady stream of documents, many of them immaterial to the analyst's thesis. The feed solves the delivery problem, but not the filtering problem.

The best place to start is with repetitive manual tasks that consume time without adding much insight. Daily checks on short-interest updates, FDA calendars, or routine filing types are good candidates. Structured numerical data tends to fit well with APIs, while document-heavy sources are better handled through RSS or simple page monitoring.

Automation does not require much technical depth. Many financial-data providers now offer no-code or low-code tools for alerts, feed imports, and spreadsheet connections. In many cases, the barrier is less about programming than about reading documentation carefully enough to understand what the tool is actually delivering.

Human judgment does not disappear when automation begins. It moves downstream. A system may flag every insider sale above a certain threshold, but the analyst still has to distinguish between a routine liquidity event and something more meaningful.

That filtering work is unavoidable. Automated systems will always surface false positives, and sometimes the more successful the automation becomes, the more carefully the human review layer has to be designed. Good systems collect automatically and interpret manually.

The strongest implementations usually grow in stages. An RSS feed for a handful of priority companies forms a baseline, then API calls add macro data, then custom rules cross-reference insider trading with compensation schedules or event calendars. Each new layer should be checked against manual review before the system expands.

Stress reveals the weaknesses quickly. APIs may throttle access when demand surges, and feeds may lag when filing volume spikes. A robust system needs fallback procedures so the analyst can verify critical developments directly when the automation falters.

The goal is not technical sophistication for its own sake. It is reliable delivery of the right information at the right time. A modest system that holds up under pressure is worth far more than an impressive one that fails when the market turns disorderly.

SEC EDGAR Alerts and Regulatory Monitoring Tools

A compliance officer gets a push notification at 2:17 p.m. The message says a portfolio company has just filed an 8-K reporting the sudden resignation of its chief financial officer. Before the market closes, the officer has reviewed the filing and started assessing the implications for trading restrictions and portfolio exposure.

That kind of speed does not come from refreshing the SEC website. It comes from a monitoring tool configured to watch specific companies and filing types. The tool turns EDGAR from a passive archive into an active stream of intelligence.

Services such as Visualping and PageCrawl do this by watching EDGAR result pages or filing pages for change. They scan at regular intervals, often every fifteen minutes during market hours, and can be set to monitor a specific CIK, a group of tickers, or a filing category such as 8-Ks or Form 4s.

The more useful versions go beyond simple change detection. They filter for material language inside the filing, flagging terms such as "cybersecurity incident," "material weakness," or "resignation." That cuts down on noise and keeps the alert stream closer to the analyst's actual intelligence requirements.

Apify's SEC EDGAR Filing Monitor pushes the idea further by assigning severity scores to trigger events inside filings. Mergers, executive changes, cybersecurity breaches, and similar disclosures are identified and returned as structured data rather than unformatted text. That structure makes it easier to integrate the alert into other research or compliance systems.

The SEC itself offers only basic feeds, and those still require the user to pull information rather than receive it automatically. Third-party tools bridge that gap with email, Telegram, Slack, Discord, and webhook delivery. The practical advantage is not just speed but the ability to route alerts directly into the place where the analyst is already working.

Those delivery channels matter. A Slack channel for filings, a Telegram bot for urgent alerts, or a Discord stream for team coordination all create a shared working surface where developments can be discussed immediately. The filing no longer sits in a queue waiting to be discovered.

Not every filing deserves the same attention. A well-built system distinguishes between annual reports, insider transactions, activist filings, and event-driven 8-Ks. The point is not total surveillance of every document. It is timely awareness of the filings most likely to affect an investment decision while the decision still matters.

There are limits to every tool. Scan intervals create latency, SEC posting delays can slow visibility, and free service tiers often impose restrictions on parsing or volume. Accuracy also varies, especially when the tool tries to interpret unstructured filing language rather than just detect the document itself.

That is why critical alerts still need human review. The automation should accelerate attention, not replace verification. A useful filing monitor surfaces the event quickly, but the analyst still has to read the source document before acting on it.

Implementation works best when it starts from the thesis. An analyst following activist campaigns may focus on Schedule 13D filings, while a healthcare specialist may prioritize 8-Ks that contain FDA-related language. The configuration should reflect the actual risks and catalysts under watch, not a generic fear of missing something.

Regulatory monitoring is most effective when it sits inside a broader system. EDGAR alerts tell the analyst that a development has occurred, but the meaning still has to be interpreted against the thesis, the risk register, and the monitoring routine already in place. The alert is the entry point, not the analysis.

No-Code Tools for Research Workflow Automation

A researcher follows twenty companies across three sectors. Every week involves checking SEC filings, tracking earnings calendars, reviewing options activity, and scanning multiple news sources. Much of the work is repetitive, and much of it does not require judgment until the raw material has already been gathered.

No-code tools exist to remove that layer of repetition. They use visual interfaces instead of code to connect data sources, apply logic, and deliver alerts or updates. The result is not a black box but a workflow the analyst can build and inspect without writing scripts from scratch.

A typical use case is straightforward. The system checks EDGAR every fifteen minutes during market hours, filters for 8-Ks with predefined language, and sends a Telegram or Slack message that includes the filing link and a short extracted summary. What used to consume repeated manual attention now happens in the background.

Platforms such as Activepieces and Creatio make this possible through drag-and-drop workflow builders. A trigger might be a new RSS item or a scheduled time of day, and an action might be sending a notification, writing to a spreadsheet, or calling an API. Between those two points, conditions can filter for relevance.

That filtering step is what makes the workflow useful. A filing may only be forwarded if it includes terms such as "material weakness" or "cybersecurity incident," or if it belongs to a priority company rather than the broader watchlist. The no-code interface does not reduce complexity so much as make it manageable.

Integration is what determines whether these tools become genuinely useful research infrastructure. Platforms such as Workato connect to hundreds of services, which allows a filing alert to populate a Google Sheet, generate an internal summary, or cross-reference the filing against a database of executives, litigation records, or prior disclosures. The workflow starts to resemble a small intelligence pipeline.

Human review still belongs inside the system. Many no-code platforms allow pause points or approval steps, so an analyst can examine a flagged item before it is pushed to a wider team or added to a live decision surface. That preserves speed without turning the process into a machine for spreading false positives.

Natural-language interfaces are pushing the barrier lower. Tools such as Vellum's Agent Builder let users describe a workflow in plain English, then generate the trigger, logic, and action sequence automatically. A researcher can ask for a system that watches FDA advisory-committee documents for a biotech watchlist and sends alerts when new materials appear.

That convenience is real, but it does not remove the need for precision. The workflow still has to be validated, and the user still has to know what outcome is actually desired. No-code systems reduce the technical burden, but they do not eliminate the need for analytical clarity.

These tools are not limited to simple tasks. Enterprise platforms such as RunMyJobs can coordinate complex workflows across multiple environments, manage dependencies, and trigger actions based on other actions completing successfully. Even so, the most useful research applications are often less ambitious and more disciplined.

Implementation should begin with process mapping. The analyst needs to identify which tasks are repetitive, which have clear triggers, and which produce standardized outputs. Weekly short-interest compilation, daily checks for new patent filings, or recurring earnings-calendar updates are all good candidates because they are mechanical enough to automate and frequent enough to matter.

Every workflow needs monitoring of its own. If the no-code system fails silently, the analyst is left with a false sense of coverage. That means regular validation against manual checks, especially at the start and during periods of market stress.

The purpose of automation is not to replace analysis. It is to create more room for it. A good no-code workflow clears away the repetitive tasks so the analyst can spend more time investigating anomalies, challenging assumptions, and deciding which developments actually change the case.

Key Takeaways

- ☐ Monitoring is not about checking more things. It is about checking the right things at the right cadence. Daily routines handle time-sensitive filings and market-moving data. Weekly reviews widen the frame to portfolio assessment and calendar planning. Monthly and quarterly reviews shift from reaction to pattern recognition and process improvement.
- ☐ Automation shifts effort from data collection to interpretation, not from work to leisure. RSS feeds for SEC filings, API calls for economic data, and email alerts for Form 4 transactions eliminate manual checking. They do not eliminate the judgment required to distinguish meaningful signals from false positives. Every automated alert still requires a human decision about whether to act.
- ☐ The practical test of any monitoring system is whether it functions under stress. Systems that work during calm markets but collapse when volatility spikes — because API rate limits throttle, alert volumes overwhelm, or the analyst abandons the routine to chase headlines — need redesign with redundancy and prioritization built in.

Fieldwork

- ☐ Implement the Appendix D monitoring routine for the next 90 days without modification. The daily checklist takes 15–20 minutes. The weekly review takes 60–90 minutes. Run it as written. After the first quarter, conduct the quarterly review and note which items consistently produced actionable intelligence and which felt like noise. Adjust only then.
- ☐ Set up EDGAR email alerts for every company you hold or actively watch, using CIK numbers. Configure separate alerts for 10-Qs, 10-Ks, 8-Ks, Form 4s, and DEF 14As. Within one week you will have a real-time primary-source feed without visiting EDGAR manually. This is the single highest-return infrastructure task in this chapter.

Apply This

If you take only one thing from this chapter, make it the filing alert stack. It takes fifteen minutes to set up and runs itself indefinitely. Everything else in your monitoring system is built on top of knowing, in real time, when a company you care about files something with the SEC. Start there.

CHAPTER 27

Real-World Case Studies and Applications

This chapter turns from framework to practice. The question is how financial-intelligence methods actually work when applied to real market events, fraud investigations, and investment decisions. The value of the discipline becomes clearer when the techniques are tied to outcomes rather than described in the abstract.

Each case highlights a different part of the FININT method. GameStop shows how retail investors combined regulatory filings, short-interest data, and options activity into a coherent market thesis. Wirecard shows what happens when financial statements are checked against physical reality through satellite imagery and on-the-ground verification.

Enron demonstrates how footnote analysis and forensic-accounting models could have surfaced manipulation years before the company failed. Archegos shows that missing data can be intelligence in its own right, and that the absence of an expected filing can signal hidden exposure. More recent applications extend the same logic through specialized software, link-analysis tools, and blockchain intelligence.

These cases share a common pattern. The strongest analysis did not rely on any one source or any one technique. It came from combining multiple streams of public information and treating discrepancies between reported numbers and observable facts as meaningful signals rather than as isolated anomalies.

That is the habit that turns public information into intelligence. The point is not merely to collect data after the fact, but to build a verification process capable of anticipating risk before the market fully prices it.

GameStop 2021: Retail OSINT and Short Squeeze Dynamics

The GameStop short squeeze in January 2021 is often described as a social-media frenzy. That description misses the structure of what happened. Retail traders identified a specific vulnerability in market positioning and used public data to build a coordinated thesis around it.

The key signal was extreme short interest. More than 140 percent of GameStop's public float had been sold short, which meant more shares had effectively been borrowed and sold than were available for ordinary trading. That condition arose because the same shares could be lent, sold, and lent again.

Retail participants tracked the setup through public short-interest reports and securities-borrowing data. They understood that if enough buying pressure entered the stock at once, short sellers would be forced to cover by purchasing shares back in the market. The vulnerability was structural, not symbolic.

The story gained a second layer when Ryan Cohen, the co-founder of Chewy, joined GameStop's board. That gave the trade a plausible transformation narrative beyond the meme-stock label. A company that had looked like a dying retailer could now be framed as a turnaround with activist backing and a digital strategy.

Retail coordination then pushed on both the stock and the options market. Traders bought shares, but they also bought call options, which gave them leveraged exposure without having to fund outright stock purchases. That mattered because market makers hedging those call sales had to buy stock as the price rose.

The result was a feedback loop. Rising prices forced short sellers, including Melvin Capital, to buy shares to limit losses, while options hedging added more demand on top of that. Each layer of forced buying made the next layer more likely.

The episode was not pure speculation detached from analysis. Retail participants were doing a rough but recognizable form of OSINT. They were combining short-interest data, options-chain activity, regulatory filings, management changes, and social distribution into a single market thesis.

They watched Form 4 filings for insider activity, followed 13F disclosures and press reports to infer institutional positioning, and used online communities to spread the information quickly. The slogan about "diamond hands" was not only cultural theater. It also reflected an understanding that the short side was vulnerable to margin pressure if enough holders refused to sell.

The case exposed limits in conventional market surveillance. The short-interest data was public, but the market underestimated the ability of a decentralized retail crowd to synthesize that information and act on it collectively. Institutions saw the data but failed to imagine the form of coordination that would emerge around it.

Once the squeeze had run its course, short interest fell back toward more ordinary levels and exchanges tightened scrutiny around reporting and risk controls. That reduced the chance of a direct repeat. The structural conditions had been exposed too publicly to remain intact.

For financial-intelligence work, the lesson is straightforward. Positioning and sentiment have to be monitored across all classes of participants, not just through institutional disclosures. Social-media coordination, options flow, and public filings can combine into a real market force long before the official narrative catches up.

Wirecard 2020: Satellite Imagery and Fraud Exposure

Wirecard posed a basic verification problem. The German payments company claimed billions in revenue through third-party partners in Asia, and those partners were described as handling large transaction volumes through substantial operating facilities. The reported business sounded complex, but the underlying question was simple: did those operations physically exist at anything like the scale being claimed?

Investigators obtained addresses for the critical counterparties from corporate records, filings, and industry sources. They then used Google Earth and commercial satellite imagery to examine those locations remotely. What they found did not match the financial story.

The images showed residential homes, empty lots, and small storefronts where high-volume payment-processing operations were supposed to be running. One address in the Philippines linked to a major partner turned out to be the home of a retired seaman's family. The mismatch between reported scale and physical reality was impossible to explain away.

That was the force of the evidence. Accounting entries can be manipulated and documents can be forged, but an empty building where a billion-euro operation is supposed to sit creates a different kind of contradiction. The imagery did not prove every element of the fraud by itself, but it broke the credibility of the reported business model.

The reporting did not stop with satellite images. Journalists and investigators cross-referenced the physical evidence with corporate registry records and found that many of the counterparties were shells or had little operational substance. They reviewed bank-confirmation letters and found irregularities in signatures and formatting that deepened the doubt.

The investigation followed a classic intelligence workflow. It began with a discrepancy in the reported financials, identified the key counterparties and assets supporting those numbers, and then tested whether those entities could be verified independently. The financial narrative was checked against observable reality.

Wirecard also showed how fraud can survive when basic verification is neglected. Auditors did not perform the kind of direct checks that might have exposed the weakness earlier. Physical verification, even at a distance, would have raised questions that the accounting narrative alone had managed to suppress.

The case also rewarded persistence. Journalists pursued the story for years despite legal threats, reputational attacks, and a short-selling ban imposed by German regulators. The resistance itself became part of the pattern. Institutions that should have been testing the claims were instead defending them.

For financial-intelligence practitioners, the principle is durable. When a company reports large revenue tied to a specific partner, facility, or region, the first instinct should be to connect the number to something tangible. Satellite imagery is only one tool for that. Shipping data, traffic counts, power consumption, trade records, and site visits can all serve the same function.

The deeper point is that elaborate frauds often fail simple verification tests. Wirecard's missing €1.9 billion was not uncovered by forensic accounting alone. It was also exposed by looking at places that were supposed to be full of activity and finding that they were not.

Enron: 10-K Footnotes and Accounting Red Flags

Enron's collapse is often remembered as a story of deception that was impossible to see in real time. That is not quite true. Many of the signals were visible in the company's own filings, especially in the footnotes, where the most revealing parts of the capital structure and accounting policy were disclosed in plain language.

One important clue appeared in the company's discussion of market risk. Enron reported a value at risk of roughly fifty million dollars, which looked plausible enough for a large energy-trading firm. But other disclosures in the same filing pointed to $6.9 billion in off-balance-sheet debt that did not appear clearly on the face of the balance sheet.

That gap between headline presentation and footnote substance defined much of the Enron story. Reported debt had tripled since 1996, but when the hidden obligations were included, the increase was closer to fivefold. The company's leverage was rising faster than the primary statements suggested.

The footnotes also revealed how much discretion management had in valuing transactions. One report stated that market prices reflected management's best estimates, which sounds technical until one remembers how much room that language creates for aggressive assumptions. When management has broad discretion in assigning value, reported earnings become much easier to manufacture.

Forensic-accounting models could have added another layer of warning. The Beneish M-Score, for example, would likely have flagged Enron's filings through several of its core components. Total accruals were persistently elevated, and that pointed to an increasing tendency to defer costs and rely on accounting entries rather than cash performance.

Other indicators moved in the same direction. The depreciation index suggested that asset write-offs were being slowed in a way that boosted current earnings, while the sales-growth index raised the possibility of aggressive revenue recognition. The numbers did not prove fraud on their own, but they formed a pattern that should have triggered deeper scrutiny.

The footnotes on special-purpose entities were particularly important. Enron used these vehicles to hold assets, borrow funds, and hedge the value of investments while keeping the associated risk and leverage out of clearer view. Even within the notes, questions remained about whether these structures complied with the spirit, or even the letter, of accounting standards.

The company also used classification changes to obscure leverage. One new accounting rule allowed $532 million to be shifted from long-term debt into other liabilities. The balance sheet was not technically silent, but the presentation made the debt load less legible than it should have been.

The operating picture was deteriorating as well. Enron's profit margin fell sharply after 1997, and the decline was not offset by stronger asset efficiency or a healthier capital structure. Return on assets stayed below three percent despite rapid asset growth, which suggested that expansion was not producing real profitability.

Some of the sloppiness was almost visible to the naked eye. In its final earnings announcement, Enron reported three-month physical transactions that exceeded the total for the preceding nine months. That kind of inconsistency should never have survived a serious reading of the filings.

The lesson is not just that footnotes are crucial. It is that they often reveal more than the headline statements. Accounting policy, contingent liabilities, off-balance-sheet structures, and classification choices all live there, and they often tell a truer story than the earnings figure carried in the press release.

Enron was not invisible. The signals were in the company's own documents, available to anyone willing to treat the notes as the main text rather than as supporting material at the back.

Archegos Capital 2021: 13F Cross-Referencing and Risk

Archegos Capital managed billions in family wealth without filing a Form 13F. That absence was legal because the firm operated as a family office and therefore avoided the registration requirements that would normally trigger public disclosure. The result was a large and highly leveraged investment vehicle operating with very little visibility.

Archegos built concentrated positions in Chinese technology and U.S. media companies through total return swaps. These derivatives gave the firm economic exposure to the underlying shares without requiring direct ownership, which meant the positions did not appear through the disclosure channels that many market participants rely on.

That structure mattered because the concentration was enormous. In some names, Archegos had effective exposure well beyond what outside observers could reasonably infer from public ownership records. The firm was massively directional while remaining largely invisible.

Prime brokers enabled the scale. Firms such as Goldman Sachs and Credit Suisse extended extreme leverage, allowing Archegos to post a small amount of capital against a much larger position. That structure worked as long as markets rose, but it turned fragile quickly once prices moved the other way.

When the positions began to fall in late March, margin calls hit across multiple counterparties. The forced liquidation that followed led to a fire sale in the underlying stocks and more than $10 billion in losses for prime brokers. The unwinding revealed risk that had been sitting inside the system without being legible through conventional disclosure.

One of the most instructive parts of the case is that the absence of a filing was itself a signal. For a vehicle operating at that scale, no 13F meant either that the exposure was not there or that it was being held through a structure designed to avoid visibility. Either possibility deserved attention.

That is what made the case so useful from a FININT perspective. Public-data analysis is not only about reading what appears in filings. It is also about noticing what should appear but does not. Missing disclosure can be a form of disclosure.

Regulators eventually focused on the loophole. Calls followed for more frequent 13F reporting, inclusion of certain derivative exposures, and tighter scrutiny of family offices managing very large pools of capital. The SEC later brought a civil complaint against Archegos founder Bill Hwang, describing how the firm used swaps and concentrated trading to manipulate market prices while remaining out of public sight.

The broader lesson is that surveillance has to include omission. Analysts who track known market participants against filing systems can identify gaps that point to structural blind spots. Archegos showed that one of the most important pieces of information in the market may be the filing that never appears.

Modern Applications of FININT Techniques

The same methods now operate with newer tools. A hedge-fund analyst may receive an alert on a private-equity-backed acquisition target that appears clean under conventional diligence. Running the company's executives through an OSINT platform configured for financial work may then surface links between a board member and sanctioned entities buried in offshore leaks or cross-border registry data.

That kind of workflow is no longer unusual. Modern FININT blends traditional public-records research with software built for link analysis, entity resolution, and structured data extraction. Tools such as Videris and Maltego give analysts environments in which corporate registries, sanctions records, leaked datasets, regulatory filings, and social media can be pulled into one searchable investigative map.

These platforms are especially strong at following relationships. An analyst can start from one company-record entry and move quickly to directors, shareholders, subsidiaries, and associated entities across multiple jurisdictions. The visual graph often reveals a structure that would be hard to see through manual document review alone.

That matters in anti-money-laundering work, supply-chain diligence, and counterparty analysis. The objective is not just to know who owns something on paper, but to understand how influence, control, and hidden association actually move through the network. Link analysis turns scattered documents into a structure that can be interrogated.

Blockchain intelligence has become another major extension of the same logic. Platforms such as Elliptic trace transactions across public ledgers, identify wallet clusters, and flag flows connected to sanctioned or illicit actors. For traders or investigators following stablecoin liquidity, exchange flows, or sanctions exposure, that can produce real-time intelligence that would otherwise be inaccessible.

Large language models have entered the workflow as well, usually not as decision-makers but as extraction and pattern-detection tools. A model such as Deepseek or Claude can process large sets of earnings-call transcripts, board materials, or financial reports and flag inconsistencies, changing tone, or repeated hedging language that merits human review.

The architecture is consistent even when the tools change. Data is collected automatically from multiple public sources, processed through techniques designed for financial relevance, and surfaced in forms that make relationships and anomalies easier to see. The goal remains the same as in older cases: connect reported claims to independent evidence and identify what does not fit.

These systems create an edge not because the information is secret, but because the workflow is organized. A trained analyst using the tools well can complete due diligence in hours that once took days. More important, the analyst can uncover risks that are distributed across many sources and would never appear clearly in any one document.

Public information has not become less useful because it is abundant. It has become more useful for those able to process it in structured ways. The modern toolset does not replace the original discipline. It simply extends it.

Lessons Learned from Historical Financial Investigations

Historical investigations tend to repeat the same lessons. The most important is that fraud usually does not appear as one spectacular false entry. It builds gradually through patterns that stretch across reporting periods, accounting choices, executive behavior, and operational inconsistencies.

Enron and WorldCom showed how footnote analysis and cross-referencing could expose billions in hidden obligations. HealthSouth showed that executive stock sales can precede the public recognition of deeper financial weakness. In each case, the individual clues looked manageable on their own, but together they formed a pattern that should have changed the level of scrutiny.

Another recurring pattern is institutional failure. Arthur Andersen's role in Enron showed how auditors can become too close to the structures they are supposed to test. Similar failures have appeared in other jurisdictions and in state-backed institutions, where the appearance of official safety can actually reduce skepticism.

Detection also tends to lag badly. Adelphia's misconduct persisted for decades before bankruptcy exposed the underlying pattern. Barclays manipulated LIBOR for years before transaction analysis and external pressure forced the issue into full view. Regulators often miss what is already visible in the data because the signals are distributed and no one process is designed to combine them.

The cases also show that successful investigators rarely rely on financial statements alone. Wirecard was not broken only through accounting review. It was broken by combining document analysis with physical verification, registry work, and persistence. The best investigations move laterally, from numbers to behavior to assets to geography, and back again.

Legal outcomes matter less for traders than timing does. By the time regulators act, courts rule, or settlements are announced, the damage to the stock is usually long done. The analytical edge lives in the period before the legal system catches up—when the signals are visible in filings, operational data, and market structure but have not yet been confirmed by enforcement.

The more useful lesson is methodological. The strongest investigations consistently connect reported financials to something outside the reporting system itself. That may be a footnote, an audit log, satellite imagery, executive trading, shipping data, registry records, or transaction flows. The verification source changes, but the logic does not.

That is what separates passive reading from financial intelligence. A discrepancy between receivables growth and cash collection is not just an oddity. A physical address that does not match a reported operation is not just an anecdote. These are not loose anomalies. They are potential indicators of a system under stress or a story that does not hold.

The most durable lesson from the historical record is simple. Reported numbers should never be accepted as self-validating. They have to be tested for consistency across independent sources, time periods, and forms of evidence. Once that habit becomes routine, public information stops being static disclosure and starts functioning as intelligence.

Key Takeaways

- ☐ Each case demonstrates that the critical information was publicly available before the market fully priced it. GameStop's short interest data was in FINRA reports. Wirecard's empty offices were visible through on-site verification and satellite imagery. Enron's off-balance-sheet debt was disclosed in 10-K footnotes. Archegos's hidden exposure was inferable from the absence of expected 13F filings. In every case, the analytical failure was not access but method.
- ☐ The absence of expected data is itself intelligence. Archegos never filed a 13F despite managing billions. That gap — a large, active investment vehicle with no public disclosure — should have prompted investigation. Missing filings, omitted metrics, and disappeared disclosures often carry more signal than what is reported.
- ☐ No single technique produced the insight in any of these cases. GameStop required combining short interest data, options activity, insider filings, and social sentiment. Wirecard required matching financial statements against physical evidence. Enron required forensic footnote analysis across multiple annual reports. The common thread is source triangulation — the discipline of checking one source against another until the picture holds together or falls apart.

Fieldwork

- ☐ Choose one of the four cases. Re-read the relevant section, then pull the actual source documents referenced: the 10-K footnotes for Enron (available on EDGAR), the FINRA short interest data for GameStop, or the 13F filing database for the period around the Archegos collapse. Work through the primary sources yourself to see whether the signals described in the chapter are visible in the raw documents. The exercise bridges the gap between reading about a technique and applying it.
- ☐ For any company currently in your portfolio, apply the "absence test" from the Archegos case. What disclosures do you expect to see based on the

company's size, structure, and regulatory obligations? Are any of them missing, late, or unusually thin? The question is not just what has been filed, but what should have been filed and was not.

Apply This

These cases are not history lessons. They are diagnostic templates. When you encounter a company with growing receivables and shrinking cash flow, the Enron template applies. When you see extreme short interest with limited float, the GameStop template applies. When physical evidence contradicts financial claims, the Wirecard template applies. When expected regulatory filings are absent, the Archegos template applies. Match the pattern to the situation and work the corresponding verification process.

CHAPTER 28

Continuous Improvement and Professional Development

Finishing this book is the beginning of the work, not the end of it. The frameworks here only become useful through application — repeated, deliberate practice with real companies, real filings, and real investment decisions. The question after your last page isn't "what did I learn?" It's "what do I do on Monday?"

This section answers that question directly. It maps a practical skill development sequence, identifies what to prioritize in your first 90 days of active practice, and describes the specific learning investments that compound most reliably over time.

What to Build First

Not every skill in this manual carries equal weight in your early practice. Some unlock everything else. Three are foundational enough to prioritize before anything:

Master EDGAR full-text search. Most analysts use EDGAR to pull a company's filings directly. Fewer know how to search across the entire database — every 10-K, every proxy, every 8-K — for a specific term, phrase, or disclosure pattern.

The EDGAR full-text search system at efts.sec.gov lets you query the content of filings, not just filing metadata. A search for "going concern" combined with a specific company name returns every filing where that phrase appears. A search for a specific executive's name returns every filing, across every company, where that person is mentioned. This capability transforms EDGAR from a document repository into an investigative tool. Spend time learning advanced search syntax before moving on to other platforms.

Build a working three-statement model. Financial intelligence work requires fluency in how income statements, balance sheets, and cash flow statements connect to each other.

You don't need to build complex projection models — you need to understand the mechanics well enough to recognize when the numbers don't add up. If revenue grows 20% but operating cash flow is flat, what does that mean? If accounts receivable days outstanding increased by 15 days year-over-year, where does that show up and why does it matter? Build a simple three-statement model from scratch using a real company's 10-K, even once. The exercise builds intuitions that reading about the concepts never will.

Learn to read footnotes systematically. Every experienced analyst says footnotes matter. Very few analysts describe a repeatable process for reading them. Build one: open the most recent 10-K of any company you're researching and work through every footnote in order, asking two questions — does this change my understanding of the headline numbers, and has this language changed from the prior year? The second question requires pulling the previous year's 10-K alongside the current one.

A side-by-side comparison, applied consistently, is where accounting red flags reveal themselves. The restatements, the revenue recognition policy changes, the related-party transactions — they live in footnotes, not in the income statement summary.

What to Add Over Time

Once the three foundations are in place, expand your toolkit incrementally rather than broadly. Adding one new capability per quarter — practiced deeply rather than sampled — builds a durable skill set faster than surveying every technique at once.

Quarter 1 after completing this book: Set up your monitoring infrastructure. Configure EDGAR email alerts for every company you hold or actively watch. Create a basic alert system for Form 4 insider filings and 13D/13G beneficial ownership changes. Build a simple weekly review routine (see Appendix D) and follow it for 90 days without modification. The routine will feel incomplete —

resist the urge to rebuild it mid-cycle. Run it, then improve it after the first quarter's postmortem.

Quarter 2: Build your first complete company dossier using the Appendix A template. Choose a company you have a genuine opinion on, not one you're indifferent to. Work through every section of the template using primary sources only — no analyst summaries, no financial media until you've completed your own analysis. Then read three or four analyst reports on the same company and compare your findings to theirs. Where did they find something you missed? Where did you find something they didn't address? This gap analysis is your most honest measure of current skill.

Quarter 3: Add one alternative data source to your regular workflow. Job posting analysis via LinkedIn or Indeed requires no subscription and takes 20 minutes per company per month. Satellite imagery through services like Google Earth's historical view, while not real-time, teaches you to think spatially about corporate assets. FDA calendar monitoring (fda.gov) costs nothing and is indispensable if you follow any healthcare companies. Pick whichever is most relevant to your current focus and build the habit before adding the next one.

Quarter 4 and beyond: Practice postmortems on paper trades or closed positions. Choose one per quarter. Write down what your thesis was, what actually happened, and — most importantly — what information was available at the time that you either missed or underweighted. Appendix E provides a structured postmortem template with the specific questions to work through. The discipline of doing it consistently is what separates analysts who improve from those who repeat the same errors at higher stakes.

What Not to Do

Three common development mistakes waste disproportionate time at this stage:

Don't chase tools before building process. Bloomberg, FactSet, alternative data subscriptions — these accelerate a process that already exists. Without a research process, they just accelerate noise collection.

Build your workflow using free tools first. When a specific capability is genuinely limiting your work — not when it would be theoretically useful — that's when a paid tool earns its cost.

Don't measure learning by content consumed. Finishing courses, reading books, and watching tutorials creates the feeling of progress without the substance of it.

The only measure that matters in this discipline is whether your analysis of real companies is improving. Run the test: pull a company you haven't looked at, spend three hours on a proper analysis using the techniques in this manual, then check your conclusions against subsequent earnings results and analyst coverage. Do that quarterly and your development will take care of itself.

Don't skip the documentation habits. Source logs, thesis memos, evidence chains — these feel like administrative overhead when you're working on a position you're confident about. They matter most when you're wrong.

The analyst who documented their reasoning can learn from the error specifically. The analyst who didn't is left with a story they've unconsciously revised to protect their ego. The documentation habits described in Chapter 25 aren't optional polish. They're the infrastructure that makes the postmortem possible.

The Compounding Skill

Every technique in this manual has a ceiling. You can only get so good at reading MDA sections, or tracking Form 4 filings, or parsing short interest data. The skill without a ceiling is knowing which technique to apply to which situation — the judgment that comes from doing the work consistently, making errors with documented reasoning, and reviewing those errors honestly.

That judgment doesn't come from any single chapter. It accumulates across hundreds of research sessions, dozens of positions, and a structured habit of looking back at your work and asking what you missed. Build that habit before you build anything else.

Building a Professional FININT Practice

Most analysts who finish a book like this feel ready. The gap between that feeling and a working research practice is about 90 days of deliberate setup. This section covers what that setup looks like — what to build, in what order, and why the sequence matters.

The Infrastructure Layer

Before you analyze anything consistently, you need infrastructure that surfaces information without requiring you to remember to look for it. Three systems form the foundation:

A filing alert stack. Set up EDGAR email alerts for every company you actively follow, watch, or have a position in. Go to sec.gov, create a free account, and configure alerts by CIK number — not company name, which can return false matches. Set separate alerts for 10-Qs, 10-Ks, 8-Ks, Form 4s, and DEF 14As. Within one week you'll have a real-time feed of primary-source disclosures without visiting EDGAR manually. This is the single highest-return setup task in this entire manual.

A monitoring dashboard. Build a simple tracking sheet — a spreadsheet is fine — with every held position and watchlist name listed by row, and columns for: last filing reviewed, next expected catalyst, current thesis status (intact / weakening / invalidated), and open PIRs. Update it once a week. The purpose isn't complexity; it's making the state of every thesis visible at a glance so nothing drifts unreviewed.

A source log habit. Every piece of information you act on — every claim you accept into your thesis — gets logged with its source, date, and file location. This takes 30 seconds per item. Without it, a postmortem three months later becomes guesswork. With it, you can trace exactly which source led you to which conclusion and which turned out to be wrong. The log is the foundation of every improvement you'll make to your process.

Your First 90 Days

The following schedule is specific enough to follow literally. Adjust timing based on how many companies you're tracking, but don't collapse the phases — each builds on the one before it.

Weeks 1–2: Set up monitoring infrastructure

- ☐ Configure EDGAR alerts for every current position and top 10 watchlist names
- ☐ Set up a Google Alert or RSS feed for each company name plus "SEC filing," "earnings," and "activist"
- ☐ Create your monitoring dashboard with all current positions entered
- ☐ Complete Appendix D's daily and weekly checklists once each — note what felt incomplete or awkward for later revision
- ☐ Pull the most recent 10-K for your single highest-conviction position and read it in full, using the footnote protocol from Chapter 8 (side-by-side with the prior year's 10-K)

Weeks 3–4: Build your first company dossier

- ☐ Select one company you currently hold or are actively researching
- ☐ Complete every section of the Appendix A template using primary sources only — no analyst summaries until you've finished
- ☐ When complete, read two to three sell-side analyst reports on the same company
- ☐ Document the gaps: what did they find that you missed, and what did you find that they didn't address?
- ☐ This gap analysis is your most accurate current-state skill assessment
- ☐ Month 2: Add sector mapping and peer comparison
- ☐ Identify the three to five closest peers to your primary focus company using GICS classification

- ☐ Pull the most recent 10-K for each peer and extract five key metrics: gross margin, operating margin, revenue growth, free cash flow yield, and accounts receivable days outstanding
- ☐ Build a simple peer comparison table — the SEC filing types quick-reference table in Chapter 5 shows which filings contain each metric
- ☐ Note where your primary company stands relative to peers on each dimension, and whether any outlier positions require explanation
- ☐ Add those explanations — or the open questions around them — to your PIR register

Month 3: Implement catalyst tracking and conduct your first postmortem

- ☐ Set up a catalyst calendar for every position: upcoming earnings dates, FDA decisions if applicable, contract renewal windows, macro data releases that affect your thesis
- ☐ For each catalyst, document in advance: what outcome would confirm your thesis, what would weaken it, what would invalidate it
- ☐ Choose one closed position — won or lost — from the past six months and conduct a full postmortem using the template in Appendix E
- ☐ Write it up. The writing is not optional. The act of articulating the error forces the precision that mental review avoids

Mapping Relationship Networks with Public Data

One of the most underused capabilities in public-source research is mapping the relationship network around a target company. Board interlocks, shared investors, and prior employer connections are all disclosed publicly — they just require assembly.

Start with the proxy statement (DEF 14A). Every director's biography lists their other board positions, their prior employment, and their equity holdings in the company. Pull this document for your target company and build a simple table: director name, current outside board seats, prior employer (most recent 2–3 roles), and ownership stake.

Worked example — mapping a target company's network:

Suppose you're researching a mid-cap industrial company. The proxy reveals:

- The CEO previously served as COO at a larger industrial conglomerate. Pull that conglomerate's proxy and 10-K filings to assess his track record there — revenue performance during his tenure, any disclosed investigations, whether he left before or after a significant business decline.
- One board member sits on the audit committee while simultaneously serving as a director of a supplier company that appears in your target's related-party transaction footnotes. This overlap is disclosed in both proxies. The question is whether the audit committee member's dual role created oversight gaps — check whether the related-party transaction terms were reviewed by independent counsel and whether pricing was disclosed as arm's-length.
- Two directors were appointed in the same year following a Schedule 13D filing from an activist investor. Pull that 13D — the purpose section will describe what the activist wanted. Did management comply? Partially comply? Did the directors brought in by the activist vote differently on subsequent proxy measures? This pattern reveals whether governance changes were substantive or cosmetic.

Now extend the network one layer out. Search EDGAR's full-text system for each director's name to find other filings where they appear — as officers, as beneficial owners, as named parties in enforcement actions. OpenCorporates cross-references director names across corporate registries globally, surfacing overseas affiliations that U.S. proxy statements may omit.

Equity holding networks add a second dimension. Pull the most recent 13F filings for your target company's top five institutional holders. Which of those same institutions also hold major positions in your target's closest competitors? Shared institutional ownership between competitors can create unusual information flow dynamics and governance pressures. When the same two or three investors own 15–20% of both Company A and Company B in the same sector, and Company A's board suddenly gains a director with deep ties to Company B, the network signal is worth investigating further.

Network density — the degree to which the same names recur across multiple companies in an industry — is itself a signal. Dense networks with extensive interlocks between competitors, suppliers, and customers suggest either a small talent pool with legitimate overlap, or structural relationships that regulatory filings may be underrepresenting. Thin networks in industries where you'd expect them, or board compositions that changed rapidly after a specific event, are equally worth examining.

None of this requires specialized software. A spreadsheet with director names, affiliated entities, and filing cross-references — built from EDGAR, OpenCorporates, and SEC EDGAR full-text search — gives you the same network picture that institutional researchers produce, at the cost of a few hours' systematic work.

What a Sustainable Practice Actually Looks Like

After 90 days of running this system, most of it becomes habit. The monitoring dashboard takes 10 minutes on Sunday evening. The EDGAR alert stack runs itself. The source log takes 30 seconds per item. The quarterly postmortem is in the calendar.

What remains demanding — and should remain demanding — is the analysis. The PIR register keeps growing with questions your system surfaces but hasn't answered yet. The peer comparison tables get refined as you understand the sector better. The relationship network maps deepen as more filings accumulate.

The practice is sustainable when it scales with your conviction rather than with your time. You don't do more research when the market is interesting — you do more research when a specific thesis requires it. The infrastructure handles the routine. Your judgment handles the work that infrastructure can't.

That's what the whole system is designed to produce: the conditions under which your analytical judgment, trained by the methods in this manual, gets applied to the right questions at the right time.

Key Takeaways

- ☐ The three foundational skills — EDGAR full-text search, three-statement model fluency, and systematic footnote reading — unlock everything else. Master them before adding alternative data sources, automation tools, or advanced analytical techniques. The sequence is important because later skills depend on the judgment these three develop.
- ☐ The only skill without a ceiling is knowing which technique to apply to which situation. That judgment develops through doing the work, documenting your reasoning, making errors with a written record, and reviewing those errors honestly through structured postmortems. No amount of reading substitutes for that cycle.

Fieldwork

- ☐ If you have not yet done so, complete the "What to Build First" exercises from this chapter: run an EDGAR full-text search, build a three-statement model from a real 10-K, and read one complete set of footnotes side by side with the prior year. These are the practical prerequisites for everything else in the book.
- ☐ Set a calendar reminder for 90 days from today. On that date, conduct your first postmortem using the Appendix E template. Choose the position where your thesis was most wrong — not the one that lost the most money, but the one where your reasoning was furthest from what actually happened. That distinction focuses the postmortem on analytical process rather than outcome luck.
- ☐ Write down the one technique from this book you found most unfamiliar or most difficult to apply. That is your skill development priority for the next quarter. Add it to your monitoring routine or dossier process and practice it on real companies until it becomes automatic.

Apply This

The infrastructure described in this chapter — the filing alert stack, the monitoring dashboard, the source log, the quarterly postmortem — takes about a week to set up and less than two hours per week to maintain. The payoff is that your research process improves with each cycle rather than repeating the same blind spots at higher stakes. Build the system. Run it. Review it. That is the practice.

Glossary

10-K — A company's annual report filed with the SEC containing audited financial statements, risk factors, business description, and management's discussion. Required within 60–90 days of a company's fiscal year-end depending on filer category.

10-Q — A quarterly report filed with the SEC containing unaudited financial statements and management's discussion of material changes. Required within 40–45 days of each quarter-end.

424B (Final Prospectus) — The final version of a prospectus filed with the SEC after pricing of a securities offering. The 424B4 variant is the definitive legal document governing deal terms, superseding any preliminary prospectus filed earlier.

8-K — A current report filed with the SEC to announce material corporate events — mergers, earnings releases, executive changes, cybersecurity incidents — within four business days of the triggering event.

13D — A Schedule 13D filed with the SEC by any investor who acquires more than 5% of a company's equity securities with the intent to influence or control the issuer. Must be filed within five business days of crossing the threshold.

13F — A quarterly institutional holdings report filed with the SEC by investment managers with more than $100 million in assets under management. Discloses equity positions held at the end of each quarter.

13G — An abbreviated version of Schedule 13D filed by passive investors who cross the 5% ownership threshold without seeking to influence management. Qualified institutional investors typically use this form.

Abduction — A reasoning technique that infers the most plausible explanation for a set of observed facts. Used in financial analysis to identify the most likely cause of unusual price movements or conflicting data signals.

Accounts Receivable — Money owed to a company by customers for goods or services already delivered. Rapid growth in accounts receivable relative to revenue can signal aggressive revenue recognition or collection problems.

ADX (Average Directional Index) — A technical indicator that measures the strength of a price trend, regardless of direction. Values above 25 generally indicate a strong trend.

AIS (Automatic Identification System) — A maritime tracking system that broadcasts vessel identity, position, speed, and heading. Used in financial intelligence to monitor shipping activity and verify supply chain claims.

Beneish M-Score — A mathematical model developed by Professor Messod Beneish that uses eight financial ratios to identify companies likely to be manipulating earnings. Scores above -1.78 suggest a higher probability of manipulation.

Benford's Law — A statistical principle holding that in many naturally occurring datasets, the leading digit is more likely to be small (1 appears roughly 30% of the time, 9 appears roughly 5%). Forensic accountants use deviations from this distribution to flag potentially fabricated financial data.

CDS (Credit Default Swap) — A financial derivative that functions as insurance against a borrower's default. Rising CDS spreads indicate the market perceives increasing credit risk for that company or country.

CIK (Central Index Key) — A unique numerical identifier assigned to every entity that files documents with the SEC's EDGAR system. Using a CIK rather than a company name ensures search results return filings from only the intended entity.

CPI (Consumer Price Index) — A monthly measure of the average change in prices paid by urban consumers for a basket of goods and services. Published by the Bureau of Labor Statistics, it is the most widely followed inflation indicator and a primary input to Federal Reserve policy decisions.

DEF 14A (Proxy Statement) — An SEC filing that provides shareholders with information necessary to vote on corporate matters including board elections, executive compensation, and mergers. Contains detailed data on governance and management incentives.

Deduction — A reasoning technique that applies established rules or known facts to reach a certain conclusion. In financial analysis, deduction confirms what must logically follow from a known regulatory requirement or disclosed policy.

Dilution — A reduction in existing shareholders' ownership percentage caused by the issuance of new shares. Occurs through stock offerings, option exercises, warrant conversions, and other equity issuances. Affects earnings per share and voting power.

DUNS Number — A nine-digit identifier assigned by Dun & Bradstreet to business entities worldwide. Used to verify company identity and trace corporate relationships across jurisdictions.

EBITDA (Earnings Before Interest, Taxes, Depreciation, and Amortization) — A common measure of a company's core operating profitability, though it excludes significant costs and can be used to obscure deteriorating cash generation.

EDGAR (Electronic Data Gathering, Analysis, and Retrieval) — The SEC's public database of corporate filings. All public companies registered in the United States file mandatory disclosures through EDGAR, which is freely searchable at sec.gov.

Evidence Chain — A structured sequence of independently verified data points that collectively support an analytical conclusion. A strong evidence chain requires each link to come from a different source type to avoid circular reasoning.

FDA (Food and Drug Administration) — The U.S. federal agency responsible for regulating pharmaceuticals, medical devices, food safety, and other health-related products. FDA advisory committee calendars and PDUFA dates are key binary catalysts for pharmaceutical and biotech companies.

FinBERT — A natural language processing model fine-tuned on financial text. Used to classify the sentiment of earnings call transcripts, SEC filings, and news articles as positive, negative, or neutral with higher accuracy than general-purpose models.

FININT (Financial Intelligence) — The systematic collection, processing, and analysis of publicly available information to produce actionable market insight. Distinguished from casual financial research by its use of structured methodologies, source triangulation, and evidence-based thesis construction.

FINRA (Financial Industry Regulatory Authority) — A self-regulatory organization that oversees U.S. broker-dealers and their registered representatives.

Publishes short interest data twice monthly, which is a primary source for monitoring bearish positioning in individual securities.

FOMC (Federal Open Market Committee) — The Federal Reserve's monetary policy-making body, composed of the seven Board of Governors members and five Reserve Bank presidents on a rotating basis. It meets eight times per year to set the federal funds rate and issue forward guidance.

Form 4 — An SEC filing that insiders — directors, officers, and 10%+ shareholders — must file within two business days of a transaction in the company's securities. Used to track insider buying and selling patterns.

FPDS (Federal Procurement Data System) — The U.S. government's database of all federal contract actions above the micro-purchase threshold. Used to track agency spending, contractor performance, and the flow of federal dollars by vendor, product, and geography. Accessible through USAspending.gov.

Free Cash Flow — Cash generated by operations minus capital expenditures. Represents the cash available for dividends, share buybacks, debt repayment, or reinvestment after maintaining or expanding the asset base. Often diverges from reported earnings when a company uses aggressive accounting.

GAAP (Generally Accepted Accounting Principles) — The standard set of accounting rules required for financial reporting by U.S. public companies. Non-GAAP metrics are voluntary adjustments that companies use alongside GAAP figures, often to present more favorable results.

GDP (Gross Domestic Product) — The total market value of all finished goods and services produced within a country in a specific period. The advance estimate is published quarterly by the Bureau of Economic Analysis and is subject to significant revision in subsequent months.

GICS (Global Industry Classification Standard) — A hierarchical system developed by MSCI and S&P that classifies companies into 11 sectors, 25 industry groups, 74 industries, and 163 sub-industries. Used to identify peers for comparative analysis.

Going Concern — An auditor's qualification indicating substantial doubt about a company's ability to continue operating for the next twelve months. A going concern flag in an audit report is a significant red flag requiring immediate investigation.

Hedge Ratio — In financial intelligence text analysis, the ratio of hedging words (may, could, might, potential, anticipate, believe, expect) to total forward-looking words. A rising hedge ratio across consecutive filings indicates declining management confidence even when qualitative language remains positive.

ICIJ Offshore Leaks Database — The International Consortium of Investigative Journalists' publicly searchable database of offshore entities, officers, and intermediaries compiled from leaked datasets including the Panama Papers and Pandora Papers.

IDIQ (Indefinite Delivery/Indefinite Quantity) — A type of federal contract that provides for an indefinite quantity of goods or services during a fixed period, with individual orders placed through task orders. Common in IT, professional services, and defense sectors.

IFRS (International Financial Reporting Standards) — The global accounting standard used in over 140 countries, developed by the International Accounting Standards Board. Foreign private issuers listed in the U.S. may report under IFRS, creating comparability challenges with GAAP-reporting domestic companies.

Implied Volatility — The market's expectation of future price movement for a security, derived from options pricing. Higher implied volatility indicates the market expects larger price swings. Unusual spikes before known catalysts can signal informed positioning.

Induction — A reasoning technique that generalizes from observed patterns to probable trends. In financial analysis, induction identifies likely future behavior based on recurring relationships seen across multiple past instances.

IPO (Initial Public Offering) — The first sale of a company's stock to the public. The process involves filing a registration statement (typically Form S-1) with the SEC, a roadshow, pricing, and allocation. The S-1 and subsequent amendments are primary intelligence sources for evaluating newly public companies.

LDA (Lobbying Disclosure Act) — The 1995 federal statute requiring lobbyists to register with Congress and file quarterly reports disclosing their clients, the issues they lobby on, the agencies and congressional offices they contact, and the fees they receive. Filings are searchable at lda.senate.gov.

LEI (Legal Entity Identifier) — A 20-character alphanumeric code that uniquely identifies legal entities participating in financial transactions worldwide. Used to trace corporate relationships and verify counterparty identity across jurisdictions.

MACD (Moving Average Convergence Divergence) — A technical indicator that tracks the relationship between two exponential moving averages of a security's price. Used to identify momentum shifts and potential trend reversals.

Market Capitalization — The total market value of a company's outstanding shares, calculated by multiplying the current share price by total shares outstanding. A basic sizing metric that determines which index categories and filing deadlines apply.

Material Event — A corporate development that would likely influence a reasonable investor's decision to buy or sell a security. Companies must file an 8-K within four business days of a material event.

MNPI (Material Non-Public Information) — Confidential information about a company that has not been publicly disclosed and that a reasonable investor would consider significant in making an investment decision. Trading on MNPI constitutes insider trading.

Mosaic Theory — The legal principle that allows analysts to combine numerous pieces of individually non-material public information to form a conclusion that may itself be material. Mosaic theory analysis using publicly available data does not create MNPI liability.

NAV (Net Asset Value) — The per-share value of a fund or investment vehicle, calculated as total assets minus total liabilities divided by shares outstanding. Used for closed-end funds, ETFs, and REITs. A persistent discount or premium to NAV can signal market sentiment about the underlying portfolio.

OBV (On-Balance Volume) — A technical indicator that uses cumulative volume to confirm price trends. Rising OBV alongside rising price confirms trend strength; divergences between OBV and price often signal reversals.

Open Interest — The total number of outstanding options or futures contracts that have not been settled or closed. Rising open interest alongside rising price confirms trend strength. A surge at unusual strike prices can indicate informed positioning ahead of a catalyst.

OpenCorporates — The world's largest open database of company information, covering over 200 million companies across more than 140 jurisdictions. Used to trace corporate ownership structures and verify registrations internationally.

OSINT (Open-Source Intelligence) — Intelligence gathered exclusively from publicly available sources including government records, corporate filings, media, academic publications, and social media. The foundational methodology for FININT.

PACER (Public Access to Court Electronic Records) — The U.S. federal court system's online database of case filings, dockets, and court documents. Used to research litigation history, bankruptcy proceedings, and regulatory enforcement actions.

Panama Papers — A collection of 11.5 million leaked documents from Panamanian law firm Mossack Fonseca, released in 2016. Provides contextual intelligence on offshore structures and beneficial ownership connections across jurisdictions.

PDUFA (Prescription Drug User Fee Act) — The statute that establishes review timelines and fees for FDA drug applications. PDUFA dates—the deadlines by which the FDA must complete its review—function as binary catalysts with specific, publicly known dates.

PIR (Priority Intelligence Requirement) — A specific, ranked question that drives collection planning. Defining PIRs before beginning data collection ensures research focuses on information that actually matters to the investment thesis.

Prime Broker — A financial institution that provides services to hedge funds and other institutional clients, including securities lending, leveraged trade execution, custody, and cash management. Prime broker relationships were central to the Archegos collapse.

PTR (Periodic Transaction Report) — A financial disclosure required of members of Congress and senior congressional staff under the STOCK Act. Covers securities transactions above $1,000 and must be filed within 45 days of the transaction.

Reg FD (Regulation Fair Disclosure) — An SEC rule that prohibits companies from intentionally disclosing material information to selected analysts or investors before making it available to the public simultaneously or promptly.

Regulatory Capture — A condition in which a regulatory agency advances the interests of the industry it is charged with regulating rather than the public interest. Surfaces as a pattern where regulatory staffing, rulemaking, and enforcement align more closely with industry preferences than with investor protection.

ROC (Rate of Change) — A momentum indicator that expresses the percentage change in price over a specified lookback period, used to gauge the speed and acceleration of price moves.

ROE (Return on Equity) — Net income divided by shareholders' equity. Measures how effectively a company generates profit from the money shareholders have invested. Persistent ROE above the cost of equity suggests genuine value creation; declining ROE may signal deteriorating competitive position.

RSI (Relative Strength Index) — A technical indicator that measures price momentum on a scale from 0 to 100. RSI above 70 generally indicates overbought conditions; below 30 suggests oversold conditions.

RSS (Really Simple Syndication) — A web feed format that delivers updated content automatically from websites. In FININT, RSS feeds from EDGAR, news services, and regulatory agencies provide passive monitoring of new filings and announcements without requiring manual checking.

S-1 (Registration Statement) — The primary SEC filing used by companies conducting an initial public offering. Contains the prospectus, financial statements, risk factors, management discussion, and use of proceeds.

Amendments (S-1/A) track changes during the SEC review process before pricing.

SAM.gov (System for Award Management) — The U.S. government's official database for entity registration, exclusion records, and federal assistance listings. All entities doing business with the federal government must register here. Also hosts the List of Parties Excluded from Federal Procurement.

SAR (Suspicious Activity Report) — A report filed by financial institutions with the Financial Crimes Enforcement Network (FinCEN) when they detect potentially suspicious transactions. SAR filings are not publicly available but their existence can sometimes be inferred from enforcement actions.

SEC (Securities and Exchange Commission) — The U.S. federal agency responsible for regulating securities markets and enforcing federal securities laws. The SEC's EDGAR database is the primary public repository of mandatory corporate disclosures.

Short Squeeze — A rapid increase in a stock's price driven by short sellers being forced to buy shares to cover their positions. Occurs when high short interest meets a catalyst that triggers covering in a stock with limited available float.

SPAC (Special Purpose Acquisition Company) — A blank-check company formed to raise capital through an IPO for the purpose of acquiring an existing business. SPAC filings—including the S-1, proxy statement, and Form 8-K announcing the merger target—follow a distinct disclosure timeline.

STOCK Act (Stop Trading on Congressional Knowledge Act) — A 2012 federal law that prohibits members of Congress and their staff from using material nonpublic information gained through their official positions for personal financial gain. Strengthened financial disclosure requirements and shortened filing deadlines for securities transactions.

Task Order — An individual work order issued under an existing IDIQ or similar umbrella contract. Specifies scope, deliverables, timeline, and price for a discrete piece of work. Represents the actual flow of federal dollars and often contains more operational detail than the parent contract.

Total Return Swap — A derivative contract in which one party makes payments based on the total return of an underlying asset while the other pays a fixed or floating rate. Used to gain economic exposure to a position without formal ownership, which can obscure beneficial ownership from standard reporting requirements.

USAspending.gov — The official public database of federal government spending. Provides searchable, downloadable data on contracts, grants, loans, and other financial assistance by agency, recipient, location, and program. The primary tool for tracking federal contracting intelligence.

USPTO (United States Patent and Trademark Office) — The U.S. government agency that grants patents and registers trademarks. Patent filings available through USPTO are used in FININT to track research and development activity, competitive positioning, and employee movement.

VIX (CBOE Volatility Index) — A measure of the market's expectation of 30-day forward volatility, derived from S&P 500 options prices. Often called the "fear gauge," it tends to spike during market stress and compress during calm markets.

APPENDICES

APPENDIX A

Company Dossier Template

Use this template as the central research file for each company you investigate. Adapt sections as needed for sector-specific requirements. Every entry should cite its primary source and date of retrieval.

Section 1: Company Overview

Company name, ticker, CIK number, GICS classification, market capitalization, exchange. Fiscal year-end date. Business description in two to three sentences from the 10-K Item 1. Primary revenue segments and geographic breakdown. Date of most recent 10-K and 10-Q reviewed.

Section 2: Financial Summary

Trailing four quarters: revenue, operating income, net income, EPS, operating cash flow, free cash flow. Key ratios: gross margin, operating margin, ROE, debt-to-equity, current ratio, accounts receivable days outstanding. Year-over-year trends for each metric (improving, stable, deteriorating). Note any non-GAAP metrics management emphasizes and the gap between GAAP and non-GAAP figures.

Section 3: Leadership and Governance

CEO, CFO, and key executives: name, tenure, prior employer, track record at prior company (from proxy and EDGAR search). Board of directors: names, outside board seats, committee assignments, tenure, share ownership. Board interlocks with competitors, suppliers, or customers. Any recent director departures or appointments (from 8-K filings). Related-party transactions from 10-K footnotes and proxy statement. Recent Form 4 insider transaction summary: net buying or selling over trailing 6 months.

Section 4: Filing Analysis Notes

Footnote findings: revenue recognition policy, any changes from prior year, contingent liabilities, off-balance-sheet items. MD&A language tracking: key phrases from current quarter vs. prior quarter (side-by-side comparison). Hedge ratio estimate for forward-looking sections. Risk factor changes: new risks added, removed, or reordered since prior filing. Auditor: name, tenure, any qualifications or going-concern flags. Accounting red flags: Beneish M-Score components if calculated, or qualitative flags observed.

Section 5: Competitive Landscape

Top three to five direct peers with tickers. Peer comparison on key metrics: revenue growth, margins, valuation multiples, leverage. GICS sub-industry classification and whether it accurately reflects the company's actual competitive set. Any recent peer developments (acquisitions, product launches, regulatory actions) that affect your target. Patent landscape: recent filings by target vs. competitors (USPTO search).

Section 6: Catalyst Calendar

Next earnings date and expected release time (BMO/AMC). Upcoming regulatory decisions (FDA, FCC, etc.) with expected dates. Contract renewal or expiration dates. Patent expiration timelines for key revenue-generating products. Scheduled investor days or conference presentations. Known litigation milestones (trial dates, settlement deadlines). For each catalyst: what outcome confirms the thesis, what weakens it, what invalidates it.

Section 7: Thesis and Risk Register

Investment thesis: one paragraph stating the opportunity, the evidence, and the expected outcome. Thesis status: Intact / Weakening / Invalidated (update with each review). Bull case, base case, bear case with probability weights. Risk register: top five risks to the thesis, each with estimated probability (high/medium/low), potential impact, and the specific data point or event that would confirm the risk is materializing. Pre-defined exit conditions: what specific developments trigger a full exit, a partial reduction, or a position increase.

Section 8: Source Log

Running log of every source document used in this dossier. For each entry: date retrieved, source type (SEC filing, court record, news article, alternative data), specific document identifier (filing type and date, case number, URL), and which dossier section it supports. This log creates the audit trail that makes postmortems possible and prevents circular reasoning.

APPENDIX B

Fraud Red Flags and Due Diligence Checklist

Use this checklist during initial due diligence or when evaluating a company flagged by other research. A single red flag warrants further investigation. Three or more in the same company warrant serious concern. Not every flag indicates fraud — some reflect aggressive but legal accounting or sector-specific norms. The checklist identifies where to look deeper, not where to stop.

Financial Statement Red Flags

- ☐ Revenue growing significantly faster than operating cash flow for two or more consecutive quarters.
- ☐ Accounts receivable days outstanding increasing while revenue growth is flat or declining.
- ☐ Inventory growth outpacing cost of goods sold growth.
- ☐ Frequent or unexplained changes in revenue recognition policy.
- ☐ Beneish M-Score above -1.78.
- ☐ Gross margin expanding while peers in the same sector show contraction.
- ☐ Non-GAAP adjustments growing as a percentage of GAAP earnings over time.
- ☐ Material related-party transactions with entities controlled by executives or their families.
- ☐ Off-balance-sheet liabilities disclosed in footnotes that substantially exceed on-balance-sheet debt.
- ☐ Governance and Disclosure Red Flags
- ☐ Auditor change, especially mid-year or following a disagreement disclosed in the 8-K.

- ☐ Going-concern qualification in the most recent audit opinion. ▢ Repeated late filings of Forms 3, 4, or 5 by insiders.
- ☐ CEO or CFO departure with no clear succession plan or vague "personal reasons" explanation.
- ☐ Clustered insider selling by three or more executives within the same 30-day window.
- ☐ Board members with undisclosed conflicts identified through EDGAR full-text search or corporate registry cross-referencing.
- ☐ Compensation structures heavily weighted toward short-term metrics with no clawback provisions.

Operational and External Red Flags

- ☐ Physical evidence (satellite imagery, shipping data, job postings) contradicts reported operational activity.
- ☐ Revenue claims that cannot be verified through supplier filings, import/export data, or industry benchmarks.
- ☐ Complex corporate structure involving multiple offshore entities in jurisdictions with minimal disclosure requirements.
- ☐ Directors or officers appearing in the ICIJ Offshore Leaks Database, PACER litigation records, or prior enforcement actions.
- ☐ Multiple suppliers or customers suing the company for non-payment within the same 12-month period.
- ☐ Short interest above 20% with a credible short thesis from an established research firm.
- ☐ MD&A language showing excuse migration — a different explanation for the same underperformance each quarter.

APPENDIX C

KEY DATABASES AND ACCESS POINTS

All databases listed below are publicly accessible.

Entries marked "Free" require no payment. Entries marked "Free with account" require registration but no subscription.

URLs are current as of publication but may change; search the organization name if a link is broken.

U.S. Regulatory Filings

- SEC EDGAR (company filings):
  - sec.gov/cgi-bin/browse-edgar — Free.
- EDGAR Full-Text Search:
  - efts.sec.gov/LATEST/search-index — Free.
- SEC EDGAR email alerts:
  - sec.gov (create account, configure by CIK) — Free with account.
- PACER (federal court records):
  - pacer.gov — $0.10/page, $3 max per document, quarterly fees under $30 waived.
- RECAP Archive (free court documents):
  - courtlistener.com/recap — Free.
- USPTO Patent Search:
  - patft.uspto.gov and ppubs.uspto.gov — Free.
- FRED (Federal Reserve Economic Data):
  - fred.stlouisfed.org — Free.
- Bureau of Labor Statistics:
  - bls.gov — Free.

- Census Bureau Economic Indicators:
  - census.gov/economic-indicators — Free.
- FDA Calendar and Approvals:
  - fda.gov/advisory-committees/advisory-committee-calendar — Free.
- SEC Enforcement Actions:
  - sec.gov/litigation — Free.

International Registries and Filings

- UK Companies House:
  - find-and-update.company-information.service.gov.uk — Free.
- OpenCorporates:
  - opencorporates.com — Free for basic searches, paid for bulk access.
- ICIJ Offshore Leaks Database:
  - offshoreleaks.icij.org — Free.
- London Stock Exchange Regulatory News:
  - londonstockexchange.com/news — Free.
- ASX Announcements (Australia):
  - asx.com.au/asx/statistics/announcements.do — Free.
- TSX Filings (Canada):
  - sedarplus.ca — Free.
- EDINET (Japan):
  - disclosure.edinet-fsa.go.jp — Free.
- European Single Access Point (ESAP):
  - esap.eu (in development) — Free.
- German Federal Gazette (Bundesanzeiger):
  - bundesanzeiger.de — Free.

Institutional Holdings and Insider Data

- WhaleWisdom (13F filings)
  - whalewisdom.com — Free for basic access.
- Dataroma (superinvestor portfolios):
  - dataroma.com — Free.
- OpenInsider (Form 4 tracker):
  - openinsider.com — Free.
- FINRA Short Interest:
  - finra.org/finra-data/browse-catalog/short-interest — Free.

Central Bank Communications

- Federal Reserve (statements, minutes, speeches, Beige Book):
  - federalreserve.gov/newsevents — Free.
- FRED API:
  - api.stlouisfed.org — Free with API key.
- European Central Bank:
  - ecb.europa.eu — Free.
- Bank of Japan:
  - boj.or.jp/en — Free.
- Bank of England:
  - bankofengland.co.uk — Free.

Policy Intelligence

- Lobbying Disclosure (Senate):
  - lda.senate.gov — Free. Searchable by registrant, client, or issue.
- OpenSecrets (lobbying, campaign finance, revolving door):
  - opensecrets.org — Free.

- USAspending.gov (federal contracts, grants, and financial assistance):
  - usaspending.gov — Free. Searchable by agency, recipient, NAICS code, and contract type.
- SAM.gov (entity registration, exclusion lists):
  - sam.gov — Free with account.
- Senate Financial Disclosures (PTRs and annual reports):
  - efdsearch.senate.gov — Free.
- House Financial Disclosures:
  - disclosures.house.gov — Free.

Geopolitical and Alternative Data

- USGS Earthquake Hazards (real-time seismic data):
  - earthquake.usgs.gov — Free.
- ACLED (Armed Conflict Location and Event Data):
  - acleddata.com — Free with registration for data access.
- UNHCR Operational Data Portal (displacement and refugee data):
  - data.unhcr.org — Free.
- Google Earth Historical Imagery (satellite time series):
  - earth.google.com — Free.
- MarineTraffic (vessel tracking, port activity):
  - marinetraffic.com — Free for basic vessel tracking; paid for historical data and fleet analytics.

APPENDIX D

Sample Daily and Weekly Monitoring Routine

Run this routine for 90 days before changing it. The goal is habit formation, not optimization. Refine it after the first quarterly postmortem.

Daily (15–20 minutes, before market open)

- ☐ Review overnight EDGAR email alerts. Flag any 8-K filings, Form 4 transactions, or 13D/13G amendments for held positions.
- ☐ Check today's economic calendar (BLS, Census, Fed speeches). Note any release relevant to an active thesis.
- ☐ Scan pre-market movers on your watchlist. For any position moving more than 3%, identify the filing, news item, or catalyst before the open.
- ☐ If an earnings call occurred after the prior close or before today's open for a held position, read the press release and note whether the initial results confirm or contradict your thesis. Full transcript review can wait for the weekly session.

Weekly (60–90 minutes, Sunday evening or Monday morning)

- ☐ Update the monitoring dashboard: review thesis status for every position (intact, weakening, invalidated) and update last-filing-reviewed dates.
- ☐ Review the week's Form 4 filings for all watchlist companies. Note any insider buying clusters or unusual selling patterns.
- ☐ Read any earnings call transcripts from the prior week for held positions. Run the side-by-side MD&A comparison if a 10-Q was filed.
- ☐ Check the coming week's calendar: earnings dates, Fed speeches, macro releases, regulatory deadlines, and court case milestones for any company in your coverage.

- ☐ Review short interest data if updated during the week. Note any significant changes in short float percentage or days to cover for active positions.
- ☐ Check the Fed speaker calendar at federalreserve.gov/newsevents. Note whether any Tier 1 or Tier 2 speakers have events scheduled and whether those events fall inside or outside the FOMC blackout window.
- ☐ Log any new source documents accessed this week into the source log for each relevant dossier.
- ☐ If you hold positions in companies with significant government exposure: check USAspending.gov for new contract awards or modifications, and scan congressional PTR filings at efdsearch.senate.gov and disclosures.house.gov for transactions in your coverage names.

Quarterly (half day, scheduled in advance)

- ☐ Conduct one full postmortem on a closed position using the Appendix E template.
- ☐ Review the monitoring routine itself: which daily or weekly items consistently produced actionable intelligence, and which felt like noise? Adjust accordingly.
- ☐ Update peer comparison tables with the most recent quarterly data.
- ☐ Review and refresh your PIR (Priority Intelligence Requirement) register. Remove questions that have been answered. Add new questions that have emerged from the quarter's research.
- ☐ Check whether any company dossiers need updating based on annual filing cycles (10-K releases, proxy statements, annual meeting results).
- ☐ For companies with regulatory or government exposure, review the latest quarterly lobbying disclosures at lda.senate.gov for changes in lobbying spend, new issue areas, or new covered agencies. Check USAspending.gov for contract award trends over the trailing four quarters.
- ☐ Assess skill development progress: which new technique did you practice this quarter, and did it improve your research output?

APPENDIX E

Research Postmortem Template

Complete this template for one closed position per quarter. The purpose is not to assign blame but to identify specific, repeatable improvements to your research process. Write your answers — the act of articulating forces precision that mental review avoids.

1. What was the thesis?

Restate the original investment thesis from your thesis memo or dossier. Include the specific claim, the expected outcome, the time horizon, and the key evidence that supported it at entry.

2. What actually happened?

Describe the actual outcome: price movement, fundamental developments, and the timeline. How did the result compare to your base case, bull case, and bear case scenarios?

3. What information was available at entry that I missed or underweighted?

Review your source log and the public record from the period. Were there filings, data points, or signals in the public domain at the time of entry that should have changed your assessment? Be specific: cite the source, the date, and what it would have told you.

4. Which data sources proved most and least valuable?

Of the sources you consulted, which provided the signals that mattered most to the outcome? Which consumed time without contributing to the analysis? This informs how you allocate research time on future positions.

5. Was the thesis logic wrong, or was the timing or execution wrong?

Distinguish between analytical error (the thesis was wrong on the fundamentals), timing error (the thesis was directionally correct but the catalyst took longer or shorter than expected), and execution error (the thesis was right but position sizing, entry point, or exit discipline was flawed). Different error types require different process corrections.

6. What single process change would have made the biggest difference?

Identify one specific, actionable change to your research workflow. Examples: adding patent database monitoring to your weekly routine, comparing MD&A language across quarters before forming a thesis, checking Form 4 filing patterns before entering a position based on management commentary. Implement this change for the next quarter and evaluate it in the following postmortem.

7. Did any behavioral bias affect the analysis?

Common biases to check: confirmation bias (seeking evidence that supports the thesis while ignoring contradictory data), anchoring (fixating on the initial entry price or valuation target), overconfidence (assigning too-high probability to the base case), and sunk cost (holding a weakening position because of prior time invested in research). If a bias was present, what structural safeguard — a checklist, a pre-commitment, a peer review — would counteract it?

About the Author

Zachary Handa is a product strategist and researcher with more than a decade of experience in digital marketing, search, and analytical systems. His work has centered on finding signal inside noisy information environments, building structured workflows, and improving the quality of decision-making through better research.

In *FININT*, he brings that same approach to the public record. Drawing on methods of source verification, cross-referencing, and structured analysis, he shows how traders and independent researchers can use filings, disclosures, and open-source data to move beyond reactive market commentary and build stronger investment theses.

Handa's work focuses on practical methodology: how to ask better questions, organize evidence, and turn scattered information into usable intelligence.

Made in the USA
Monee, IL
05 November 2026

67914376R00233